Living Happily Ever After

Because your family matters ...

Family matters is a brand new series from Wiley highlighting topics that are important to the everyday lives of family members. Each book tackles a common problem or difficult situation, such as teenage troubles, new babies or problems in relationships, and provides easily understood advice from authoritative professionals. The *Family Matters* series is designed to provide expert advice to ordinary people struggling with everyday problems and bridges the gap between the professional and client. Each book also offers invaluable help to practitioners as extensions to the advice they can give in sessions, and helps trainees to understand the issues clients face.

Titles in the series:

Living Happily Ever After

Putting Reality into Your Romance

Bob O'Connor

Professor Emeritus,
Licensed Marriage and Family Counsellor

JOHN WILEY & SONS, LTD

Chichester · New York · Weinheim · Brisbane · Singapore · Toronto

Other Wiley Editorial Offices

John Wiley & Sons, Inc., 605 Third Avenue,
New York, NY 10158-0012, USA

WILEY-VCH GmbH, Pappelallee 3,
D-69469 Weinheim, Germany

John Wiley & Sons Australia, Ltd, 33 Park Road, Milton,
Queensland 4064, Australia

John Wiley & Sons (Asia) Pte Ltd, 2 Clementi Loop #02-01,
Jin Xing Distripark, Singapore 129809

John Wiley & Sons (Canada) Ltd, 22 Worcester Road,
Rexdale, Ontario M9W 1L1, Canada

British Library Cataloguing in Publication Data
A catalogue record for this book is available from the British Library

ISBN 0-470-84134-6

Project management by Originator, Gt Yarmouth, Norfolk (typeset in 11.5/13 Imprint)
Printed and bound in Great Britain by Biddles Ltd, Guildford and King's Lynn
This book is printed on acid-free paper responsibly manufactured from sustainable
forestry, in which at least two trees are planted for each one used for paper production.

Contents

About the author

Professor Emeritus Robert O'Connor taught college and university undergraduate and graduate level courses in mental health and marriage and family for 35 years. He has been a licensed Marriage, Family and Child counsellor in California since 1971 and has been a director of councelling centres in both the college and the private sectors. He has authored a number of college textbooks, but this is his first book on relationships for the general public.

To Kelsi Michelle Wells, my first granddaughter, born on the day that the final proofs and corrections were submitted and the book went to press.
May she have all the abilities for loving and caring that her parents have shown to her brother and to each other. And may every reader's child be similarly blessed

Acknowledgements

Thanks first to Dr Vivien Ward, the editor of this series, for her faith and direction throughout the process of writing.

While I had thought of writing a book such as this for some time, it was the interest and stimulation of Oprah Winfrey's program planning and interviews which clarified the need and stimulated the process of beginning it.

The cartoons were done some years ago by George Moran for a college textbook I wrote which was published by Holt, Rinehart & Winston. Many thanks to the publisher for passing the copyright to me.

Helen Ilter was the person doing the leg work for Wiley. Thanks Helen.

Bruce Shuttlewood and all the competent people at Originator Publishing Services who were in charge of copy-editing and typesetting. Thanks for an outstanding job.

Solving the problems you have now

You've probably realised already that living happily ever after is about more than choosing the right person, otherwise you wouldn't have picked up this book. You may know that there are certain things about your relationship or partner that are less than perfect. Or perhaps you just feel less happy than you once did, but don't know why, exactly.

This section (and the section at the start of each chapter) is to help you pick out which bits of the book to read first, such as wanting solutions to problems rather than stopping the problems from happening in the first place. Once you've sorted out the things that are bothering you most, you'll want to read the rest of the book to make sure that the fairy-tale ending you've always wanted, really *is* going to happen.

Chapter 1   Planning for 'happily ever after'
(Have I looked at my complex relationship?)

Read this chapter if:

- You see your relationship changing
- You wonder where your relationship problems may lie
- You want to know the basic ingredients of your relationship
- You wonder if you are getting married for the right reasons
- You haven't thought about the changing nature of your marriage
- You are wondering how to make your relationship better
- You think that your, or your partner's, understanding needs some adjusting
- You are seriously considering marriage

Chapter 2   Am I still in love?
(Have I looked at the realities of loving?)

Read this chapter if:

- You think that love is only a warm feeling in your underwear
- You think you can fall in love at first sight
- You think you love your partner or your child because you tolerate their alcohol or drug abuse
- You think that giving 'quality time' is enough

- You believe your relationship needs more intimacy
- You think you love someone because they are sexually attractive
- You want to know if you really love someone

Chapter 3   In the contract – Who are you?
(Do I really know me?)

Read this chapter if:

- You wonder about the maturity of yourself or your partner
- You wonder about your self-esteem – whether you have it or you want to know how to develop it
- You or your partner are controlling
- You want to clarify your or your partner's values

Chapter 4   Understanding our adjustments
(Do I really understand us?)

Read this chapter if:

- You are interested in why you or your partner need to control the other (in finances or other decisions)
- You or your partner believe you are controlled by fate
- Stress is a factor in your life

- You wonder if your behaviour, or your partner's is normal
- If your behaviour is helping your relationship
- You are feeling depressed

Chapter 5   The psychological contract in marriage
(The obvious and the hidden aspects of our relationships)

Read this chapter if:

- You wonder whether there are things you don't know about your relationship
- You want to get an idea as to why you and your mate don't think alike
- You want to get a glimpse of the deeper aspects of your relationship
- You want to see how you can develop a greater intimacy by sharing unshared thoughts and ideas
- You think a committed relationship is simple and can be easily shared

Chapter 6   What do you want from your relationship
(Are my needs being met?)

Read this chapter if:

- You think your relationship isn't as satisfying as you thought it would be

- You are concerned with the intimacy of your relationship
- You wonder if you are both mature enough for a modern marriage
- You think your mate isn't helping you toward your goals or satisfying your needs
- You are wondering whether you and your mate are on the same wavelengths (take the self-test)
- You wonder where your real interests lie (take the self-test)
- You are contemplating marriage and wonder what the major issues should be

Chapter 7   Understanding the sexual contract

(Have things changed sexually for you?)

Read this chapter if:

- You are having a sex problem
- Your reduction of sexual activity seems to be causing problems
- Your sexual activity has reduced since your marriage
- You don't know why your sexual activity has become less frequent or less fun
- Your sex life needs some spicing up
- You wonder how you and your partner differ in your thinking about sex (take the self-test)

Chapter 8 Biological forces and your sexuality
(What controls and stimulates your body and mind?)

Read this chapter if:

- You wonder why you want more sex
- You wonder why you want less sex
- You wonder why you ejaculate too quickly
- You wonder how to reduce your ejaculation problems
- You wonder what happens chemically in your body when you are touched tenderly
- You wonder why your body chemicals affect your sex life for better or worse
- You wonder what happens in your brain to create your orgasm
- You wonder why your sexual desires fluctuate during your menstrual cycle
- You wonder how smoking reduces your potential to have an orgasm
- Your mate has taken an approach to sexuality which you don't think is normal

Chapter 9 Effective communication
(Why can't I get through to my mate?)

Read this chapter if:

- You think there isn't enough positive communication in your relationship

- You or your mate don't say 'I love you' enough
- You think there is too much negative or controlling communication in your relationship
- You think your relationship needs to get on a more positive track
- If you think something needs to be done to bring your relationship up to what it once was
- You want to re-kindle your romance
- You need to clarify your relationship understandings
- You want to understand how to communicate more clearly and effectively
- You need some help in communicating your concerns
- You want to learn to listen more effectively

Chapter 10   Problem solving with love and respect

(Is there really a way to solve our problems?)

Read this chapter if:

- You want to know how to effectively solve relationship or personal problems
- Your mate irritates you with his or her habits
- You want to explore a new avenue to solving problems
- You want to judge whether your anger with your partner is justified
- You want to know how to make your criticisms more easily understood

Epilogue: Realistic romance

- YES – It's possible to be happy!
- YES – It's possible to love and be loved!
- YES – It's possible to be in a romantic and fulfilling relationship!

Introduction

When a princess kisses a frog and it becomes a prince or when a prince kisses a sleeping princess and she awakes – we expect 'happily ever after'. But that magic kiss isn't always enough.

The glow of romance may keep you going during your engagement and maybe the first year or two of marriage – but then you had better be equals – and equally committed to the relationship. It is a shame that so many people become disillusioned with a relationship which held so much promise. Fairy-tale endings in films make us expect the unrealistic. Hey guys, this ain't Disneyland!

When entering a marriage or a 'live in' relationship you can *hope* for the best OR you can plan and nurture. The second option is far closer to a 'guarantee' of satisfaction. It allows for a firmer commitment because you know the terms of the agreement – your relationship contract. With this in mind, your romance can develop deeper roots in reality.

If you are already married or in a close relationship, you may need some re-direction. All relationships do. So

let's take a deep look into the most complicated relationship yet invented. You think that IBM or AT&T are
complicated? They are nothing compared to the potentials
for joy and the possibilites for problems of a modern
marriage.

Although some people have stated that the death of
the family is fast approaching, Margaret Mead, the
famous anthropologist, believed that the family is 'in
fact, the only institution that doesn't have a hope of dis-
appearing.' The jury is still out deciding the state and
future of marriage. Looking back at our basic needs and
drives, we can easily see why close relationships are essential for most people. (Being alone is good only if you have
chosen it!) We all have needs for emotional security, for
love, and yes! – even for sex. These make it psychologically imperative that most of us pursue close committed
relationships.

As biological and medical science continues to unveil
the essential interactions of our brains and bodies and as
psychology probes deeper into our minds to find out what
makes us 'tick', we discover that we are extremely complicated individuals. When you put two complicated individuals together, you have an even more complicated
relationship. So to understand how to increase our romantic potentials, we should know about our deeper physical
and biological realities. They can help us to bring a more
profound level of contentment and romance into our
relationships.

Did you know that the good feelings of tender touching are caused by a hormone – oxytocin? Did you know
that a reduced desire for sex can be caused by another
hormone – prolactin? Did you know that some of the
factors that cement our bonds or problems that rock our
relationships can be caused by memories or desires from
deep in our unconscious minds.

Whether or not you think that men and women come

from different planets or whether you believe that under-standing some simple communication techniques will bring you closer together – it's not quite that simple.

For those who are interested, let's look at some of the possible problems and joys which can come with marriage and from other types of committed relationships. Each disadvantage of marriage can be countered with an advan-tage. Each detractor of marriage is challenged by a defen-der. We might then surmise that an intimate relationship can be either good or bad, depending on the people in-volved and the type of relationship which they have achieved – and particularly how they have planned for and negotiated in the relationship to make it function well.

Modern egalitarian marriages must acknowledge the dynamic realities of our relationships. Our understandings and our agreements are ever-changing. Our romance is fueled by how we initiate and how we respond to the myriad of opportunities which a close relationship offers. Romance is based on reality!

That's what this book is about.

Planning for 'happily ever after'

Have I looked at my complex relationship?

Read this chapter if:

You see your relationship changing

You wonder where your relationship problems may lie

You want to know the basic ingredients of your relationship

You wonder if you are getting married for the right reasons

You haven't thought about the changing nature of your marriage

You are wondering how to make your relationship better

You think that your, or your partner's, understanding needs some adjusting

You are seriously considering marriage

She asked him how to find the station. He answered 'If I were you, I wouldn't start from here.'

But in life we must start from where we are. Often, our direction is much less clear than our aim to get to the station. In our lives, we must be clear about who we are and where we are going – otherwise we won't know it when we get there!

We must start with the *I, you* and the *us* in the *now*. It is the 'now' that gives us the basis for our futures. When we lay the foundations for our relationships, we don't know just how high and wide the relationship will be. But it can't be any higher and wider than its foundation. Aim high! (Figure 1).

Let's not kid ourselves, the reason that any of us live together is for what it does for us – or, at least, what we think it will do for us. But while the 'me' is the starting

Figure 1   Our reach must exceed our grasp.

point, it is not the ending point in a good relationship. A good relationship will make us happier and will strengthen our ties to that 'significant other' making the 'we' more and more important. A good relationship does not mean that you lose the 'me'. In fact, the 'me' should become stronger and more complete. We therefore have to be conscious of the three parts of any relationship – the *me*, the *you*, and the *us*.

The statistics relating to divorce are scary. With about half of first marriages, 60% of second marriages and 70% of third marriages ending in divorce, we are faced with some sobering negative facts. The chance of either living in an unsatisfying union or ending that relationship in a divorce is well over 50%. On the other hand, the potential for happiness in a well-thought-out union is better today than it has ever been, *IF* the two people are mature and handle their relationship sensibly. So while the chance of failure looms large in our marital futures, our hopes for the ecstasy of a harmonious and blissful relationship can usually be fulfilled if we will but understand the dynamics of the egalitarian marriage which is generally the ideal in today's Western world.

Since a huge majority of people say that marriage and family are very important to them, it is imperative that we understand how to work together in the rapidly changing institution which has been the foundation of our civilisation. Its importance today is even more greatly amplified than at any time in the past, because the extended family of the past (grandparents, parents, aunts, uncles, cousins, along with a number of siblings) is generally giving way to the nuclear family of today – living away from other family members and possibly without children. Psychologically, most of us need a close intimate partner more than anytime before in history. We seem to recognise this, but too often we are not sure of how to participate in an intimate partnership.

Be ready to change for the better

Alvin Toffler, in his book *Future Shock*, said that not only are things changing – but they are changing at an ever faster rate. This idea can certainly be seen not only in how those of us in the Western world see ourselves, but also in what we expect. We have a world of exciting occupations to choose from. We have travel opportunities never dreamed of by our parents. We have unlimited avenues for further education. These are some of the realities which can help to make us better people and which can make our relationships more stimulating and satisfying.

On the other hand, as we leave the farms and small towns for the big cities, as our extended families become smaller and as we feel the frustrations of being more alone in our technological world – we often experience greater psychological needs than did our parents. Our forebears often lived in emotionally secure settings with large numbers of siblings and friends to nourish their souls. This setting, said psychologist Erich Fromm, gave those people a feeling of being loved. But our near social isolation today, according to Fromm, makes us feel alone – and being alone is a major cause of unhappiness and mental illness.

Today's adults have often chosen the excitement of modern city life, rather than the serenity of the past. Nevertheless, just as in bygone days, our emotional needs must still be met – and we usually expect that our marriage will fill that void. However, today, a deeply satisfying relationship in a marriage is more difficult to achieve than it was in the past, because we expect so much more from that age-old institution.

But a deeply satisfying and growth nurturing relationship is not only possible, it is probable – if we approach it with intelligence. Relationships today have far more potential because we have knowledge of how relationships work and we have more recreational time to enjoy our friendship. This is the reason for intelligently planning for that relationship, rather than hoping that the brothers Grimm will write our storybook ending.

Planning is the key

When you are developing a long-term relationship you shouldn't go in blind – yet most people do (Figure 2). While couples generally know what kind of movies they like, their favourite foods and some general life goals –

Figure 2   Life is what happens to us while we are making other plans.

there is much more to developing a mature permanent relationship. This holds true just as much for people who decide to live together, without the benefit of marriage, as it does for those taking the more serious step in matrimony. Whether homosexual or heterosexual, young or old, previously married or not – there are goals to achieve, issues to negotiate and compromises to make.

We have expectations in many areas of the relationship. Intimacy, friendship, sexual fulfilment, economic needs, the possibility of parenthood and the self-actualisation of education, career and travel. Many of our expectations are clear to us. Some are muddled. And some are not yet known at all because we have not thought about them or we can't think about them because they are deep inside our unconscious minds.

We are obviously not robots. We are thinking, feeling, human, beings. We are continuously changing – both biologically and psychologically. Our relationships are changing and our world is changing. The bonds of traditional culture are rapidly being loosened. So we must prepare to fly with the freedom now possible.

You may remember American president Abraham Lincoln's favourite story. An ancient emperor of China asked his wise men to tell him something which would always be true. One said 'Our country will always be the greatest in the world'. The emperor could not be certain of the veracity of that hope. Another said 'The sun will always rise in the east'. But the emperor was not certain that this would be eternally true. A third said 'And this too shall pass away.' 'That,' said the fascinated emperor, 'must always be true.'

We all know that our world is changing – far faster than any time in history. We may be able to adjust to computers and the Internet, to interplanetary exploration and to heart transplants, but we often can't see that these rapid changes are affecting our relationships.

Finding our way in the relationship maze

Let's fly to Tahiti.

I need a vacation house. I feel too cooped up here all the time.

Our son is addicted to crack cocaine.

Both desires and problems which were unthinkable 50 years ago now are often commonplace (Figure 3). As science affects our lives, intelligent changes are often made. For example, the science of nutrition is doubling its knowledge every three years. Are you still eating the way you did when you were growing up, or are you reducing animal fats, eating more fish and pasta and supplementing your diet with antioxidants? Science is showing us better ways to live. Whether it is our nutrition, our careers or our relationships – science often gives us a better option to choose.

Figure 3 Much happiness is overlooked because it doesn't cost anything.

The changes in our world are affecting our relationships – sometimes for the worse, but often for the better. We are having fewer children. We are seeking more fulfilling careers. We are increasing and satisfying our material desires. And often we are returning to a spiritual life which had been abandoned by the 'me' generation of the 1960s and 1970s.

Our rapidly changing ideas of relationships demands a continual rethinking of our goals, needs and values. This requires more fundamental communication on relationship issues to keep our intimacy growing and our partnerships moving positively. Today, more than ever before, knowledge exists to allow us to increase the positive aspects of our marriages and to reduce or eliminate the negatives. Theorists in psychology and in marriage counselling are giving us specific ways to make our relationships more dynamic and fulfilling. Are you ready to use them?

There are several critical areas in making a relationship work better:

1   We must be mature individuals – not self-centred, insecure, emotional skeletons.

2   We must understand who we are and what we must have as well as what we are willing to give up in order to have an ideal partnership.

3   We must understand that our partner is not exactly the same as we are in terms of needs, values and the ability to communicate – and that our partner's desires should be on an equal footing with our own.

4   We must understand the methods of effective communication and understanding. Men and women generally see things differently. You and your partner won't always have the same views of what communication is all about.

5 We must understand that our relationships are a series of negotiations and contracts and that our needs and those of our partner may be found in our unconscious as well as our conscious minds.

6 The relationship must be of primary importance. A purely selfish person cannot be a part of an effective partnership – a partnership based on what we call 'commitment'.

7 We should understand what 'love' means in terms of how we develop our relationship.

8 We should not begin a long-term relationship with major issues unresolved.

Each of these critical areas will be examined in detail to assist you in understanding our modern relationship workings – and potentials. There has never been as much need for effective relationships as there is today. And there has never been as much potential for fantastically fulfilling relationships as we have in our middle-class Western World. Let's take advantage of our opportunities.

Just getting married is not the answer

For whatever reason, a large number of people just want to be married. Marriage is a status symbol. *At least somebody wants me!* Because of this overriding desire we often go into marriage blind. If merely being married is more important than having an ideal relationship, then we get what we deserve. Just check the divorce courts to see how many of the people who got married did not have a relationship.

The United States has the highest marriage rate of any industrialised society. Not all countries have the same attitude towards marriage. The 'romantic' French and the 'sensual' Italians marry at only half of the US rate. And Scandinavians are much more likely to live together without the marriage ceremony. In Norway only 50% of couples under 35 who live together are officially married. But by age 50 only about 5% are unmarried.

While in agricultural countries, such as India, marriage is an economic asset, in the more developed countries marriage is not essential for our economic survival. In Scandinavia, for example, marriage is not economically required. Most men and most women have jobs, whether they are single or married. Living together, unmarried in a truly egalitarian relationship, is much more common. Marriage is a far more solemn commitment, usually made when parenthood is planned or imminent, or after the relationship has evolved into a deeply satisfying bond.

Also, in the Scandinavian countries, equality of the sexes is more of a fact of life than it is in other countries where the ideal of gender equality is talked about but seldom acted upon. Just count the number of women in the British, Italian, American or French national legislative bodies, then count those in the similar bodies in Norway or Sweden. In Scandinavia, you are more likely to find 40–50% of the legislators being women. A figure of 10% would be quite high in most other countries.

Life is a series of contracts

For better or worse, for richer or poorer, in sickness or in health, 'til death do us part.

That's a contract. It is a verbal contract which could be just as valid as a written one. That's why you have witnesses to your promise at your marriage ceremony. However, lawyers doubt the legality of the terms of this traditional contract because they are so vague and their terms last until death. So, if that marriage contract were ever tested in court, it would probably be tossed out as unenforceable. A binding contract must be more specific – and it must be fair.

Part of our marriage contract is emotional, part is about unselfishly loving, part is about values, some of it is conscious but some of it is unconscious – we don't consciously know what we want because it is deep in our unconscious mind. We will discuss these ideas as the book unfolds.

In legal terms, contracts can be 'expressed' or 'implied'. An expressed contract could be written, as when buying a house, or can be verbal, as the traditional verbal contract in a marriage ceremony. Another type of verbal contract could be a promise between the two people to act in a certain way. But this isn't necessarily 'legal' if other people were not there to hear the promise being made.

The 'implied' contract is symbolised by our actions. When a couple has had sex every day for two years before the marriage ceremony, there is an implied contract to continue that level of sexual activity. If one of the partners reduces the level of activity, there is a breach of the implied contract.

Of course, the implied contract can be verbally amended. 'I have a headache' may allow for a break in the sexual activity until the headache is over. But sometimes that *headache* occurs over and over again, just when the other partner wants to play sex games.

Another implied contractual term might be that the partners had dinner at a restaurant every week prior to getting married. It might continue into the marriage or it might be changed. The *dinner every week* contract might be amended because the couple decides to save for a house or to have the money necessary to have a child. They would therefore reduce the frequency of their restaurant outings.

We all operate under a number of contracts. At work, we may be protected by a collective bargaining contract between our union and our employer. When driving your car, you operate under a contract with the government. If you violate the contract you may pay a fine, have your licence taken away or spend time in jail. When you borrow to buy a house, you promise to pay the money back to the bank or the bank can repossess the house.

It would seem that, in a relationship as intimate and long term as a marriage is expected to be, the couple would insist on a written contract which would cover many of the situations which we are quite sure will occur. But the romantic ideas which accompany a marriage usually make each person believe that life will just get better and better *because* they have participated in a marriage ceremony. Based on our knowledge, this is a highly fanciful idea.

If you are married now, you have a contract. It tells what reasons can be used to end your marriage, the financial consequences of a break-up, and it will indicate what the state considers to be the most important considerations in determining child custody.

One misunderstanding about the marriage contract is that, while the couple is usually looking for a deep friendship and usually a sexual relationship the government usually sees the marriage almost totally in terms of a financial agreement. The contract terms expressed at the wedding ceremony – that we will love and cherish each other for ever – doesn't mention what the relationship means in terms of money and property. Perhaps, to be more honest, we should add a sentence or two after 'until death do us part' and add the financial terms of the contract. So if your government has decided that your incomes are community property, the financial terms might be 'and half of all you earn once you are married belongs to your spouse.' With the exception of lawyers (solicitors) and judges, most of us don't have a clue as to what is really included in the unspoken and unwritten terms of our contracts.

We may understand the basic reasons for being able to divorce. For example, in the UK, you should be able to obtain a divorce if: your partner is adulterous, your partner has exhibited unreasonable behaviour (such as cruelty), you were deserted at least two years ago or have been separated for at least two years and your partner also wants a divorce, or you have been separated for at least five years (even if your partner did not want a divorce.) A number of years ago, in California, the grounds were: adultery, mental or physical cruelty, insanity or abandonment. As in the UK, these charges had to be proven and guilt shown. In 1960, it was simplified to be merely 'irreconcilable differences' in which guilt is not a factor. So, while in some jurisdictions a person must prove that the spouse did something legally wrong, in other places it is enough to say 'I've had enough.' Once that happens, the court can grant a divorce.

Every relationship is a contract

Not only every marriage, but every relationship, is a contract. Friends can break up their long-term relationships. One of my clients was stunned when his best friend of nearly 60 years broke up their friendship after my client's divorce. Although the friend was not particularly close to my client's ex-wife, he sided with her on the divorce and decided to end the friendship.

We enter every relationship with expectations as to what we will give and what we will get. Often, we change our expectations. If the other person in the relationship does not change, the friendship may be weakened or broken. For example, if I am a teenager moving into a new area and am accepted by a group of people who use alcohol or other drugs, I will use the drugs if I want these people to be my friends. If, later on, I find that the drugs were a negative influence on me, perhaps I have gone to jail or have failed my classes, I can either ask others in the group to give up their drug use or I can leave the group.

Even parenthood is somewhat of a contract. In some cases, children can 'divorce' their parents when the parents don't fulfil what is expected of them. You may remember a few years ago that Gregory Kingsley, a 12-year-old in Florida, divorced his natural parents because they had mistreated him and abandoned him. Some governments have allowed older children, usually 14 to 16, to get a legal separation from their parents and become 'emancipated minors'.

It goes without saying that adults living together should have clear understandings about their expectations and their responsibilities in any 'live in' situation, whether married or unmarried, heterosexual or homosexual. In adult relationships, there is nearly always a financial assumption on which the relationship is based. There is also a friendship foundation. Quite often, these come into conflict. That is why every live-in relationship should have a written contract. It is quite common for both married and unmarried couples to argue about things at their break-up which they had thought to be settled by verbal agreements, or unsaid understandings, earlier in the relationship:

We should split everything equally.

But most of it was bought with my money.

I bought the BMW with my money.

But both of our names are on the title.

I want to keep the condo.

But I found it and put up the down payment.

One unwed couple spent over £25,000 in solicitor fees and court costs settling these questions which could have been settled prior to and during the relationship without any costs at all. Some celebrities have spent hundreds of thousands of pounds in settling the financial arguments which result at their break-up. And, of course, divorce costs for married couples have occasionally topped the hundred thousand pound level – even though their 'contract' is written in the laws of their government.

The point is that, if there is any possibility that financial concerns may enter into your relationship at any time in the future, there should be a written understanding and agreement. But far more than finances, there are other areas within your intimate contract which must be clarified. What you really want, what are willing to give, how you will talk to each other, as well as the day-to-day issues of in-laws, sex, spending money, household chores and child raising are all part of the contract which will develop as your friendship matures. All of these concerns, and more, will probably enter your alliance. How you handle them will determine whether your relationship weakens or strengthens.

Yes, you can make your relationship better

It has been said that marriage is like eating a mushroom – you never know until it's too late. In actuality, because the relationship contract is not written in stone, it can be continually amended, as long as the parties to the contract agree to the changes.

This is what marriage counselling is all about. Too bad it usually isn't resorted to until the problems are large and the contract needs massive changes.

It would make so much more sense to discuss important issues and agree, or agree to disagree, before 'tying the knot'. It is appalling how few people really discuss and plan for their futures. According to the professional journal *Family Relations* (January 1996, **45**(1), 80) only 30% of married couples have even one or two hours of formal preparation for their marriage. That is not nearly enough!

As we move through this book, you will be aided with some 'do it yourself' methods to develop and to change your relationship contract, if it needs to be amended. Solve the little problems as they occur, then you won't need massive surgery to save a nearly dead relationship. If we are to live intelligently, we must be concerned with the future – because that's where we're going to spend the rest of our lives.

A few hundred years ago, the English writer Samuel Johnson mused that the reason people re-marry is 'the triumph of hope over experience'. We do much more hoping and romantic dreaming than we do analysing and planning. That's not so difficult to understand, when we are courting. The enjoyment of 'kissing the face and hugging the body' during courtship is certainly

Figure 4 'He that will not look forward must look behind'
(Irish proverb).

less challenging and more fun than looking at the realities
of a relationship. But intelligent people will understand
that if there is a future for the relationship – it must be
planned for. As the Irish proverb goes 'He that will not
look forward must look behind' (Figure 4).

In relationships, such as marriage, the contract provisions are generally not so clearly spelled out. Some people
have developed written contracts before marriage – a pre-
nuptial agreement. In the past, these have generally been
used entirely to settle questions on the financial side of the
relationship:

My kids get my money and your kids get yours.

*If we get a divorce you get $10,000 a year for
every year we were married but none of the other
money earned will be community property.*

Without such pre-arrangements your marriage is subject
to the contract which your government, and particularly
the judges, have determined to be the law for you. Various
governments and judges take quite different approaches
to what is fair in settling the financial aspects relating to
ending a marriage. Quite possibly, your judge will not

agree with you on what is fair! In spite of the laws, judges have their prejudices. Some years ago, in the San Fernando Valley area of Los Angeles, there were two divorce judges. Both were Jewish, one was a man and one a woman. The woman was actually pro-man. She felt that women needed to get out and go to school and work after a divorce. The male judge was pro-woman. As a good Jewish boy, he knew that mothers could do no wrong. The local attorneys knew that she got the odd-numbered cases and he got the even-numbered cases. If they represented a man in a divorce they would wait until they knew their case would be odd numbered. It might take hours of standing in the filing line to wait for the correct number – but it came close to guaranteeing a favourable verdict.

Contracts for marriage are not new

In Babylonian times, nearly 4,000 years ago, contracts were used to set the value of a bride. Some 500 years ago, Queen Elizabeth had her wedding plans collapse after a disagreement with her betrothed. He wanted to be crowned King of England right after the wedding. These historical situations dealt with both money and power. These are still the major factors, but not the only factors, in the stresses and discussions of living together.

When I recently told Berit As, perhaps Norway's most prominent social psychologist, that I was writing a book on marriage and contracting, she was amazed. When she was married, 46 years ago, she and her husband worked out a marriage contract. But then the Scandinavians have always been ahead of the rest of the world in the area of gender equality.

The well-thought-out-agreement – before and during the relationship

Everyone getting into a partnership should have a clear understanding of what is expected and what is to be given. The more permanent the partnership is expected to be, the more the discussion is critical. If you just met someone and want to go to a movie together, you don't need their opinions on child raising or the status of their finances. But if you are getting married, especially a second time and have children, you had better do some serious thinking and talking. If both of you are in competitive careers, where late nights at the office or extensive travelling are a part of your lives, you had better talk about it. The realities are that every marriage and live-in relationship is both a business and a friendship partnership. Agreements are understood. But do you both understand what is supposed to be understood?

A major problem in marriage is that the couple doesn't understand what the terms of their contract are. They may have decided that they don't want any children and that they will pursue their own careers. (A verbal contract.) But perhaps he expects his wife to make dinner for him whenever he comes home, just like his mother did. (This is an expectation, but not a contract, because she had not agreed.) She may expect him to play tennis with her at least once a week because he had done that when they were dating and engaged. (This is an implied contract assuming that what has gone on before will continue.)

Many misunderstandings occur because what one person expected to happen after the marriage has stopped happening or never did happen once the marriage took place. The couple may have discussed their future

education and careers, whether or when they would like
children, and where they would like to live. But they may
not have even thought about: whether they will shop or
cook together, how their incomes will be handled
(separate or joint bank accounts), what are the household
cleaning expectations and duties, or when they would be
able to see their individual friends without the spouse
accompanying.

It goes without saying that the contract for a 'live-in'
partnership or a marriage is a bit more complicated than a
contract for buying a car. The potentials and the problems
or relationships go far beyond just choosing a model and a
colour!

A former client signed a post-nuptial agreement a few
years into the marriage. She agreed that she would get
$5,000 for each year that she had been married up to
five years. After five years she would be entitled to the
full community property laws of the state and share 50%
of the profits which her husband's multi-million dollar
bakery brought in. She signed. He divorced her four
months before the five-year period had elapsed. She had
changed her religion. Part of the implied contract of their
marriage was that she would stay in the same religion in
which he was an active member. That aspect of 'the contract' had never been discussed – but it ended the marriage and left her with few financial resources.

Two lawyers of my acquaintance were quite afraid of
the consequences of a divorce. Being realists, who handled
both contract problems and divorces in their law prac-
tices, they decided to make a very specific contract.

• He would do the shopping and cooking on Mondays,
  Wednesdays and Fridays and she would do the dishes.
  On Tuesdays, Thursdays and Sundays the roles
  would be reversed. On Saturdays they would dine out.

- On the first weekend of their marriage he would clean the kitchen and bathroom. She would clean the living room and bedroom. These jobs would alternate each week.
- They would take three weeks of vacation. He would choose the first. She would choose the second. If they couldn't agree on a third week they would take separate vacations during the third week.

Friends said that it wouldn't work, but before long they were helping each other with the shopping, cooking and dish washing. They helped each other with the cleaning. And they had no vacation problems. By laying out the ground rules for the relationship relating to what each expected there were fewer surprises.

Another set of lawyers in Berkeley, California have lived together, without being married, for over 20 years. They also have a written agreement on their rights and obligations throughout the relationship.

Several years ago, two female legislators in the USA attempted to get a law passed which would require couples contemplating marriage in their state to address the problems which they knew would come up and draw up a marriage contract. Problems to be discussed could include:

- Who does what housework?
- Who does the shopping and cooking?
- If and when should we have children?

The male legislators refused the idea, saying that it would 'take all of the romance out of marriage.' What those men didn't seem to see was that women have traditionally done the housework, even if they have full-time jobs. Men have been content to take out the garbage, wash the car and make some repairs around the house. This unequal sharing of household and parenting duties grates on most women who hold full-time jobs. And the men wonder why. After all, housework is women's work! (Even in egalitarian Norway, working women do twice the amount of work in the home as the men.) Some wives don't seem to understand that their Saturday cleaning and shopping chores are not really as difficult as her husband's Saturday job – of walking around the golf course and hoisting a few beers afterwards at the 19th hole, or the stress and strain he endures having to watch TV sports for most of the weekend.

Only a few people have so far designed specific pre-nuptial contracts which look at many of the realities which face a relationship. Rex and Theresa LeGalley of Albu-querque, New Mexico developed a pre-marital contract a few years ago. Rex, twice married, and Theresa divorced once, realised the importance of having an understanding before going into the marriage. In their 16-page contract, which has been filed with the court, are such agreements as:

- we will have healthy sex three to five times a week;
- nothing will be left on the floor overnight;
- we will buy only Chevron unleaded fuel for the cars;
- when the fuel gauge shows 'half full' the driver will fill up the tank;
- Theresa will be responsible for the inside of the house; and
- Rex for repairs and for outside cleaning including the garage and the cars.

The fact that it's easier to get a marriage licence than a driver's licence is probably the reason that we have more divorces than deaths in traffic accidents. Since the government doesn't seem very concerned about our understanding the dynamics of our marriages, perhaps we need to take it upon ourselves to understand and control as many of the elements of our marriage contract as possible.

The fact is that pre-nuptial agreements are becoming more prevalent – especially in situations in which a family business is involved or in second marriages where children are involved. These financial situations are obvious. Understanding the terms of your relationship will prevent many problems later. Whether you want to put the agreements in writing or not, they should be discussed. But writing them down gives you a record to which to refer. It makes logical sense. The problem is that we are generally not logical. Sadly, most of us human beings are romantic dreamers – not romantic realists.

So let's take a look at some of the major and minor problems of relationships and see what can be done about them. We will look a little deeper into the implied contracts which often develop and how they can be more effectively understood and agreed to. We must be able to clearly see the potentials and the problems, and to find agreement on at least some of them so that our relationships can become more positive.

Unless you have been through a marriage or two, you may not realise that things may change after the wedding ceremony. It is not uncommon for newlyweds to continue to 'date' for a year or so, but eventually some hard decisions will have to be made. It is impossible to go through a 30–50-year marriage without having a few problems come up:

- Should we have another child?
- Should I take a better job a thousand miles away from our friends and family?
- How do we get our drug-dependent daughter into treatment?

These are not uncommon problems faced in a marriage – but they are *not* the kinds of situation you are likely to encounter, or discuss, while dating.

But there are deeper needs and drives, and there may be unspoken values which will become a major part of your relationship. We need to look at these, also. The foundations of our relationship are well below the conscious levels of our thinking. They are there and they are often controlling our behaviour. To understand the dynamics of a relationship, these also must be explored.

Many people are afraid that the honest exploring of issues will break up the relationship. If that is the stuff from which the relationship is made, it doesn't have much hope anyway. A committed relationship, if it is to be effective, must be able to face the issues and to fairly work out compromises. Such communication and negotiation is a major ingredient of real intimacy and trust.

Fairy-tale endings may happen in Gothic novels and in Disney's films – but we live in the real world. It is therefore better to look forward to a relationship which has been based on understanding, intelligence and faith than to have to look back with sorrow. Sorrow in the way the marriage has evolved or sorrow in the fact of the divorce. Show your concern before the marriage, learn to communicate on the tough issues as well as the exciting goals, then the future has a much better chance of being rosy because it was intelligently planned for. Base your romance on reality.

Marriage is a partnership for *living*. You must therefore look at all of the issues involved in 'living' in order to have the best chance for success. People generally ignore the realities or make poor decisions by not discussing the real issues because they are overconfident in their hope of marital success. Or, possibly their short-term goal of 'being married' is more important to them than the long-term goal of developing the abilities to handle the real communication of the issues as they arise. Intelligent people will choose the more difficult but more rewarding approach.

Whether you are already happily married, are married and having some problems, or are going into a marriage, you must understand the basics of such an intimate relationship. You must understand that the relationship is a dynamic entity. Every success or failure of one of the people in that relationship changes the relationship – for better or worse. Each year of marriage changes it – for better or worse. Each child affects it – for better or worse. Every career move, every educational achievement and every recreational hour changes it – for better or worse. By understanding the dynamics of our relationships, we can better develop our relationships into sources of joy and love.

What are the areas which generally need understanding – and possibly negotiation?

We are most likely to need common understandings in these areas:

- Our personalities, our needs and wants which are specific to us need to be accepted by our partner.
- We must be able to love in an unselfish way, helping our partner to be the best that he or she can be.
- We need a common understanding as to what our particular marriage should entail. No two relationships are the same.
- Most modern marriages should be based on a relationship of equals.

- We must be able to share both positive and negative feelings with healthy and effective communication.
- We must be able to accept or solve the problems which confront us – either by ourselves or with the help of others who are trained in the area of solving marital problems.
- The financial area is a major concern in most marriages, how we will spend or save the available money is a critical area for understanding and action.
- Household responsibilities are a major issue in two-income families.
- Which leisure-time activities will we share?
- What is a satisfactory sexual relationship for each of us?
- How do family and friends fit into our lives and our relationship?
- Will religion play a part in our lives, and if so how important will it be?
- If we choose to have children, how will we raise them?

Many of these will be discussed in the following chapters. You can then take what you want and discuss the areas of common concern in developing your understandings for your relationship. There is no question that a strong, dynamic and happy relationship can occur. But it doesn't just happen. *Happily ever after* really does take more than just kissing a sleeping princess – or a frog.

If we don't do it, will the government require us to develop contractual agreements?

With the great increase in divorce rates since the 1950s and the accompanying result of children living with only

one parent, often in poverty, the government will probably eventually step in and require people to seriously
think about what their marriages mean. Marriage will be
a bit more difficult to enter, but the chances of divorce for
that marriage will be greatly reduced. At the same time,
the issues of divorce will be largely answered at the time of
the marriage. When the financial issues are addressed
before the marriage, there will be less need for the fights
in the divorce courts. When the determination is made to
have or not to have children, that issue will become less of
an issue as the time for parenthood approaches.

When the issues, which experts know are important,
are discussed and agreed to before the marriage, many of
the issues which have continually been found to cause
break-ups will be brought to the surface. Some legisla-
tures in the USA already require those under the allow-
able marriage age to have some counselling. That
requirement could certainly be extended to all adults.
We already have to obtain driver's licences, dog licences
and permits to build a fence around our yard. Each of
these is probably a bit less important than making prospective lifetime mates be aware of the realities of their
lifetime commitment.

Prior to the time that the government forces us
to think through the issues of marriage or other live-in
relationships, we should have the maturity to do it
ourselves. Now, let's take a look at some of the critical
issues involved in any close relationship.

As we wind our way through the concepts in this
book, we will continually encounter four principles
which we MUST understand if we are to choose a
partner wisely:

1 All of us have both conscious and sub-conscious needs
and values.

2 The need to show 'power' and control is nearly universal. It is probably the major psychological drive in most people – and it keeps showing up in our relationships.

3 The higher psychological accomplishment is found in those who can actually 'love'.

4 In every area related to gender differences and relationships, there is a continuum of feelings, needs, desires and abilities. These may be genetically influenced or socially ingrained.

If we were to take a continuum of men on one line and a continuum of women on another, we would find some women both far above and far below the average man. The same would be true for men, if we compared them with the average woman. So while men, on the average, may have more sex drive than the average woman, many women are far above the average man. Whether we look at height, strength, running speed, interest in football or sexual desire – many women are far above the average man. Similarly, if we look at the average woman's superior ability to communicate, to show her emotions, to express tenderness or even to 'shop' – many men rate much higher than the average woman. While most men may be from Mars and most women from Venus, there are women from Mars and men from Venus. In every trait and need, we will find people of both sexes along the continuum from 0 to 100.

While it is often the differences that attract potential mates, the similarities of our places on the various continua of personality abilities and traits may reduce our potential problems and make them more solvable, if they do occur. This is particularly true in terms of our desires and abilities to be close or distant, intimate or private, spontaneous or reserved, communicative or stand-offish, aggressive or passive.

My favourite old professor said that 'If you don't know everything you don't know anything.' When we look deeper at what and why we believe, we will often be looking at unconscious motivations – both our own and those of our partner. The unconscious parts of our minds will never be totally known to us, but, because of a hundred years of psychological studies, we are getting a glimpse of some elements which are quite important in how we behave. When we try to understand ourselves and our partners, we will often be more realistic if we can see the reasons behind the reasons. Why does he want to control the purse strings? Why does she want a baby? Why does he avoid housework? Why does she want a fulfilling occupation?

Conclusion

Committed relationships today are the most complicated in history. Yet, our need for a committed relationship is greater today than at any time in history. Every committed relationship needs agreements and understandings. Planning and sharing together is the best guarantee of continuing the romance which began with that first kiss.

Box 1   Some divorce statistics

From the *United Nations Demographic Yearbook*
(1993–last year available):

United Kingdom

	Number of marriages per 1,000 people of marriage age	Average age at marriage		Divorces per 1,000 marriages
		Male	*Female*	
1950	166.4	22.8	20.3	10.3
1975	118.5	23.5	21.1	20.3
1992	88.2	26.5	24.4	21.2

Statistics from various sources for 1996

	Divorce rate per 1,000 people	Divorces as a % of marriages
UK	3.08	53
USA	4.95	49
New Zealand	2.63	—
Australia	2.52	—
Italy	0.27	12
Norway		43
Sweden		64
Belarus		68

Am I still in love?

Have I looked at the realities of loving?

What is this Thing Called Love?
Love is a Many Splendored Thing.
Love Makes the World Go Round.
All is Fair in Love.

Song titles

Read this chapter if:

You think that love is only a warm feeling in your underwear

Your think you can fall in love at first sight

You think you love your partner or your child because you tolerate their alcohol or drug abuse

You think that giving 'quality time' is enough

You believe your relationship needs more intimacy

You think you love someone because they are sexually attractive

You want to know if you really love someone

Western society has an obsession with the idea of love.
When the King of England gave up his throne for the
love of a divorcee, the British were aghast, but the
world was enraptured. When Prince Akihito, son of the
Emperor of Japan married a commoner, the Japanese
were embarrassed, but the world was joyous. When, in
the days of the Iron Curtain, the Olympic champion in
the women's javelin from Czechoslovakia fell in love with
the US Olympic champion in the men's hammer throw,
she was allowed to marry and move to America –
apparently love can be more powerful than politics!

The ballads of the medieval minstrels stirred passionate desires with the ideas of romantic love among the
knights and ladies. The *Kama Sutra* graphically desribed
the love-making techniques of the ancient Hindus. Drs
Masters and Johnson have utilised the method of
science to learn more about the most effective techniques
of love-making. We find love as the central theme of the
arts, music and the theatre. Love is the cause of our birth
and the goal of our life. But what is this thing called love?

Let's first dispel the notion that people marry for love.
They don't. They marry for infatuation and 'what can you
do for me.' Jeanne Moreau, France's leading actress, said
that 'love is just the desire to take hold of somebody – it is
possessiveness.' While this is too often true, there is such a
thing as love and it can and often does find its way into
relationships.

But what is love? Can it be defined? When we say, 'I
love steak', or 'I love my wife', or 'I love my country', do
we mean the same thing? There seems to be a great confusion in our society regarding the true definition of love.
We 'make love' when we have sexual intercourse. We 'fall
in love' when we have an immediate, strong attraction to a
particular person. We 'love' ice cream because it tastes
good; and often we equate love with lust.

Many of us are so intellectually lazy that we often use

a word without precise meanings. Its real definition then becomes more and more obscured. Probably, no word is more often misused than the word 'love'. Like the other four-letter words we use, it is often misunderstood:

- I love apple pie.
- I love Tom Cruise.
- I love my wife.

The first statement means 'I enjoy apple pie'. The second may mean 'I idolise Tom Cruise' or 'I think he is a good actor'. The third may mean 'I want my wife for what she does for me'. It might also mean 'I want to help my wife develop to her fullest potential'.

Most people have some fuzzy idea of what human love is. This idea usually relates to some romantic notions developed from an exposure to the fantasies of fiction in literature and other expressive media. Psychologists have recently separated the real roots of love from the images romance writers usually associated with it. It is, therefore, now possible to more precisely define love, it is also possible to see the essential relationships between real love and mental health.

It is often difficult, if not impossible, to comprehend an idea or an emotion, if we have not experienced it. If we have not been loved as a small child, or have not been involved in a real love relationship, such as a mature husband–wife or parent–child relationship, it may be somewhat difficult to relate to the ideas developed in this chapter.

The idea of love can be based primarily on the knowledge of science, but it is tempered by insights and speculations of philosophers, religious thinkers and poets. What will be examined is the definable, solid aspects of a love relationship and separate them from the romantic feelings which so often cloud our minds. Hopefully, that most misused four-letter word, **l-o-v-e**, can be defined ... or, at least, made clearer.

What is love?

Ashley Montagu, writing for the *Encyclopedia of Mental Health* (New Year 1963, **3**, 950) has attempted to solve this enigma with his definition that:

> *Love is the communication to another person of one's deep involvement in that person's welfare, of one's profound interest in him as a person, demonstrated by acts that support, stimulate, and contribute to the realization of that person's personality and its fulfilment.*

With this definition in mind, he then echoes Freud's idea that, 'Mental health is the ability to love and the ability to work.' This is exactly what modern politicians are asking of their countries' citizens, today. All our recent national leaders have been very clear in their desire that people should take responsibility for their own lives and that they should work to improve the lives of others in their communities.

We can better understand what Montagu meant by breaking down the definition into its component parts: 'Love is the communication to another person.' How *do* we communicate? If I say 'I love you, baby.' to a newly born infant, the idea would vary according to the tone of my voice. If I coo it softly, the baby will receive a positive message; if I snarl it sharply, the baby will receive a negative message. So, it is not only the actual words spoken that reveal the message, but also the tone of the voice used and my body language.

There is evidence that non-verbal communication may account for as much as 90% of all communication. Communicating love non-verbally may be shown in hugging, pleasant facial expressions, various kinds of touching, or in actions which are not seen, but whose effects are experienced – a wife surprising her husband with a batch of his favourite cookies, or a father buying a book for his child. Even certain negative experiences, such as a child's spanking, may show a positive love effect to the child.

The person who 'loves' must communicate a concern for, and an interest in, the persons he or she loves. And that communication should be in the form of actions that help the loved ones to achieve their fullest potentials. It is easier to illustrate loving actions from adults towards children than between adults – but that is also possible. Let's begin by looking at adults and some things they might do which are loving – or which appear to be loving, but are not.

I remember a sixth-grade classmate, Marvin, whose grandmother used to hold his hand as she walked him to school. She would meet him before lunch and walk him home, then back to school with him after lunch. After school, the same ritual took place. Grandma's overprotection of poor Marvin was bad enough, but the fact that he lived only three houses from the school compounded grandma's overzealous actions. While she was certainly concerned with him, her actions were not actions of love. The truly loving person would have seen to it that Marvin walked home by himself, for there comes a time in every young person's life when independence must be realised. The truly loving person will see to it that children begin to exercise their independence at the right time.

Adults often cannot actually love because their inferiority complexes and power drives get in the way. Real love between adults is shown where each person helps the other to be the best that he or she can be. It means helping them to fulfil worthwhile goals, helping them to eliminate harmful habits, saying things which make them feel good and making them feel worthwhile. But love is not so much what you *say*, but rather what you *do*. How often have we said, 'I love you', when we really meant, 'I want you'. Our basic selfishness must be overcome before we can be a real 'lover'.

Other definitions of love

One of the problems encountered in defining love is that it is sometimes defined in terms of marriage love and sometimes in terms of the generalised ability to love. A typical definition of 'marriage-type love' is found in Alexander Magoun's classic book *Love and Marriage* (Harper & Row, New York, 1956):

> *Love is the passionate and abiding desire on the part of two or more people to produce together the conditions under which each can spontaneously express his real self; to produce together an intellectual soil and an emotional climate in which each can flourish (that is) far superior to what either could achieve alone. (Figure 5)*

Frank Hoffer defined love as involving an integration of personalities with a:

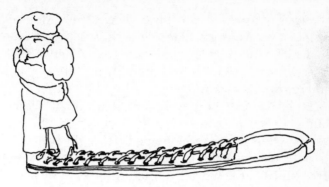

Figure 5 Love is not blind. A person who loves sees the loved one's faults and shortcomings but cares anyway.

passionate interest in the other's ideas, hopes, and aspirations; interchange of thought; respect for the other's dignity and worth. The physical relationship is assumed to possess the greatest degree of intimacy. While this in one sense may be true, I wish to stress that the ultimate in intimacy may occur in a congenial conversation, looking at a sunset together, partaking of a meal. The sense of intimacy does not arise from mere physical contact. It is mental rather than physical.

This definition also implies an 'adult' relationship.

A brief definition of love, not necessarily applicable only to adult humans, was offered by Dr Harry Overstreet:

The love of a person does not imply the possession of that person. It means granting him or her, gladly, the full right of unique humanhood. One does not truly love yet seek to enslave by bonds of dependence or possessiveness.

Overstreet expressed the same generalised idea of love developed by Montagu. Here it is the quality of relationship which can be found and recognised between a man and a woman, an adult and a child, or between persons who are friends or strangers.

Here we see the psychological intimacy which can occur between persons. It may be the Good Samaritan, who knew not the man he helped. It might be a husband and wife team working together such as the scientists, Pierre and Marie Curie or the authors, Will and Ariel Durant. It might be a teacher with a student, a nurse with a patient, a parent with a child. In any case, it is a feeling of involvement, helping the other person to become the best that he or she can be. It is a psychological intimacy between people. Here we find, in the understandable terms of science, those feelings and ideals which poets and prophets have expressed for so many centuries.

The kinds of love

There have been many words and meanings from other cultures that have been translated into the English word 'love'.

Romantic love

The words *eros* (Greek) and *cupido* (Latin) originally meant a sentimental attachment between people. 'Love' can also mean desire (*libido* in Freudian terms). The gods of love, Eros and Cupid, were sources for these ideas of love. Our word, erotic, stems from Eros, and we all know about Cupid shooting his magic arrows to bind the hearts of passionate lovers.

The history of erotic or romantic love influences our imaginations. Our minds are often clouded with the myths and love stories of our culture which sets us up to fantasise a 'love' relationship, when it is often merely our own needs which our loved one is meeting. Our need for self-esteem is often mistakenly placed into a person who meets our current needs – and we think that we are 'in love'. (Ethel Person, 'Romantic love: At the intersection of the psyche and the cultural unconscious'. *Journal of the American Psychoanalytic Association*, 1991, **39**, 383–411).

While, in early civilisations, marriage was an economic arrangement, this is changing. As the idea of romantic love evolved, more people were allowed to follow the paths of their hearts, rather than the call of financial security, in choosing a mate. Today, in 147 of 166 cultures studied, romantic love is practised and is the major consideration for marriage (Paul Bray, 'What is love?' *Time Magazine*, 15 February 1993, 45).

Brotherly love

This is a second meaning of 'love'. It comes from the Greek word *philia*, which originally meant friendship or brotherly love. This is the type of love shown when people help others. Giving to a charity, assisting with a special group (such as a youth sport or Boy Scouts), or just being a good neighbour, are examples of this type of love. Our word 'philanthropist' comes from the same Greek word.

Altruistic love

This is seen as the highest form of love, utterly unselfish. It could be seen in the love of God for humanity or in the

unselfish, sacrificing love of a person for others. The word
'love' in this sense is often expressed by the Greek word
agape. Many of the Nobel Peace Prize winners exhibit this
type of love. Albert Schweitzer or Mother Theresa are
such examples.

Tough love

This is a concept heard recently as a way of handling
wayward children. When a child has become an addict,
such as through alcohol or other drugs, and the parent
continues to support the child – that parent is not
looking after the best interests of the child. The 'tough
love' approach has the parents tell the child to 'shape up or
ship out'. Often this works. It lets the child know that he
or she can no longer control the parents and get approval
for actions which the parents do not approve. To be loving
requires doing what is best for the loved one – not merely
being nice.

Erich Fromm, in his classic book *The Art of Loving*
(Harper & Row, 1956) on the importance of, and the
ability to, love, spent a good deal of time analysing the
kinds of love which people might show towards others.
The kinds of love were differentiated according to: the
qualifications of the persons who were to be the subjects
of the loving actions (intelligence, sexual attraction or
simply the fact that they were human beings) and the
relationship to the person doing the loving (such as a
spouse or a child).

   Fromm believed that, in today's society, people have
become too far removed from the closeness and concern of
earlier families. This has resulted in a feeling of 'aloneness' which can only be remedied by people becoming

more concerned with each other. He said that learning to love is 'the only satisfactory answer to the problem of human existence'.

While Montagu defined the characteristics of concern and behaviour necessary in *any* loving relationship, Fromm found some overlap and some differences depending on the type of relationship. So we might look to Fromm for another point of view and, perhaps, a broader perspective on the kinds of relationships in which loving behaviour can occur.

The types of relationships in which Fromm found that love can exist include:

1 Unconditional love, the ideal 'mother love' in which the person is loved, no matter what that person has done. This is also called 'unconditional' love. Not all mothers exhibit this type of mother love. Many fathers do exhibit this unconditional love. Some years ago, there was a radio interview with a woman whose son was about to be executed for the slaying of two police officers. The mother kept repeating that, 'her son was such a good boy'. She 'loved' him in spite of what he had done. But one wonders how he would have turned out, if she had really loved him early in life in the sense that Montagu describes in his definition.

2 'Conditional love' is dependent on a condition in order for 'love' to occur. In other words, the person is loved if that love has been earned somehow. It can be viewed as a kind of approval of a person because they have acted in a certain way. Sometimes, parents 'love' their children, when they perform. The star athlete is 'loved'; the smart student is 'loved'. Fromm associated this type of love with fathers,

although he noted that many mothers also love 'conditionally'. With this kind of 'love', it is really 'What have you done for me lately' that is the key. This really isn't love in the sense which Montagu defined it.

3   Spousal love is defined by Fromm as 'evaluation and emotion'. It has been similarly and aptly described by the prominent European philosopher, Sophia Loren, as being 'amorous reciprocal esteem'. Fromm and Loren are saying the same thing – that loving a person of the opposite sex consists of liking the qualities of that person and being 'turned on' by them in a sexual way.

4   One can also 'love' friends, a positive feeling for them and a willingness to help them if needed.

5   One can love one's country. When President John Kennedy said, 'Ask not what your country can do for you, but ask what you can do for your country', he was pointing out that people can feel and act for their country in a positive way. Immigrants often love their adopted country far more than the native-born citizens. The immigrants have standards by which to measure and can appreciate what their adopted country has done for them. They may be more eager to help that country develop its potential.

6   Love of humanity is the broadest application. This type of love is probably found most often in those who are religious. Jesus may be said to have been such a person; Albert Schweitzer in his ministry in Africa might be another; some missionaries might fall in this category. Many people who assist in developing countries might also qualify. Those who love

their neighbours as themselves exemplify this type of love.

Fromm has defined types of love, based on the natures of the love objects and the attitude shown by the person who loves. In so doing, he has gone far afield of the Montagu definition, which is concerned with the acts that a person does which develop another person's potential. Yet, Fromm's idea that 'love is an unselfish attitude and a psychological closeness' (as Montagu identified it) permeates his work. Certainly, his book *The Art of Loving* is a classic and should be read by anyone who wants a better understanding of this often nebulous idea of love.

Because of the various meanings of 'love' brought to our language from other languages, it is understandable that we are confused about its meaning. But now, as modern psychologists have begun to understand the nature of love in the 20th century, they have been able to identify the essential elements which make up a 'loving relationship'. Yet with all of the thinking which has occurred in finding adequate definitions of love, many people still believe that they are in love when they merely have hot pants.

We might ask 'Are there really different kinds of love or are there really only degrees of love?' Both Montagu and Buscaglia in his book *Love* (Fawcett Crest, New York, 1972, pp. 96–100) would hold that there is only one kind of love, but that it can be shown in many situations and to many degrees. I would agree.

The need for love

If Erich Fromm is right, humans have a basic need for love. However, the needs that a person feels (such as the need to be popular or to be needed) may not indicate the basic needs in the person. People's basic needs (to be loved, to be able to love, to feel secure) may be overshadowed in their own minds by other needs which they feel more strongly (to make money, to be popular, to get married). We should keep in mind that it is our real needs, not those which we feel, which are essential in developing our mental health and happiness.

Overcoming our aloneness

Albert Schweitzer said that 'We are all so much together but we are all dying of aloneness.' This is exactly Fromm's point. Fromm has continually emphasised that our greatest need in modern society is to overcome our aloneness. Modern economic necessities and the pursuit of wealth have separated us from the extended families which we had in earlier days – where people lived close to many relatives and friends. In those days, there was more interdependence on people. There was therefore a human warmth which surrounded most people. As people moved to the cities, they often left the emotional cosiness of the family and entered the emotional cold of a detached existence. This is a major psychological reason for having a nurturing relationship such as marriage.

There is nothing wrong with being alone. When we need to be alone to relax, to create, to 'recharge our batteries' we can call this 'solitude' – a creative and necessary type of being alone. However, when we do not have warm human relationships, we often are shrouded in a depressing existence. It is then that we need to be loved–to have friends and family for our emotional support. (See Erich Fromm, *Contemporary Psychoanalysis*, April, 1990, **26**,

305–330 – originally appeared in *Psychiatry*, February 1959, **22**.)

How love develops

In terms of love between people, Erich Fromm's *The Art of Loving* stressed the point that most people see love primarily as the problem of 'being loved' rather than that of being the person who 'does the loving'. Then, he emphasised that being able to love depends on our capacity to love. This is an ability which we learn. We 'learn to love by being loved.' Love does not come naturally, it must be cultivated. Therefore, the best thing that parents can do for their children is to teach them how to love. This is done by example.

Fromm was probably the first to point out how the capacity to love is developed, noting that, while people believe that loving is natural and easy, the development of the capacity to love is actually a very difficult task. And when a person has learned to love, that person does not just love one other person, but rather he or she develops the generalised ability to love.

Self-respect

This is the basis for developing an ability to love. It is primarily the job of parents to make their children feel worthwhile. As small children, if needs are met, cries answered, tummies fed and bodies cuddled, we get a feeling of being worth something. We develop self-respect. Children should be encouraged and praised, not continually chastised. On the other hand, children should

not be overindulged or appeased by being given too many
material things or letting them do whatever they want. It
is the quality of time, not the quantity of money, that
registers on the mind of the child. This self-respect
should be developed in a child before its fourth or fifth
year, if it is to be an effective basis for the child's mental
health and the ability to love.

Self-love

This is the second stage in the development of the ability
to love, according to Fromm. He makes it clear that
self-love is not selfishness. Selfishness is seeing ourselves
only – excluding other people. Self-love is seeing ourselves in relation to other people. It can occur only if the
person has developed self-respect which is fundamental to
a feeling of self-esteem.

Fromm notes that when a person 'loves one's neighbour as one's self', it implies that the loving person's own
uniqueness and integrity are respected. An understanding
and appreciation of our selves is necessary before another
person can be understood and appreciated. It is now
much more often realised by psychologists that, while
love is often identified as a relationship with a particular
person, it is essentially a matter of caring for our selves
and others. (Denis O'Sullivan, and Eleanor O'Leary,
'Love – A dimension of life'. *Counseling and Values*, **37**,
October 1992, 32–38.)

Dr Robert Felix, then director of the US National
Institute of Mental Health, said self-love occurs when
'one has a feeling of dignity, a feeling of belonging, a
feeling of worthwhileness, a feeling of adequacy – yet a
healthy sense of humility'. Such an attitude requires that
if we have the right feelings towards ourselves, are kind to

ourselves, and forgiving of ourselves, we will have the basis for exhibiting those attitudes towards others.

As long as we're talking about self-love, we should emphasise that we should also love ourselves. We must be concerned with our own potentials, too. Remember, self-love is essential to love. So, in a love relationship, we must also love ourselves. In an ideal love relationship, there should be elements of both self-love and selfless love. That is, we must be concerned with our selves and concerned with our partner. Of course, our partner should feel the same way.

The generalised ability to love

This is the culmination of the development of love. When people feel real 'self worth' and 'self love', then their self-esteem and self-confidence make them sufficiently secure to be able to show this same attitude toward others. People who have developed this potential to love do not just love one or a few people, they love 'generally'.

Dr Leo Buscaglia, one of America's foremost advocates of 'love', emphasised that 'if you have love, you can give it ... It's a matter of sharing ... I don't lose it because I still have it'. (Leo Buscaglia, *Love*, Fawcett Crest, New York, 1972). If we love, we cannot be ambivalent to others. We understand that the opposite of love is not hate – it is indifference.

A true 'lover' must be concerned with others – with the young and the old, with those of different ethnic and religious backgrounds, with those who possess mental or physical disabilities. Another best-selling writer, Dr Harry Overstreet, expressed it this way, 'If what we call love in relation to one person creates in us no added capacity for goodwill toward many, then we may doubt that we have actually experienced love.'

With this generalised ability of love understood, it is easy to see how we can love more than one person at a time. In fact, we may love many people at the same time. That is, we may do many things for these people to help them to be the best that they can be. A loving nurse or teacher can also be a loving partner, parent and community leader.

It goes without saying that we can have sexual attractions for, or infatuations with, more than one person at a time. The question is how much do you pursue that attraction? And what if you are successful in developing a deeper relationship with that person or stumbling into bed with him or her? What effect does that have on your other relationships? You don't have to act on every infatuation. When President Reagan was shot by a man who said he was trying to impress actress Jodie Foster – that was carrying an infatuation more than a bit too far.

The point is that we must be intelligent enough to be able to know when that great feeling can be coupled with a deep friendship and a mutual ability to love each other. If we can't do that, we should probably remain single and indulge every sexual obsession which entices us.

The ingredients of love

Time is a necessary ingredient of love. We cannot show love without devoting a certain amount of time to the object of our love. In evaluating how much you love a person, you must honestly judge both the quantity and the quality of time spent with and for that person. A father might spend a great deal of time with his son coaching him in sports. But, if the natural interest and inclination of the boy is to play the piano, the father is not helping the boy toward his natural fulfilment. The father spent a great quantity of time, but the quality of time was not too meaningful for that particular boy. What if a girl wants to spend more time in sports? Will her parents spend as much time fostering her interests as they would do for her brother?

More often, it is the quantity of time that is lacking. Ralph Waldo Emerson once wrote that, 'Rings and jewels are not gifts, but apologies for gifts; the only true gift is a gift of oneself.' How often do we see the successful business executive working as many as seven days a week, playing golf with business associates during free time, seldom seeing his or her family. But he or she buys them off with gifts. Son gets a new car. Daughter is sent to the finest boarding school and the best summer camps. This person has put time into what he or she values – the job. The money earned is then traded to 'buy off' those whom are supposed to be loved. We can tell what people value by the amount of time they spend in various activities.

A person is what he or she *does* – not what he or she *says*. Perhaps it is better said that we can identify people's ego needs and drives best by noting where they spend their time. There are not enough hours in the day for most people. Where do you spend your waking hours?

When people date, they generally spend a great deal of time together. During engagement, the same relationship continues. But what happens after marriage? Do they go separate ways? Do we watch a great deal more television than before? Do we go back to school a few nights a week? Do we follow an athletic hobby and not include the other? Or, do we spend a good deal of time together? Do we hold intimate conversations on their plans and problems? When marriage partners continue to give each other a good amount of quality time, the marriage generally prospers.

Time can be used effectively in many ways. We might use time by showing consideration for a loved one. A husband or wife might buy a bouquet of flowers for the other. A person might cook a favourite meal for a loved one. The idea here is that it is the thought that counts. The loved one understands that he or she is important to the other.

A second use of time is showing interest in the other person, helping him or her to achieve their greatest potential. A married couple might go to school one or two evenings each week, each pursuing his or her own interests. Often, husbands would like to thwart their wives' intellectual pursuits when the wife's achievement minimises the husband's supposed superiority. This would only be true if her husband had an inferiority complex. Does a husband show an interest in his wife's work or a wife in her husband's work?

Deep and meaningful communication

This is another way of giving time. Does the father take his daughter out for dinner so the two can be alone to try to understand each other? Does the mother take her son on a hike with the objective of getting to know him better? Do the husband and wife ever really try to get to know each other; to know what is positive or negative in their lives?

Communication is a necessity for love and romance. Most people are aware of this, but far too few try it, and far fewer ever succeed. It is tragic that so often it is difficult to get emotionally close to those to whom we should feel closest. A man or woman may tell their co-workers about the faults of a mate. But they fail to communicate these problems to each other. They thus fail to accomplish that necessary first step in solving the problem. Perhaps, it is because they are afraid of hurting each other's feelings, so they bite their tongues and internalise their anxieties. But such actions only magnify the problems and widen the gap between the two. True lovers can speak their innermost thoughts to each other, secure in the belief that such communication will strengthen rather than weaken the relationship.

Intimacy

This is an essential in a romantic type of love. It requires acceptance of the other person to such a degree that our innermost secrets can be shared. Women are much better about sharing feelings than are men. Men often have trouble because, if they reveal fears or weaknesses, they feel they lose control and sacrifice some of the strength which is supposed to be a masculine imperative. So, when secrets are shared they must be held in strictest confidence. It breaks a sacred trust to tell them to anyone – ever!

Intimacy also means sharing at least some interests. Some couples share everything and may grow in the process. Others go different directions, hopefully growing, then come back to share their experiences. It is important to grow just as it is important to share. Intellectual, psychological and recreational areas give us fertile opportunities for personal growth which can be shared.

We might consider that there are three parts to a love relationship – each partner and the couple. Many of the most successful couples, today, have lives which are quite separate from the relationship. It's not like the old days when both people worked on the farm and totally shared a life. In the modern world, especially in the two career relationships, there are two lives – but those lives meet often. And depending on their needs and their capabilities for loving – there is often a dynamite relationship.

To evaluate our love

We should evaluate the respect, care and responsibility which we show the other person. Are we seeing and respecting each person for what they really are? Do we show an active concern for the life and growth of the people we love? Do we respond voluntarily to the needs of other people? If so, we are exhibiting the characteristics of being a person who loves. Each of these characteristics takes time – time for reflection and time for action. It takes time to be considerate to others. The quality of time spent with a loved one is probably the major factor in a love relationship, whether it be husband–wife, parent–child, friend to friend, sibling to sibling.

As great a genius as was Albert Einstein, his love relationship ended as a failure. In his student days, he was wildly and passionately in love. The couple had a child. Then they married and had two more children. But, as he became more involved in his work and fame, his wife felt rejected. His work 'gets the pearls and I get only the shell,' she lamented. This change of focus in young lives is not a rarity, so we must be prepared for it or guard against it.

Mistaking infatuation for love

Up to now, this chapter has dealt with the form of psychological intimacy called 'love'. The attempt has been made to show how attitudes, abilities and behaviours called love can occur in any human relationship. But since we generally hear and think of the word in a romantic sense – usually between a man and a woman – this section will deal more specifically with the romantic illusion compared to real love. So, here we will look more at what love 'is not' rather than what it 'is'. Before getting into a relationship, you certainly want to be confident that your future mate is capable of honestly loving – and is not just playing a game. The same goes for you. Most of us think we can love – but when the chips are down, it is not always that common.

The confusion about what love is and how it can be accomplished has been fostered by romantic movies and novels. In the 100 minutes of a movie, boy meets girl, boy loses girl, then boy gets girl and they live happily ever after. Usually the notion developed is that a pretty face or a handsome body is the primary requisite for someone to be lovable.

Sexual attraction is not love. Physical intimacy does not produce love, but can give the appearance of what we think is 'love'. But the media confuse us and call mere infatuation *love*. Most human beings can provide *physical* intimacy. But how many can provide the deep mental and intellectual intimacy which is essential for real love? How do you think that you and your partner measure up in both the romantic and the true love aspects of your relationship?

It is not uncommon to mistake the romance of infatuation for the romance of love. The glamour of a face or physique, the charm of a personality or a feeling of sexual desire should not be confused with love. We often confuse our approval of someone with a belief that we are in love. Being realistic, any or all of these approvals and desires may also be a part of a mature love relationship. The danger begins when we confuse our approval of a person with our ability to love that person – or their ability to love us. While most of us would not kiss a fool, we are often fooled by a kiss.

Infatuation is 'what can you do for me.' Love is 'what can I do for you.' Both are necessary in a deep romantic relationship. Certainly, you should be infatuated with your mate. But there is no sense spending time on that idea because nobody is going to walk down the aisle to marry somebody who doesn't turn them on. So infatuation is a 'given' in our relationships. The big question is whether both of us are capable of unselfishly loving the other person. When most people say 'I love you', we see that love is the middle word in the sentence. But we often forget that the remaining words are arranged in the order of their importance to the speaker.

If love requires that we aid a person in helping him or her to achieve their full potentials, then mere approval is not enough. As pointed out earlier, we may approve of a person merely because we need them. We may then do whatever they want in order to keep the relationship alive. We may even measure our actions against the criteria which Montagu set out and find that we are doing things to help their potentials. But are we doing it out of an unselfish desire or are we doing it to get them to do what we want – to be accepted by them?

'Jumping in love'

This is a term that should be used in place of 'falling in love'. Falling sounds a bit passive, but jumping implies an active rush towards the ridiculous. Theodore Reik (*Of Love and Lust*, Aronson, New York, 1974) brought out the possibility that only people who are discontented are susceptible to 'jumping in love'. The 'need to be needed' often clouds our thinking and masquerades as a feeling of love.

An unhappy home life is a common reason for a person to develop a strong desire to change lifestyles. If another person can be found upon whom we can be dependent, a good feeling will result. That good feeling may be confused with 'being in love'. The next step may follow when this romantic feeling pushes that person into marriage. Unfortunately, this is not uncommon. The obvious problem is that the person was too weak to stand alone so he 'jumped into love', then stumbled into a long-term relationship, and assumed that life would be 'happy ever after'. But the probabilities are that such an insecure personality will not be able to love or to sustain the relationship necessary for a happy long-term relationship.

Such an insecure person can easily become jealous. But jealousy is not a sign of loving. It is an indication of possessiveness. It is more often a sign of insecurity and a need to be loved than an indication of being able to love. The stronger the jealousy, the greater is the amount of insecurity.

'I've fallen into something – I hope it's love'

Falling in love at first sight is impossible. We may fall into 'approval' at first sight because of a physical or psychological attraction to another person. This relationship may then grow into a loving relationship in which both people care for and feel responsible for the other's needs. But this situation might be more properly called 'an evolution into love'.

Those who 'fall in love' or are 'swept off their feet' are those who tend to believe that 'fate' controls their lives.

These people often believe in luck and have more un-realistically romantic ideas about love. On the other hand, people who consider themselves to be masters of their own destinies are far less likely to think of love in the idealistic, romantic way.

And so?

Research has indicated that for a large number of happily married people the keys are companionability and respect. As partners, you are friends and friends must be equal – and have the respect of each other. But both people must want to help each other to be the best that they can be. This is the most critical qualification for a marriage. You must be capable of loving. Your partner must be able to love. When these two necessities are present, you have the absolute essentials for a deep and meaningful relationship. We must also remember that in a relationship kindness is more important than perfection.

Self-test on love

Tick the box, if you think the following are true for you:

1 Love should be unselfish ☐

2 Being jealous when your loved one seems interested in someone else is a sign of love ☐

3 In love relationships, people should spend nearly all of their time together ☐

4 You can fall in love at first sight ☐

5 Infants and small children have great capacity for loving ☐

6 In order to be able to love others, you must be able to love yourself ☐

7 If you are really in love, you will do anything for the person you love ☐

8 Accepting a person's alcoholism or drug addiction is a sign of unconditional love ☐

9 Loving a young child requires that you spend a great deal of 'quality' time with the child ☐

10 Romantic notions of love are always harmful to a relationship ☐

Answers

1 *True*: The deepest meaning of 'loving' requires a desire to do what is best for the loved one.

2 *False*: Jealousy is a sign of insecurity.

3 *False*: Adults are independent people and a mature adult needs some space. Needing to spend all of one's time with another indicates insecurity.

4 *False*: Love takes time to grow. Infatuation can occur at first sight.

5 *False*: Being able to love takes maturity.

6 *True*: Self-esteem and self-love are essential ingredients to the maturity necessary to be able to love unselfishly.

7 *False*: Since you need to love yourself also, you must take time to develop your own interests. Wanting to do everything for another may be a sign of manipulating that person so that they will stay in the relationship. This is also a sign of insecurity.

8 *False*: If you truly love a person, you will want

what is best for them. Addictions are not best, so you must work to get the person off of drugs if you really love.

9 *True*: A loving parent will spend both 'quantity' and 'quality' time with a child who is loved.

10 *False*: There is nothing wrong with romance; however, it is the frosting, not the cake. Adult loving sexual relationships should have romance as an exciting ingredient in the relationship.

Exercise

WHO AND WHEN HAVE YOU LOVED? List the times that you have done unselfish things for people. When did you last visit grandma. When did you do something nice for a friend. When did you do something nice for your mate? What about your children? What have you done for charitable causes?

WHAT CAN YOU DO FOR THOSE YOU SAY YOU LOVE? List those you say you love, and think about what you could do to love, them according to Ashley Montagu's definition. What could you do for your mate that he or she really needs. What can you do for grandma? What about a neighbour?

List those who you say you love	What unselfish things have you done for them — to develop their potentials?*	What loving things could you do for each person?

* Their potentials can range from helping your child learn to cross the street alone to making grandmother feel that you care about her.

In the contract – Who are you?

Do I really know me?

Read this chapter if:

You wonder about the maturity of yourself or your
partner

You wonder about your self-esteem – whether you have
it or you want to know how to develop it

You or your partner are controlling

You want to clarify your or your partner's values

All serious thinkers, philosophers, scientists, theologians
and other intelligent people start by asking questions. As
an intelligent person, you must ask and answer essential
questions about yourself – your goals, your needs, your
personality and your values. Thinking intelligently about
us is difficult because our emotions and rationalisations
often get in the way of sound evaluation and logic.
However, it must be done if you are to understand yourself and your relationships.

The real 'stuff' which is our selves is largely unknown by scientists. We know a little about brain chemistry, we know a little bit about how the brain works, we have examined some theories about how we are motivated and why we behave as we do. But we don't know very much about the science of what we are – the science of psychology. We also don't know that much about how we function in our society – the sciences of sociology, social-psychology and anthropology. However, we do have some theories. We will look now at some of the factors, which may influence how we see ourselves.

If we are going to understand how we function alone and how we function in a relationship, we must look for a few moments at what some of the leading psychologists say motivate and control us. Hopefully, we can then apply that knowledge to how it can affect our relationship. It is here, in our heads, that most of the delights and the problems of relationships develop. It is not whether we are of different races or religions, it is not whether we like to play tennis or sit at home, it is not whether we are fat or thin. The key to relationships is in our own heads and the heads of our lovers. So let's take a look at what some psychologists say about who and what we are.

One way to look at ourselves is to look at our sex, our gender and how we function in society because of the gender expectations of our society. Another way to look at ourselves is to see us according to our age. Each age seems to have tasks, which must be accomplished in order for us to mature as we age.

Before you think of making an intimate long-term commitment with somebody else, you really must know who you are, what you want and what you are willing to give. It goes without saying that you want certain things from your relationship. But who are you? And are you the person you think you are? There are a number of needs and values, which propel us as we move through our lives.

As we understand ourselves and succeed in our lives, we are more likely to become honestly mature. *AND UNLESS YOU ARE MATURE YOU CANNOT MAKE AN HONEST COMMITMENT OR A LEGITIMATE CONTRACT.* Insecure immature people marry for security, not for the right reasons, such as developing a committed and satisfying relationship. If you are selfish and immature you will want a slave, not an equal companion.

We must realise that we are responsible for our own lives. It is common for people to blame others, when things don't go the way they want. Such blaming often takes the form of rationalisations. A rationalisation is a reason, which we believe is true, but which is actually not true. Often, but not always, they are used as excuses for our failings:

- If you didn't make such big dinners, I wouldn't be so fat.
- If the government would only increase my welfare payments, I wouldn't be so poor.

If you know that whatever you are saying is not true, that is a lie. If you don't know that what you are saying is untrue, it is a rationalisation. If we are to be mature people, we must look at our true selves and take responsibility for the direction in which we are going and the changes necessary, if we are to alter our course in life. This means seeing the truth and avoiding the rationalisations.

Let's start with looking at our mental health and the necessary requirements for being a mature adult. The evidence of modern research into marriage makes it clear that we must understand our own needs and desires. If we can get an accurate picture of ourselves, we have a much better

chance of determining what we really want out of life –
and whether that includes a mate. And if so, what type of
mate.

Self-esteem

In popular psychology, there are several terms which are
commonly used related to our idea of 'self'. *Self-identity*
means 'who do you think you are?' If you have *self-efficacy*,
it means that you are an effective person – that
you can learn, think and make effective choices and decisions. *Self-respect* indicates that you think that you are
OK and that you deserve the success, friendship and relationships, which you have enjoyed. And *self-esteem*
means that you like yourself because you have the identity, efficacy and respect which you have learned and
earned (Figure 6).

Probably, no one has their self-esteem completely
intact. We all have some doubts about ourselves. Just
look at the confessions of Fergie, the Duchess of York,
and Diana, the Princess of Wales, relative to their own
insecurities and problems with self-esteem. You'd think
that, when you marry a prince, your troubles would be
over. We can have no doubt that Prince Charles has his
own problems with self-esteem. Maybe, the Queen has no
problems with self-esteem – but with her record as a
parent perhaps she ought to?

People with legitimate self-esteem seek valuable goals
in their lives. They want to communicate, to be understood and to understand. They are also capable of loving
in an unselfish way.

People with low self-esteem are insecure. They are
afraid of challenge and change. They are not able to

Figure 6 The greatest conquerers are those who conquer themselves.

communicate effectively because of their fears. Of course, they can't love unselfishly because their own insecurities make them self-centred and unable to honestly reach out to another. They want others, for what the others do for them. And, often, they want to control the other person and so enhance their feeling of self-worth.

You should have a clear and accurate idea of your assets and liabilities. People with inferiority complexes don't think they are as good as they are. People with superiority complexes think they are better than they are. Do you have an accurate picture of yourself? Here are some areas of personality, which you should consider in getting a clear picture of who you are. One of the major aspects of our personalities is where we are in the power–love–meaning triangle. We can all find ourselves at some point in the controlling–helping–creating experiences triangle:

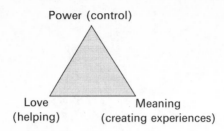

We should understand where we are now, but we must also understand that, as we stumble through our lives, most of us will move, often significantly, in a different direction relative to our primary motivation, such as moving from a 'love' person to a 'power' person. As you change, it is going to affect your relationship contract – your understanding of who you are and what you need, as well as what you can give.

The basics of our personalities

Research indicates that perhaps as much as half of our personality is genetically derived. But, obviously, many of our traits are learned and can be unlearned. When 'learned', they can be held in either our conscious or our unconscious minds. You may remember the enjoyable holiday rituals of your family. They are not only in your conscious mind, but you expect them in your life. You may not consciously remember being sexually abused as a toddler, but that abuse may haunt you through your adult life as a feeling of inferiority and a revulsion of sex.

Here are a few aspects of personality which we have observed. They can be held to either a great or a minimal degree. But take a look at yourself and your partner to see

where you fit – where you are alike and where you are
different. What probable joys and problems might result
from your similarities and your differences?

We might look at the major approaches to life as:

1   being power and success driven;

2   having a need to be loving and helping others; or

3   having a need to find new meanings in life.

These traits will probably never be found to be 100% in
any one person. Most of us major in one and minor in the
others.

The doers – the power people

Power people have a great need to achieve in some area.
This can be either mentally healthy or unhealthy. The
person who wants to rise to a leadership position in business or politics probably has a healthy power drive. One
who uses sarcasm, who races his car from the stoplight or
who is physically violent definitely has an unhealthy
power drive.

The power people are either self-confident or appear
to be self-confident as a cover for their inferiority feelings.
Aggressiveness is often a tendency in this group. Those
who do not have a real feeling of self-esteem may be very
guarded and wary of the potential power of others. It is
nearly a certainty that many of the forces that motivate

your life will be in this area. It is the most common motivator in the Western world.

Typically, men exhibit this drive. In fact, a test of his manhood is often how well he succeeds in the areas of work, sport or sex. Men, typically, need to be in control of themselves not only in the social and economic areas but in their control of their mental make-up. This idea of control, while useful in some areas, is counterproductive in the negotiation mode of a relationship where finding equitable solutions, as opposed to winning, is the objective. Happily, today many men are finding their loving sides and realising that a productive and satisfying relationship is generally more important than getting another promotion at work or winning another game of tennis.

But power is not only a man's domain. It is also found in abundant amounts in the psyches of women. While, in the past, just having a man choose her was a big boost to her power drive, today most women, especially those in the higher social classes, want to succeed in the same ways that men have traditionally done – power, sports and sex. As this metamorphosis has occurred, women have become more overt in their drives for control.

The drive for power can be satisfied by having power *over* someone or some people or by having the power *to* do something – such as to be successful in sports, to develop computer programs, to make national policies. So power 'over' is often a negative use of the power drive, but power 'to' is quite often positive.

The feelers – the loving people

Caretaking is needed in our increasingly hostile world. A truly caring person is indeed a pleasure to be around. The caution is that the person may be caretaking because of inferiority feelings and may be doing these 'good things' for approval. So, behaving as an unselfish person, for some people, may really be a way of handling our power drives.

On the other hand, a person who has honestly been loved when growing up may have a great capacity for giving. Many of the foremost psychologists believe that this caretaking ability is a fundamental for good mental health.

The more intelligent men and women are recognising the importance of nurturing this softer side of their minds. Both partners must recognise that the caretaking aspect of our beings is needed, if we are to have truly successful relationships.

The experiencers – the meaning people

Meaning-seeking people want new experiences. It can be the adventure of a trip across the country or a visit to the local museum. There is a sense of adventure in either creating or experiencing more of the world. These are the people who travel to distant lands or who climb Mount Everest, those who continually seek excitement. But this drive is also found in the quiet philosopher, the poet or the artist whose adventure begins in the mind.

A problem for those busy exploring the world is that they might be reckless – and that is a negative! So while an adventurer may be able to have a truly interesting life, recklessness will often invite trouble.

Those who seek adventure in their minds may be introverted and unsociable. They may be so involved in their preoccupations of thinking and creating that letting other people into their world may be an unwelcomed intrusion into their privacy. So, the meaning-driven people can be quite interesting, but if their interests become all absorbing they may not be good partnership material. However, you can imagine that two artists, two philosophers or two adventurers might make perfect mates for each other.

What do these mean to a relationship?

There is no hard-and-fast rule about being similar or different. A marriage between a power-driven success-oriented person and a loving caring person may work out just fine. The monetary success of the one may take care of the financial-security needs of the caring person. Meanwhile, the caring person can handle the ego needs of the power-driven person. On the other hand, two power people might fare very well together. Their success and interests may make them highly respectful of each other and outstanding dinner companions. As long as they leave their needs for dominance at the office – there may be no problems. But if one tries to dominate the other at home – *PROBLEMS!*

Two loving caring people should do quite well together. They might not gather too many possessions from the generally low-paying jobs for lovers, such as nursing or elementary-school teaching, but their psychological treasures and their families should more than make up for their lack of furs and Ferraris.

The problem with the drive for power is the need for control. In a marriage, this can mean trying to control the finances or any and all other aspects of the relationship. Often, the power-driven people who have not achieved in other areas must exert their control over their children or their mates. It is not uncommon that whatever the mate says is contradicted almost before it is out of the mouth. This is a very common kind of control – and one which can often be eliminated through good communication.

Our drive for power makes us want to be right all the time. The question is – is it more important to be fulfilled and happy in your relationship or is it better to be right in every situation? If he is driving and goes two blocks farther to get to a destination is it really important to tell him? If she is cooking and he tells her to add more sugar because that's the way his mother made it – was it necessary to say? Generally, in management, when we give a person the responsibility to do a job, we also give them the authority to make the decisions necessary to do that job. Continually correcting and advising them puts them in an inferior position in terms of the equality of power in the relationship.

Jealousy is a power-drive problem. If your mate is actually hustling others it is one thing. If you think your mate is hustling, it is quite another. Imagined intentions of our mate is related to our insecurities and desire to control.

Power versus love

The noted psychologist Alfred Adler had a theory that we are all seeking power in life in order to overcome our inferiority complexes. He believed that early in our lives we developed these complexes because we really were inferior! As a baby, when you can't talk, can't walk and can't feed yourself, you don't have much going for you. You *are* inferior. We then spend the rest of our lives trying to overcome our inferiority complexes by achieving power in one or more areas of our lives.

The feeling of insecurity, usually unconscious, drives many people into marriage. The 'need' to have someone can lead us to marrying alcoholics, spouse beaters or other insecure people. In order to be able to have a sound and meaningful relationship, a person must be mature – and have that power drive in check.

As a therapist, I have noted that, in almost every case, personal problems and marriage problems stem from feelings of insecurity which we all have – and which we are all trying to overcome. Why do you laugh when a comedian slips on a banana peel? Because you didn't – so you are better than him. Why do we read those scandal-sheet tabloids? Because we are better than the public figures mentioned who are going on their sixth divorce or who have been caught in unseemly situations.

In Chapter 5, we discuss a very important level of our relationship contract – the psychological contract. This idea of inferiority and the need to control (satisfying our power drive) will be more fully discussed. It is a well-known theory among marriage counsellors, but is almost unheard of in the general public.

So – how are you going to fulfil your need for power? Is it bossing around your wife – or hitting her? Is it being in total control of the children? Is it telling your husband how to drive, where to turn and pointing out all of his mistakes? Is it achieving success at your work, at the tennis club or as the social secretary of your charity group?

It is essential to understand that you have a drive for power, for control, for success – and how you plan to handle that urge. You must also realise that your focus for control may change. For a young woman, it may be first either to succeed in a profession or to get married – or both. A young man probably has the same ideas. But his drive has been traditionally focused on success in his field, while a woman's has traditionally been on marriage and family concerns. These two traditional goals are changing somewhat as the gender barriers to women in business have been lowered and as more men have found the importance of the joys of a successful marriage.

There is another deep psychological need which most of us have, that is the need to love and be loved. As noted in the last chapter, love is an unselfish ability which is quite counter to the generally selfish need for power and control. It is a need that more and more people are coming to understand as being essential in their lives – especially since so many of us have moved from the extended family of the relatives and friends of our early lives to the nuclear family (mom, dad and the kids). Because of our moving far from home, to complete our education or to find a better job, our immediate family often becomes, for many of us, our only family. So the caring which we could once find from a large number of friends and relatives is now often found only in our small nuclear family.

The rapid changing of our society

This often takes away our traditional-role expectations. In the 'olden days', a man was expected to be successful enough in his job to make the money that the family needed. If he was lucky enough to have a job that he honestly enjoyed and had a large degree of success in that occupation – he was indeed a lucky fellow. His wife, on the other hand, was to be content with making him happy, keeping the house and raising the six children. His life was in the 'power and control zone' while hers was in the 'love and caring area'.

For a number of years, those gender boundaries have been crossed so that, today, we have most married women working – many in high-paying challenging jobs. Similarly, some men have moved into the traditionally female areas of nursing, elementary-school teaching and house-keeping/child raising as 'househusbands'.

One of the problems, which we commonly see in marriage counselling, is the 40–50-year-old woman who has lived in the traditional pattern of wife–mother, perhaps also working outside the home, now being without anyone to control as her children become more independent or leave home. She may have had the ability to 'love' and care for her family when she was younger, but, as she 'grew up', she needed to express her drive for success in another area. The children, long the object of her need to control, are no longer around. How can she handle that drive for power? She can go back to school and work towards a profession or she can pick up on the profession she once had. At home, who is there to pick on? Only her husband! Tell him to control his weight or he might have a heart attack. Complain about his watching too much TV. Tell him how to drive. The loving caring woman of the earlier marriage has changed. Her psychological need to control must be met.

Let's make it clear that there is nothing wrong in having a drive for power and success. There is nothing wrong with wanting to be the prime minister, with wanting to start your own business or with wanting to win at tennis. There is something wrong when we step on people to become a manager or legislator, when we are not honest with our clients in our business, or when winning at tennis becomes a major factor in our suburban lives. It becomes a major problem when we are physically violent – especially towards our mates and our children. That primitive physical use of power cannot be a part of a *loving* or an egalitarian relationship.

Having an honest feeling of self-esteem

This translates into several positive attributes. Because we feel good about ourselves, we don't need to 'put down' others in order to make ourselves feel good. It is the truly inferior people who need to be sarcastic, to order others around or to be physically violent towards others.

Because we are content with ourselves we can become 'lovers' – people who can help others to be the best that they can be. A person who has not effectively worked out the inferiority complex, which started in childhood, will continue to be self-centred. While this person may do good things for others in order to become acknowledged, these things are not done with the genuine motive of love, but these actions appear to be loving.

A couple of the good things that happen when women become more independent, especially when they are young, is that they don't need a man for financial security. Having an interesting job which pays well greatly increases a woman's self-esteem. As this happens, she is able to choose men whom she really likes – because she is choosing out of strength, not weakness. This then translates into more enjoyable sex because, with a higher self-esteem and a man she honestly likes and is on an equal footing with, she can be more free in her sexual expression.

With an honest feeling of self-esteem, it is easy for you to back off from a position or a plan which you have suggested. It is easier to apologise. Having to have it your own way all the time is a sign that your inferiority complex is in control and you are exercising your power in order to show that you are not inferior. But you don't fool many people with that attitude – and it is impossible to have an open and honest relationship. Real self-esteem

comes from doing (success: at your job, in sports, in educational areas) not from talking to yourself telling yourself
that you are worthwhile. You must DO!

The consequences of low self-esteem

These are often that we go too far in either being aggressive or in withdrawing from the world. It has already been
mentioned that spousal and child beating is one aspect of
this violence, but so is gang violence and abusive verbal
behaviour.

It is actually more likely that a person will withdraw
from reality, when there are great feelings of inferiority.
Drug and alcohol dependence are common forms of such
withdrawing. In using substances which act on the brain,
the person is trying to forget the real world through
alcohol, marijuana, heroin or other downer drugs which
reduce physical or psychic pain. Others try to escape by
taking a drug which gives great pleasure – instant orgasm.
Cocaine, in its many forms, or other upper drugs, such as
methamphetamine, give intense 'highs' which make up
for the unsatisfying lives which these people are living
and for the depressive feeling which results from their
low self-esteem.

While honestly feeling good about yourself is a fundamental of good mental health, there are other important
considerations which are of a more intellectual bent. We
all hold values in many areas of our lives. These are generally quite clear to us. However, we often don't understand just exactly what our values are, how deeply we hold
them and how they may fit into another person's value
system. These are essential qualities of ourselves and
others and must be considered when choosing a mate.
And when there are significant differences in values.

there are likely to be problems so they must be addressed. Sometimes our values change as we become older.

Understanding your values

A large part of our make-ups and the forces which motivate us are found in the things which we value. We are motivated to fulfil our values just as we are motivated to handle our psychological drives and needs such as power, love and meaning. Evaluating our value systems is much easier than understanding our drive for power or our need to love and be loved. As with our drives and needs, our values can be found in both our conscious and our unconscious minds.

Economic values

When we're young, and know everything, most of us are liberals. 'Tax the rich. Take care of the homeless. Stop charging me college tuition.' When we are older and earning more money, many people change and want to keep more of what they have earned. They are no longer the 'have-nots' of their earlier days.

A large number of the radical–liberal demonstrators and hippies of the 1960s have become business leaders, lawyers, doctors, stock investors and politicians. Some have continued in their liberal bent, others have become much more economically conservative. '*Reduce the taxes. Send the illegals home.*'

In the Western world, we seem to be thinking more and more about making money and less and less about enjoying life. Much happiness is overlooked because it

Figure 7   This time is a very good time if we but know what do
do with it (Emerson).

doesn't cost anything. So when we look at our economic
values, we will want to balance them against other values
which may be more important to us. Everything takes
time. Making money takes time. Playing tennis takes
time. Raising children who are loved takes time. Where
do you want to put *your* time? (Figure 7)

Our economic views are one type of value which we
may share with our partner in our early marriage days.
But they can certainly change as we age. But there are
many other areas of value: religion, recreation, social consciousness, the family style we desire, personal independence needed, etc. We should know where we are at the
beginning of the relationship, but we must understand
that these ideas may change as our relationship matures.

Another aspect of economics is that sometimes one
person, usually the man, wants to control the purse

strings. This is one way that an excessive power drive can be found in the financial area of the relationship. Most people, today, say that they want an egalitarian marriage with a 50/50 sharing plan. If this is true there needs to be some real discussion on the monetary aspects of marriage. The most commonly mentioned problems in marriage have to do with money. One partner may want a bigger house. One may spend a lot on clothes shopping. One may use too much money on alcohol or gambling. All of these indicate different values relative to finances.

Having children will also financially impact a couple. Among the possible financial problems are that the wife stops working so that she can spend time with the children. *There goes one salary!* You may need a bigger house or apartment so that the baby can have its own room. *Up goes the rent!* There may be doctor's bills which were unexpected. Of course, there is the increased cost of food and clothing. Perhaps the money spent earlier in the marriage for dining out, recreation and vacations is now unavailable. That puts another stress on the couple. These are not problems for those who are financially well off – but most of us are not quite so financially fixed.

Even when you have plenty of money, one person may become upset by the spending habits of the spouse. Excess spending by their wives were factors in two divorces of rich friends of mine.

Recreational interests

A lawyer of my acquaintance discovered tennis when he was about 50. He left the office nearly every day at 2 and played tennis until dark. His wife joined him. They became tennis 'junkies'. It gave their lives new meaning – one-dimensional though it might have been.

Recreation is important to re-create our non-working selves. Whether it is making pottery, painting, attending concerts, reading; or playing golf, fishing, hiking or travelling – recreation should re-energise us either by fulfilling our continuing interests or by giving us new interests.

The recreational pastimes of our youth, going to the beach, playing team sports or doing other group activities will generally give way to family recreation when children arrive. As we age and the children go their own ways, our interests may change to the more intellectual pursuits of enjoying the arts, reading or creating in our own choice of the artistic realm – painting, writing or continuing our education. If we are inclined toward the more physically active pursuits, jogging, cycling, skiing, golf and tennis may be our choices. However, there is almost always a change in our recreational values as we age. This also changes our understandings for our relationships.

Religious values

Our religious beliefs often change as we age. We may start our relationships as irreligious infidels, then become 'born again' as we get older. The opposite also can happen. In terms of the marriage contract, it isn't important as long as we change together. When one person changes, a revision in the relationship contract will be needed. Can the spouse accept change or will it totally disrupt his or her life? It seems that when Jane Fonda became a re-born Christian, it was too much for her billionaire husband Ted Turner to handle.

A number of years ago, I had some interesting neighbours. They had been born Jewish, but had become atheists. By the time I met them, they were ardent practitioners of the Eastern meditative faiths of Hinduism and

Buddhism. Since they changed together, there were no changes needed in their relationship contract.

A religious commitment can be very shallow, '*Well, it's Easter so maybe I'll go to a sunrise service,*' or very committed. It is the deep religious belief area which can cause problems, if the partners don't see eye to eye on the belief. There is nothing more basic than a deep religious concern for those who hold such values.

For some people, the religious commitment is essential. Conservative religions often insist on it – as do marriage-minded adherents to the faith. Conservative Catholics, Orthodox Jews, 'born again' Christians, devout Muslims, as well as Hindus are all likely to hold deep-seated religious values, which are so fundamental in their lives that a marriage with an outsider is unthinkable.

Keeping your identity and pursuing your own goals

A common problem, today, is balancing the need for the security of someone to love and the need for freedom to be what we can be. Our expectations for the emotional security of having someone to love and to love us is probably greater today than ever before. Our extended family of the past, with grandparents, parents, siblings, cousins and interested neighbours has been replaced by a disinterested society which forces us to find our emotional needs met in a small nuclear family. It's just us – our mate and possibly our children and a few friends. Our emotional needs for security and love must now be met by our chosen partner. This is a big order. At the same time, our modern society has allowed us to pursue careers and interests undreamed

Figure 8   All parents should remember that some day their
children will follow their example, rather than their advice.

of a few years ago. We need the freedom and the support
of our mate to effectively spread our wings and soar to our
chosen heights. So, we have a greater need for security,
yet a greater need for freedom and they both have to be
handled by our chosen partner. We therefore expect more
than did our parents – and we are expected to do more
than our parents (Figure 8)

Because we are more complicated people today and
our relationships reflect that diversity, we cannot expect
that both partners will always want to do the same things
at the same time. The realities are that one may want to ski
while the other hang-glides, or that one wants to study
history while the other studies literature. No problem.
Having and pursuing different interests can strengthen
the bonds of the relationship, as long as both people are
secure in themselves.

This dilemma of the possible conflict between the

nearly universal need for human companionship and the more modern need for self-fulfilment and self-actualisation may puzzle us and cause us concern. Most of us need a warm human being to share with, to love – and to cuddle. At the same time, our need to experience life more fully than it has been possible in any earlier generation requires that we have freedom to be what we can be. The solution to this situation is going to take serious consideration and possibly deep communication.

Because of the increase in the two-career marriages and the myriad of recreational possibilities open to us – we can expect a great divergence in interests. As an example, at this moment my wife is taking a riding lesson while I am typing away on my computer. Tomorrow, I will be coaching football (my special hobby) while she prepares a speech for a conference in Lisbon. We are two people with quite different backgrounds – she from Norway and me from California. We have a common interest in sport. But we have quite different interests and qualifications in other areas. She is probably the leading authority in the world in the area of women and sport – from a psychosocial perspective. I am quite interested in her quest for true equality in that area. Meanwhile, she understands my passion for educating young people through sport, travel and history.

Does that mean that we live lives that are quite separate? No! We both love to ski and do so often, sometimes right from our apartment in Oslo. We both enjoy travelling and tennis. I tolerate her interest in golf and play occasionally. While I share her interest in good eating, I'm a klutz in the kitchen – but I do a mean dishwashing act. Since my retirement, I not only fix the cars but clean the house. Her professorship takes long hours each day, so does my writing. But when we're together – *dynamite!!*

The point is that each of you should understand yourself well – your drives, needs and values. With this knowledge you should be able to make better career choices,
approach your recreation intelligently and decide
whether and when to have children. Plan for doing
things that you like to do – career, parenting, recreation,
visiting friends, reading or going to school. You should
not be handcuffed to your mate. You should think now
about what your desires are for your own growth and
discuss these with your mate or your intended mate.
Even when children are involved, you should each have
a life of your own. This doesn't mean that you always do
what you want. It means that you take responsibility for
yourself – and your relationships. If you have decided to
have children, they are a prime responsibility – especially
when they are very young. But they are not a prison. You
need to take some time for yourself, alone – and with your
mate, just the two of you. You have to keep yourself sane
and your relationship solid. Your kids will be the better
for it.

Self-evaluation of the love–power–meaning areas

To get an idea of where you are in the power–love–meaning triangle, here is a way to get an idea of what motivates you

Make a list of the times in your life in which you have experienced a great feeling of joy:

_____

_____

_____

_____

_____

Now try to find the motivation which was satisfied when you experienced that great joy – power, love, meaning. Perhaps you felt great just because a stress was reduced. (Stress reduction is not a satisfaction of a psychological drive.) You certainly don't want to spend your life just reducing stresses. Just look at the happiness rating of those who do: alcoholics, drug-dependent people and spouse beaters.

Perhaps you listed a Hawaiian sunset. The joy from that experience would be the satisfaction of the meaning drive.

Maybe you listed the time that you got your driver's licence or your first car. That would obviously be a satisfaction of the power drive. (Don't say that it was 'love' because you loved your new car. Love, remember, in our definition is giving and making another person better or happier.)

Did you list getting a special job or getting a high mark in a difficult class in school? That would be a power-drive satisfaction.

Did you list 'helping a child' or 'helping a friend with a problem?' If so, it could be the satisfaction of a love motivation, your joy came from giving, or it could be a power-drive satisfaction because you were in control and were successful. (Being your own psychologist isn't so easy, is it?)

Did you list seeing the Eiffel Tower in Paris? Well, you may 'love' Paris, but this isn't a love-drive satisfaction. It might be a meaning-need satisfaction, because it is a very special sight and you are finally experiencing it. Or it could be a power-drive satisfaction, because you are there and you are responsible for taking the trip.

There are some other factors which might have given you a great joy but don't fall into the power, love or meaning areas. Perhaps you listed an orgasm or the feeling you got using cocaine. These both are felt in the same area of your brain – the medial forebrain bundle. If Sigmund Freud were here, he would say that this is exactly what he was talking about in satisfying our drive for sexual pleasure. But experience shows us that if we spend our whole lives stimulating our medial forebrain bundles with orgasms, cocaine and methamphetamines, our lives will not be truly joyful or satisfying.

Another source of joy can be experienced when you have reduced a stressful experience. My brother-in-law was the head of the military police in Shanghai after World War Two. After his tour of duty was over, he was sent on a crowded ship on the six week trip to San Francisco. He was seasick for six weeks. When he got off the boat, he knelt and kissed the ground because he was so happy to be home. That's stress reduction. No more six weeks of seasickness. No more foul-smelling Shanghai streets. He finally got to taste mom's cooking again. No more stress!

Another type of stress reduction can occur:

- when you walk out of a courtroom after having been a defendant or a witness;
- when you walk out of a classroom after finishing your last final exam in college; or
- when your last guest has left your party after overstaying his welcome.

As good as stress reduction may feel, we don't want to spend our lives merely reducing stress – eliminating the negatives. Life should be positive. We should be looking for what the psychologist Abraham Maslow called 'peak experiences', times when we are 'surprised by joy'. Our longer lasting joys occur, not in orgasms (as good as they always are), but in building a business, helping our spouse and child to grow, painting a picture or reading a poem. So where are you in this puzzle of passion called life?

Self-test on similarities and differences in our backgrounds

1 I was born in: country   _____
in the city   _____
or in a rural area   _____

2 I was raised until I was at least ten years old in (see above list)   _____

3 From age 10 to 20, I lived in (see above list)

_____

4 I have lived the last 10 years in (a big city, a small city [under 300,000], a large town [100,000–300,000] people, a smaller town, in a rural area)   _____

5 My religion is   _____

6 My parents are (recent immigrants, first generation, later generation)

_____

7 The highest income my family earned per year was   _____

8 The highest grade (position in form) I have completed in school was

_____

9 How many years of schooling do I expect to complete? _____

10 My father's highest grade level finished (form position) _____

11 My mother's highest grade level finished (form position) _____

12 The number of children in my family was

_____

13 I was the first, second, or third child born

_____

14 My parents' marriage was (happy, unhappy)

_____

15 My parents are now (still married, separated, divorced, separated by the death of one of my parents) _____

16 How many divorces have there been among my grandparents, parents, aunts and uncles, cousins, brothers and sisters)

_____

17 Who raised me primarily (family, other)

_____

18 I believe that my upbringing was (happy, sad)

_____

19 When I was young the three activities I liked best were:

(a) sports, camping, reading, being alone

_____

(b) doing school work, religious activities, being with other people

_____

(c) arts and crafts, music and dance

_____

20 Up to the time I was 12, I had (no friends, few friends, many friends)

_____

21 In high school, I had (no friends, few friends, many friends)

_____

22 When I was a teenager, my communication with my parents was (very good, fair, poor, almost non-existent)

_____

Self-test on how I feel mentally and socially

1 My physical health is (perfect, pretty good, not too good right now, always poor)

           _____

2 My mental outlook is (very happy, not too happy, fairly insecure and unsure, quite sad)

           _____

3 Over the next several years, I feel that (things will get much better, somewhat better, stay about the same, be a little worse, be much worse)   _____

4 I prefer (being alone, being with just one person, being at a party, being surrounded by many people most of the time)

           _____

5 My career (is secondary to having a secure family relationship, is secondary to my having children, is of primary importance to me)   _____

6 Having children (is out of the question for me, might be a possibility if I feel that I can become a good parent, is absolutely essential in my life)

           _____

7 Being married now is (not all that important, very important, only important because I am in love)   _____

Understanding our adjustments

Do I really understand us?

Read this chapter if:

You are interested in why you or your partner need to control the other (in finances or other decisions)

You or your partner believe you are controlled by fate

Stress is a factor in your life

You wonder if your behaviour, or your partner's, is normal

If your behaviour is helping your relationship

You are feeling depressed

We have dealt with the idea that we all have some inferiority feelings and that these feelings are major factors in the relationships between people in close relationships. Inferiority feelings can be shown in a large number of ways. In one person, they can result in a greater than normal drive for success, such as in business, sports and even housecleaning and child raising. There are some housekeepers who clean compulsively – sometimes not even letting their families into a room because it might get dirty. Child raising is a much more common area to find the effects of inferiority, because the child is smaller and 'more inferior' than the adult. The child is therefore easier to control and can become a tool of the parent whose unconscious mind does not rest on a foundation of love, success and a true feeling of self-esteem.

Often the effects of the feelings of inferiority include a strong feeling of loneliness. This can develop an overwhelming need to be wanted and to have somebody who will support you. That loneliness needs to be cured. The problem is that the inferiority feelings still exist, even if someone is taking care of you. Maturity cannot be gained just by saying 'I do'.

Another common kind of effect of inferiority, often rooted in men who have lost their mothers early in life, is the need to control another person. These people are often successful in business or in other fields, but this success is not enough to eradicate their inferiorities. They must still control all who are around them. It may seem very masterful when we see it in a person whom we need – but in a marriage it is intolerable.

Another type of inferiority behaviour is often seen in women who have had dominant mothers and psychologically inactive fathers. They may dress well, be flirtatious and have bubbling personalities with many social skills. Some merely flaunt their sexuality, others act on it. This is sometimes a source of nymphomania. These women are continually seeking social approval to fill the emptiness of their inferior psyches.

A feeling of inferiority is also commonly found in the financial area. One person wants to control by handling all, or most, of the money. It can also be shown in people who must continually increase their wardrobes, buy flashy cars or spend lavishly on things which are not really important.

When we have stresses of different sorts, we make adjustments to them. This is part of our real psychological self. When we make unhealthy adjustments, it definitely affects our relationship and our romantic feelings. If we make unhealthy adjustments, our partner is highly likely to react negatively. If our partner makes such adjustments, it is then likely to affect our feelings of romance toward that partner. While it would be nice to be able to say that we are all good and we are all able to control every action we do − that isn't the way our minds work. Consequently, to understand the realities in each of us and how they affect our relationships is essential if we are going to progress toward the ideal and romantic relationship that is possible. Sometimes, we can understand how we react. Sometimes, we can change it for the better. Sometimes, we need competent therapy to do it. This chapter is a bit more negative. But we have all often seen relationships which have negative aspects to them. By understanding the negative forces, we should be more able to see them, eliminate them and replace them with behaviours which are positive for our relationship.

Do we have control of our own lives?

How we see ourselves

Self-view determines a great deal of our behaviour. Our selfview is important in our choices of adjustment patterns. People may be classified as internalisers (those who believe that they are responsible for their own fate) and externalisers (those who believe they are merely pawns of fate and are controlled by creatures or forces over which they have little or no control).

Studies of the 'externalisers' indicate that they are often limited in their outlook: rigid, prejudiced, uncreative and conforming. These people function reasonably well in a highly structured authoritarian social system such as is found in military life or in a strongly religious community. They are usually intolerant of change and sometimes strongly resist any attack on the authority to which they have surrendered control. In general, they are more motivated by the social system than by their internal drives.

Psychiatrist John Sims and geographer Duane Baumann were intrigued by the fact that many more Southerners than Northerners have been killed by tornadoes, even though the twisters of the South are less frequent and less intense. They checked several reasons why this might be so and concluded that the people of the South were more externally controlled. Southerners tended to believe in fate, luck and the will of God far more than did the people of the North. Northerners tended to believe that they controlled their own lives. They were far more likely to listen to the news and watch a barometer when tornadoes approached. They were also more likely to warn their neighbours of the impending peril.

Our view of ourselves and our world is learned early in life

Our adjustments to the stresses of life are also learned when we are young. The behaviourists believe that our views of ourselves and our reactions to stresses are determined by the type of reinforcement (rewards and approval) we have had. So if a parent encourages defiance in a child, that child will tend to become more defiant when faced with a problem. If a child is rewarded for crying or running away, then those are the types of responses we would expect from that child in a stress situation.

Stresses

There has been some concern of late that many jobs may be stress producing

A doctor may feel a certain stress in having to manage a medical practice or deciding on the necessity of a serious operation. But, usually, doctors are quite happy in their line of work. Certain jobs may, however, cause stress just from sheer boredom. The ten most boring jobs, not necessarily in this order, have been found to be: an assembly-line worker, operator of an elevator with pushbutton controls, typist in a clerical pool, bank guard, copier operator, keypunch operator, highway-toll collector, car watcher in a tunnel, file clerk and housewife. If you are in a job which you view as boring, it is not going to do much for your feelings of self-esteem. A move to a new occupation may also help your relationship because *you* will be happier.

Stresses are going to occur in everyone's life. It can be job stress (including raising your children), social-life stress, a disease, unhappiness with the political situation or problems in the relationship. When you feel stresses, you will adjust. Often, that adjustment is made in our relationship – because that is the safest place to react. Remember that our adjustments to our stresses are seldom done consciously. We often don't know that we are adjusting while our behaviour is changing.

Adjusting to stress

How you and your partner adjust to stressful situations can have a positive or negative effect on the relationship. We adjust to stresses by attacking the stress or by withdrawing from it. This is often called the 'fight or flight' response. We hope that our responses will be socially acceptable and mentally healthy:

There's a fire in the kitchen. Call the fire department. I'll get the fire extinguisher.

If you really think we have a problem with our marriage, why not go to a marriage counsellor. Perhaps then, we can understand the roots of the problem and find out how to cope with it.

I've tried everything I can think of to be friendly to Mr Jones. Everything else here at work is really great and I don't want to quit. So, I guess I'll just stay out of his way.

This air pollution bothers me as much as it does the rest of the family. I think I'll take that job away from the city. We'll probably be happier and healthier there.

The first two responses indicate an intelligent way of attacking a stress situation. The third and fourth responses indicate intelligent methods of withdrawing from a stress-ful situation. But often we use non-intelligent, mentally unhealthy ways of adjusting to a problem:

This is the house that belongs to the guy that fired me. Let's burn it down.

You fat slob, ever since we got married it's nag, nag, nag. You're a stupid idiot, and I've had enough of you.

That blasted Jones. He gets me so uptight that every night I've got to drink five or six beers just to relax and forget him.

I really hate this city living, the air pollution, the violence and all. I must spend at least 20 hours a week just dreaming about what it would be like to live in western Canada, the Arizona desert or the Swiss Alps.

Here we have similar situations, but the people made unhealthy adjustments to their stresses. The first two at-tacked abnormally. The second two withdrew abnor-mally.

Our bodies can't help but make adjustments to stresses. When our noses are tickled, we may sneeze. If germs invade us, we may develop a fever. When poisons are ingested, vomiting and diarrhoea result. Similarly, our minds make adjustments to stresses. We may develop physical problems such as ulcers or high blood pressure, we may become neurotic, overeat, get drunk, rationalise or use other such unhealthy adjustments. When we have problems in our lives, whether from the unconscious level

Figure 9 I try awfully hard to relax.

(from our earlier life) or from the conscious level (family, job and other stresses), we will make adjustments.

The way we adjust, generally, in our lives will tend to be the way we adjust in a relationship. If a person has had success in attacking as a means of adjustment, yelling at or hitting one's spouse may be utilised. If withdrawing from problems has been the norm in other areas of life, in the relationship it may show by abusing alcohol or other drugs, by withdrawing from sex or by being uncommunicative (Figure 9).

Normal and abnormal behaviour

Normal behaviour

This is determined by the society in which a person lives. It is based more on what is average behaviour (the norm) rather than on what might be ideal behaviour. An Englishman who chooses a strict vegetarian diet is not in the 'norm' of British eaters. In India, a vegetarian would be in the norm because those of the Hindu and Jain religions are generally vegetarians. In an inner-city ghetto, violence might be the norm for teenage boys. But at a senior citizens' home in the suburbs of the same city, violence would definitely be outside of the norm.

A society need not be thought of as a whole country or a culture but may be thought of as a smaller group of people with similar interests. So what might be 'normal' for an Orthodox Jew might not be in the norm for a Reformed Jew. What is the norm in London might not be the norm for the Lake District. And what is normal behaviour for a prizefighter in the ring would not be normal behaviour if he were attending a university class.

We can look at behaviour possibilities as being on a continuum with 'fight' (attacking reality) on one side and 'flight' (withdrawing from reality) behaviour on the other. Normal behaviour would be in the middle:

Fight (attack)				Flight (withdrawal)
(Abnormal)		(Normal)		(Abnormal)

When we encounter a stress, we typically adjust by attacking or withdrawing – fight or flight. Attacking can be as simple as standing up for yourself. But it can include yelling, physical abuse – and even murder. Withdrawing can be as simple as crying, daydreaming or retiring to your room. But it can include drug use, such as alcohol or sleeping pills, developing a neurosis or more serious mental problem – and the ultimate would be suicide.

The stresses which can bring on the fight-or-flight reaction can be as simple as being in slow traffic or burning the dinner, to losing our jobs or having a death in the family. In relationships, the stresses can be brought on by doing something or neglecting to do something.

Neglecting a loved one, forgetting a birthday or anniversary, or neglecting to do our responsibilities can be every bit as negative as storming out of the house or coming home too late.

If we are confronted by a problem or stress and choose to use 'attack' as a means of solving it, we might discuss the problem ourselves, with a friend or with a therapist. These would be in the ideal normal patterns for behaviour. If you were attending school and did poorly on a test, studying more diligently would have been a good type of attack, so your behaviour would be in the ideal–normal type of behaviour. If you were to meditate after a stressful situation, this would be an ideal type of withdrawing behaviour in coping with the situation.

Among the less desirable, more emotional, attacking adjustments we might use would be: yelling, arguing or slamming a door. These attacking behaviours would be closer to abnormal but probably still be in the normal range. We might also resort to criminal activity such as fighting or raping. These would definitely be in the abnormal area of attacking reality. Mass murderers, neo-Nazis, hate-group activists are all examples of emotional and senseless attacking as means of satisfying their huge inferiority complexes. Spousal and child beating also fall into this area of severe unhealthy adjustments to stress. They signal real problems in the personality of the perpetrator. The media have made us more attacking than before – more hitting, knives and guns. The media have given us permission to attack, even savagely.

If we choose to withdraw, we might either avoid an antagonising situation or keep quiet rather than arguing as an acceptable means of adjustment. We might resort to daydreaming or making excuses (rationalising). Or we might become drug addicts or alcoholics or commit suicide, as grossly abnormal types of withdrawing adjustments.

Everyone makes adjustments

The question is when do you or your partner make an adjustment that has gone past the bounds of normality. Psychiatrists and psychologists are often in disagreement as to where we leave normality and enter into an abnormal adjustment. The same actions may be normal or abnormal depending on the age of the individual or the cultural factors involved. For example, a nine-year-old living in a ghetto area might be involved in a fight once a month and be quite normal for his age and culture. However, when a celebrity, in a non-violent setting, gets in a fight, it may be seen as rather abnormal. But if a professional hockey player, the same age as the celebrity, gets in a fight during a game, it may be within the norm for the situation and many spectators are quite pleased.

Similarly, a normal 13-year-old might spend a good deal of time daydreaming about becoming popular on campus or being an outstanding athlete. But a 35-year-old who spent the same amount of time daydreaming might well be abnormal. A person might drink a fine wine with a delicious dinner and be quite normal. But a young person who gets drunk once a month may have some problems. An adult who handles problems by going on a drinking binge would definitely be making an abnormal adjustment.

If we are emotionally mature, we will be able to recognise when we or another person, especially our partner, is overadjusting to a stress. If we use alcohol or other drugs excessively, it is a danger signal. If we daydream too much or eat compulsively, it is cause for concern. If we cannot take the blame for our own failures, it might be time to take stock of our adjustment patterns. If we drive too fast or too recklessly, gamble compulsively or do anything else which might be considered to be an intemperate type of behaviour, there is probably some psychological problem that we are not successfully solving.

Some common patterns of adjusting

Everyone makes adjustments to stresses. Some of these adjustments are called 'defence mechanisms' by psychologists. The adjustment reactions are unconscious methods we use to deny or change our idea of reality. Our unconscious minds use the methods which have been found useful to reduce our anxieties. Since these mechanisms operate at the unconscious level, it is often difficult for us to see whether our behaviour is normal or abnormal. In fact, we usually see ourselves as being normal all the time. The list, at the start of the next section, will give you an idea of how you or your spouse might react to stresses. Normally, we can see these behaviours in others. The major problem is to determine how serious they may be in the relationship. Then, there is always the challenge to see which of these behaviours we are using. Such self-diagnosis takes both knowledge and insight.

Our adjustments to our stresses may be socially approved, socially tolerated, socially criticised or socially disapproved. For example, a person who works very hard is approved of by many people; one who watches television most of the time may be tolerated; one who is always making excuses may be criticised; and one who drives while drunk is disapproved.

Sometimes, it is the action which is approved or disapproved, other times it is the setting in which the action takes place and, sometimes, it is the degree to which the action occurs which makes it socially desirable

Figure 10   Fear carries you further than courage – but not in the
same direction.

or undesirable. A man who picks a fight in a pub is socially
disapproved. But the man who wins an Olympic gold
medal for boxing is socially approved. This would be an
example of the same action, fighting, in different settings.
An example of differences of degree in an adjustment
would be the person who cleans the bathroom once a
week as opposed to the person who cleans the bathroom
30 times each day (as happened in one of the classic cases
in the history of psychology).

If we use our defence mechanisms to an abnormal
degree, we can be diagnosed 'neurotic'. When we use
them to such a degree that we lose contact with reality,
we can be called 'psychotic'. A neurotic person is, by
definition, mentally ill. A psychotic person is severely
mentally ill (Figure 10).

One method of staying mentally healthy is to be able to
see when we are making an adjustment which may be

bordering on the abnormal. If we can see this in our behaviour, we may then be able to look for the cause of our anxiety. Once we find that anxiety, we can begin to work toward changing or eliminating it and we can begin to solve our problems more effectively using healthy adjustments and intelligent actions.

The following list of defence mechanisms or other types of adjustments will be categorised according to how the individual uses them to relate to the world. Some will be quite normal, some will be very abnormal. For clarity, they will be categorised according to whether the individual is attacking reality or withdrawing from reality.

Attacking reality – the fighting approach

Attacking reality can include such normal behaviours as:

- laughing;
- singing;
- nail-biting;
- thinking;
- working;
- playing;
- dancing; or
- swimming.

Some of these are constructive activities, some are meaningless. Being:

- overly aggressive in the use of a motor vehicle;
- fighting;

- beating a child;
- raping;
- robbing; or
- murdering

are signs of the 'fight' syndrome done to a harmful degree.

Traditionally, boys and men have been more overtly violent in their attacks on reality. They have fought, stolen and killed. Other men were not as violent in their harmful attacks on reality. They might have become bad-cheque passers, con men or exhibitionists. When women have used attack as an abnormal means of adjustment, they have usually been nonviolent in their attacks on reality. They might have shoplifted, become sexually promiscuous or resorted to prostitution, but they seldom became physically violent. Recently, however, it has become more common for women to involve themselves in physically violent activities – bomb making, gang fights, kidnapping, robbery, spousal beatings and murder. During the last ten years, the rate of arrests for violent crimes has risen twice as fast for women as for men.

There is very strong evidence that the violence shown in movies and on television has given us permission to be violent (L. Berkowitz, 'Some effects of thoughts on anti- and pro-social influences of media events', *Psychological Bulletin* (1984) 95–410; see also R. G. Geen, and E. I. Donnerstein, (eds) *Aggression: Theoretical and Empirical Reviews*, Vol. 1, Academic Press, New York). Not only have the media given permission, but they have shown us how to become ever more violent. Some years ago, after a movie depicted some boys pouring gasoline over an old man and burning him, the same scene was played out in real life, once with another old man being burned to death and a second with a social worker being set afire. Other violent scenes in the media have been copied by maladjusted people soon after they saw the action on television.

On the other hand, a sensitive portrayal of a violent act may make thinking people re-evaluate their ideas and behaviour. In a large study in which date rape was portrayed in a movie, many of the subjects in every age group changed their view of who caused the aggressive act. Most blamed the man, older women who had earlier thought that it was the woman's fault often changed their minds, but older men often reacted against the woman in the film (Barbara Wilson *et al.*, 'The impact of social issue television programming on attitudes toward rape', *Human Communication Research*, **19**(2), December 1992, 179–208). So the media can be used to increase or reduce violence – but the reality is that violence sells. Consequently, while such violence has anti-social outcomes, the belief of many that 'freedom of speech' includes saying and showing nearly anything will undoubtedly continue to give maladjusted people more methods of gratifying themselves by conquering others through violence and other means of attack. This is, increasingly, finding its way into family relationships as spousal and child beating.

Types of attacking behaviours

The major attacking or 'fight' adjustments are:

Displacement

This occurs when a person releases strong emotional feelings against something, or someone, who was not the actual cause of the anxiety. A student might throw a rock through a school window after failing a test. An adult might yell at a spouse or child after having had an argument with the boss at work.

One of James Thurber's cartoon characters indicated this very well. We find him lying on a sofa with his telephone pressed against his ear and saying 'Well, if I called the wrong number, why did you answer the phone?' Like so many people – he couldn't be wrong!

Hate groups are common vehicles for senseless attacking. Whether they be white (as with the Ku Klux Klan, Nazis or skinheads), black (as some in the Nation of Islam) or Jewish (as the Jewish Defense League), the displacement of feelings against unknown others because of a different race or religion is a sign of severe abnormality. People, who at the unconscious level, believe themselves to be inferior, can consciously feel superior when they join a group and can feel superior to all those in other groups which they are against.

Attacking reality can be seen as power motivation which is misdirected. The beating of a spouse or a child, the rape of one who is either an acquaintance or a stranger, a drive-by shooting, a car jacking are examples of criminal behaviour in which one uses physical force to attack reality. If estimates are correct, perhaps the most common site for physical attacks is in the home. Estimates are that 2 million women in the USA are severely assaulted by their male partners each year. Further estimates are that between one in three and one in five emergency-room treatments on women are for battery (*University of California Wellness Letter*, April 1994, citing a study by the Council of Scientific Affairs of the American Medical Association). Of all battery cases, 10% involve the woman beating her male partner. Furthermore, women make up 40% of the cases of spousal murderers (Department of Justice report cited in *Los Angeles Times*, 21 July 1994) (See Box 2).

Box 2 Recent statistics of women being beaten

		% of adult women beaten during the last year	*% of adult women who have ever been beaten*
Australia	1993–1994	22.4	Not available
Canada	1993	3.0	29
UK	1993	12.0	30
USA	1998	1.3	22.1

The profile of male batterers indicates that: they lack problem-solving skills, are somewhat hostile and that they are likely to act out their hostility. They also tend to be self-critical with lower self-esteem. In addition, their perception of their relationships tended to change from seeing their partner earlier as highly valued, then later as having a very low value. As expected, uncontrollable anger is also a factor in the personality of the batterer (*The Menninger Letter*, 1 : 9, September 1993, p. 1, reporting on a study by LaTina Else). Batterers come from every social class and every ethnic group.

The violent use of the automobile is a common method of attacking reality. Frustrations which build up in one's mind or feelings of inferiority can often be released behind the wheel. It may be done legally while bouncing over sand dunes in a Jeep. But, it is much more likely to be done illegally in unauthorized drag races, highway speeding and generally unsafe driving.

Many people attack by the way they drive their cars. There seem to be three major types of hazardous drivers:

1 The selfish or proud driver will not let another person pass or will not yield the right of way because it makes him or her feel inferior.

2 The person with sudden fits of temper (a sign of immaturity) is inclined to feel intimidated when another driver tries to pass; this angry person may cut in on another driver or tailgate when frustrated.

3 The third type of neurotic driver is the one who is withdrawing from reality through the use of drugs such as alcohol. This driver is a danger because of the slowed reaction times.

Do any of these reactions fit you or your partner?

Jealousy and envy

These can also be seen as examples of aggressive behaviour, which is not warranted. Envy is often an effect of inferiority feelings. The envious person has destructive impulses toward a good object. It differs from jealousy in that jealousy involves a third person or an imagined third person, who may be a threat to a loving relationship with another person. Envy involves only two people, the self and the envied person. The envy may be exhibited solely by thoughts or talk about the person, but, in its extreme form, it may emerge as homicidal actions. As with other adjustments, it doesn't make sense logically, but our unconscious minds do not work on logical principles.

Passive aggressive behaviour

This occurs when a person is being aggressive by being passive. A husband or wife may show displeasure with the other by consciously not touching the other or by not talking. Withdrawing sex can also fit into this pattern.

If you see in your mate, or your potential mate, any of these types of behaviours, you should be wary. While driving recklessly or yelling may seem 'normal' at times, they indicate some insight into their behaviour. You don't want those aggressive tendencies to be taken out on you.

Types of withdrawing behaviour – the fleeing approach

Withdrawing from reality is probably our most common type of adjustment. We might overeat, smoke, cry, sleep a great deal, daydream or use alcohol or other drugs. Even working on a hobby is a type of withdrawing. Some of these are good, even necessary and healthy adjustments. Others can be carried to an abnormal degree. In each of the following types of adjustments, it is always the degree of adjustment that determines whether or not a pattern of behaviour is in the healthy or the unhealthy area.

We can categorise the types of withdrawing behaviour which we might use as:

- *forgetting reality* (such as daydreaming);
- *distorting reality* (such as rationalising in which the truth is distorted);
- *atoning for reality* (making up for real needs by compensating in other ways); and
- *retreating from reality* (such as is done when resorting to drugs or suicide).

Forgetting reality

Forgetting the real world by fantasising or daydreaming can be carried past the boundaries of normality. In fantasising the person looks to what might be and forgets what is. Another type of forgetting is called *repression*. Here, we repress or forget painful thoughts which are attempting to enter our consciousness. We don't like to think that we have been hated by our parents. So, we might repress our memories of when we were severely beaten or neglected.

Daydreaming can be a problem or an aid. Healthy fantasies can help us define our goals, but they are worthless if we don't act on them.

The defense mechanisms which a person might use in 'forgetting reality' are:

Denial of reality

This can occur to inward or outward stimuli. It is denial when a person does not acknowledge something which he or she knows to be true. A person may deny that there is a risk of pregnancy when engaging in heterosexual intercourse. Another may deny that there are problems in the marriage when such problems really exist. Still another may deny the reality of danger in riding motorcycles by riding with street shoes and no helmet. Alcoholics and other drug users commonly deny that they have problems.

Fantasy or daydreaming

This occurs when we delight in imagining ourselves to be other than we are: a professional athlete, a glamorous personality or a person unusually successful in any field.

Repression

This occurs when we do not allow unwanted thoughts to enter our conscious minds. Feelings such as shame, pain or guilt are likely to be repressed because we are embarrassed by them.

Distorting reality

Distorting reality is done by 'transferring' our feelings or by 'rationalising'; that is, giving reasons for our behaviour which we believe to be true, but which are not really true. We must be careful not to talk ourselves into believing something which is not true. We can generally give a reason for what we did. But was it the real reason or a 'rationalisation' – an excuse:

> *I like being fat because fat people are jolly. And I'm really happy this way. [Is this the real reason or is it that I can't control my impulse to have 'pleasure now'.]*

> *When another person acts antagonistically, he's ugly ... When I do it, it's nerves. When she's set in her ways, she is obstinate ... When I do it, it's firmness ... When he doesn't like my friends, he's prejudiced ... When I don't like his friends, I'm showing good judgement of character ... If she takes*

too much time to do something, she's lazy ... When I do it, I'm deliberate ... When he continually finds things wrong, he's cranky ... When I do it, I'm discriminating. I'm just like Mary Poppins ... practically perfect.

The defense mechanisms which can be categorised under the area of 'distorting reality' are:

Rationalisation

This is a very common type of behaviour excuse. In using this, we give a reason which sounds good to us and to others, but it is not the real reason for our behaviour. Yet, we believe ourselves when we rationalise (Figure 11):

Figure 11 Everybody's wrong but me and thee, and sometimes even thee is a little queer.

I bought a new car because my old one needed new brakes. [The real reason might have been to enhance my need for esteem from others.]

I hit you because you needed it.

More than likely, we are responsible for our own situations. But it is so much easier to find someone else to blame. Since we tend to think of ourselves as perfect, it is difficult to see ourselves as occasionally inept – only the mature person can realise a personal failure or admit to a mistake.

'*Sour grapes*' is the name applied to the rationalisation which a person gives when depreciating that which cannot be attained; that is, making something good (such as a grape) appear to be bad (sour):

I don't mind that I failed medical school. I didn't want to be a doctor anyway. They're all too money hungry.

I wouldn't want to get married, even if somebody asked me.

In the 'sweet lemon' type of rationalisation, something which is really bad is made to appear good:

I'm glad I got fired. I didn't like that job anyway.

I'm glad we broke up. She was too perfect. There wasn't anything wrong with her. She probably wouldn't have liked me after she really got to know me.

Projection

This is a type of rationalisation. When we blame another person for our own inadequacies or failures we are projecting:

> *That teacher doesn't like me. That's why I flunked the exam. [Is it possible that I hadn't studied?]*

> *She's really stuck-up. That's why she won't go out with me. [Could it be that my personality turns her off?]*

> *The police killed somebody of our race – let's burn down the city.*

> *You never want to go out. I have to sit home day and night.*

> *If you weren't on my case all the time, I wouldn't have argued with the boss and lost my job.*

Reaction formation

This means that the person says or acts in a manner exactly opposite of what is felt. A person may be nice to another while actually disliking that person.

Idealisation

This occurs when a person thinks too highly of another. Believing that a mother or child, husband or wife will take care of you for ever, because they are perfect and they will love you for ever. The 'madonna–prostitute' syndrome is a neurosis in which a man cannot make love with his wife because he loves her like his mother. There are only good girls and bad girls. You can't have sex with good girls.

Denigration

This is just the opposite. Here a person sees another as bad, when it is not the case. A parent may be blamed for a child's failure. The child sees the parent as responsible for everything that has gone wrong in life.

Atoning for reality

Atoning for reality is another major type of withdrawing from reality. In this major-adjustment category, the person tries to make up for the problems, such as an inferiority complex, by doing something to excess in another area – usually a non-productive area.

Transference

This occurs when we transfer our positive or negative feelings from one person to another:

> *It was love at first sight. She looked just like my mother.*

> *He is from Oxford, and you know I've never trusted anyone from there. Once, I heard of one who was a bookie.*

Figure 12 When you're in a rut, but you think you're in the
groove – you're an egotist.

Egocentrism

This is the name given to behaviour in which the person is
overly concerned with himself or herself. Bragging,
throwing a temper tantrum, or showing off are examples
of this mechanism (Figure 12):

> *I'm the flashiest dresser in this town.*

> *Nobody has a car faster than mine. I am the greatest.*

Negativism

This is the name of the behaviour which people use when
they continually thwart constructive ideas or the power of
legitimate authority.

> *I'll tell you Wright brothers, you'll never get this
> thing off the ground.*

I don't want to go to that party. There probably won't be anyone interesting there anyway.

Last time we went on a vacation it was terrible. Let's just stay home.

As a member of a partnership you should continually be thinking of affirming your partner's self-esteem. The development of the relationship is the objective – not satisfying your power drive. Forget the put-downs.

Identification

This occurs when we see another person as an ideal, then make some psychological link with them. When a child adopts some of the values or behaviours of a parent in order to avoid the wrath of the parent, the child is using this mechanism. An adult may also adopt characteristics of a departed parent or loved one. Some people identify with an institution such as a professional sports team, as a means of developing a feeling of importance. Others identify with people by collecting pictures, autographs or records of an 'ideal' person:

United is my team, win or tie. We can beat your team any day of the week and twice on Sunday.

I have a personally autographed picture of Tom Cruise. I've seen every film he's ever made. I even write him at least once a week.

Substitution

This occurs when a person enters one activity because of the fear of failure in another. Having a number of children may be a way of avoiding having to go to work.

Perfectionism

This is a type of substitution. However, the person feels that, in order to be adequate, it is necessary to overachieve at the chosen activity. It is the adjustment mechanism in which a person attempts to escape blame by being perfect. Being perfect sounds fine, but it can be overdone.

> *I vacuum my house every day. I just can't stand any mess at all. People are always complimenting me on how nice my home is.*

Compensation

This occurs when a person tries to make up in one area what is lacking in another. Helen Keller, who was blind and deaf, compensated by developing a great depth of character which was exposed in her writings and speeches. This was an admirable kind of compensation. Some people become 'workaholics'. They spend a great deal of time at their jobs. This may be desirable, sometimes. But it may occur because the hard-working person does not know how to relate to his or her home and family. In this case, it is undesirable.

Another type of undesirable compensation is compulsive eating. In this, a person tries to use food as a way of compensating for what is lacking in another area of life.

Overeating to compensate for a feeling of inferiority is a common example.

Sympathism

This is used when a person seeks the sympathy of others when problems or failures occur. The sympathy gained helps to bolster the person's feeling of worth. Often, when problems develop in a relationship, one of the partners, usually the woman, will seek sympathy from others. This sympathy can bolster their ego. A better approach would have been to seek counselling.

Fixation

This occurs when a person stops developing in one or more areas of psychological growth. It can happen because the person was either frustrated, or experienced a great deal of pleasure at that age. The pleasure of childhood masturbation might 'fix' a person at that level of sexual enjoyment and not allow more advanced levels of sexual fulfilment to develop. Or 'daddy's little girl' or 'mama's little boy' may want to stay dependent on their mate after marriage, as they were with their parent, instead of growing up and being an adult partner.

Compulsive gambling

While not a defence mechanism, this is another common method which people use to compensate for reality. Dr Robert Custer, a New Jersey psychiatrist, has been studying compulsive gambling for many years. He found that

80% of these people suffered severe parental deprivation as children. Commonly, the mother was severely mentally ill, often alcoholic, and the father was often a gambler who was absent from home a great deal. Furthermore, he found that 96% of compulsive gamblers had developed this adjustment by the time they were 21 years old – often, by the time they were 15.

While financially, gambling is generally a losing proposition, for the gambler it can be a psychologically satisfying activity. Since the drive for power is so often primary for maladjusted people, gambling can satisfy that drive. If you win, you obviously have had a 'power' experience. On the other hand, if you lose, the odds were stacked against you anyway so you cannot be held to blame.

While gambling on sports, horse racing and games of chance are the most common, many people have taken to gambling on the stock market. Even some of the top dogs in the stock exchanges have found the fascination of speculating on high-risk options too much to pass up.

Retreating from reality

Retreating from reality occurs when a person tries to avoid the real world. It may be done by developing physical symptoms which separate the 'ego' from the world (such as is done in psychologically induced blindness or paralysis), developing multiple personalities, by committing suicide, by running away or by retreating from the world through drugs of various types (Figure 13).

The adjustment pattern associated with retreating from reality is called avoidance.

Figure 13   The greater our unhappiness, the greater our need to
escape.

Avoidance

This is a common method of coping with threatening
situations. By avoiding the situation, it cannot threaten
you. People who refuse to ride in commercial airliners
use this technique. We might avoid seeking a job, even
though their relationship needs more money, because of a
fear of failure. Phobias (unwarranted fears) are a type of
neurosis which falls under this behaviour pattern.

Running away from home is a far too frequent form
of adjustment for unhappy teenagers. But it is also a
relatively common method in adults who desire to
leave a family situation. In the past, it was most likely
to be the man who would run away from a relationship.
Now, however, mothers often leave their families in
search of the happiness which has eluded them in the
traditional role of a housewife. And a few years ago, two
professors left their very prestigious universities in the
USA. One was found months later working as a shill in

Las Vegas. The other was a stable boy at Hollywood Park racetrack.

Fearing success

This is another type of avoidance. Because of their own inferiority complexes, some parents or teachers may 'put down' children and make them believe that they cannot be successful. When that child does achieve success in one area, he or she may unconsciously look for failure in another area. For example, a student who passes a test with a high grade may argue with a friend so that the relationship fails, at least for a while.

Drugs, including alcohol

These are probably the most serious type of retreat from reality. They can aid a person in retreating from reality by depressing the brain, stimulating the brain or by causing hallucinations. Alcohol and 'downers' depress the brain and make you forget your problems and stresses. Uppers, like cocaine and amphetamines, give a 'high' that over-powers the depression which is being experienced.

Procrastination

This is a common method of avoidance. We certainly see this type of avoidance when we are in school. Studying for tests or writing research papers are not always as interesting as talking with friends or going to parties. When the reality hits us that the exam is tomorrow or the paper is due in two days, we will have to cram and will probably not be nearly as effective as if we had put the same number of hours into the effort over a two-week period. Procrastination attacks us all when we have unpleasant tasks which we must do, whether it is doing a business report, doing our taxes or cleaning the house – procrastination is a frequent visitor to our lives. People who plan for the future and don't procrastinate certainly have progressed along the road to maturity.

Shyness

This is another example of avoidance. A feeling of inferiority due to perceived inadequacies of a person's body or a lack of self-esteem make many people shy. This shyness is more likely to be evident earlier in life, especially during the years before and during high school. As we enter college or succeed in a profession, it is more likely that the shyness passes as we become more sure of ourselves. Shyness can often be conquered by forcing ourselves to function in situations where we would ordinarily be shy, such as at a dance, party or a business meeting.

Suicide

This is now responsible for 20% of the deaths of young people in the UK. The highest rates are for men 25–45 and over 75. Young white women have a risk only about 25% of that for men and black women have a risk only half that of white women. Its rate has doubled during the last 30 years. Suicide is the ultimate retreat from reality (Box 3).

The foregoing brief survey of psychological manifestations is certainly not complete nor in depth. But the

Box 3   Recent suicide statistics from
the World Health Organization

Rates per 100,000 people in 1997

UK	3.2
Canada and Australia	5.1
New Zealand	5.9
USA	4.4
Hungary	14.7
Sri Lanka	16.8

reality is that we all adjust, and our adjustment patterns are not infinite. We tend to react in somewhat similar ways – either attacking or withdrawing from reality. As mentioned, most of these 'defence mechanisms' or adjustment patterns can be done within a normal range, or to an abnormal range to a neurotic or even a psychotic degree.

Sometimes, we bring these adjustment patterns to the relationship. Other times, they develop as a result of problems during the time we are in the relationship. They may be due to the relationship. They may also be due to forces outside of the relationship, such as our jobs, our relatives or our neighbours. Whatever the cause of their development, they will undoubtedly affect our relationships when they occur. Consequently, we should be on guard against excessive behaviour adjustments in our partners before and after the marriage. Whatever behaviour adjustments have worked will continue to be used.

The person who gets relief by using drugs and alcohol will tend to continue to use them more and more. The person who gets his or her ego satisfied because people feel sorry, will continue to seek sympathy. We will all use some of these adjustment patterns, do we yell and scream, do we work harder, do we cry? Whatever the pattern of adjustment we each use, it should be understood – and controlled. Certainly, we must be aware of these psychological patterns in our relationships.

It is heart-warming to see how often a young lover can get a potential spouse to give up alcohol or other drugs. The 'it's my way or the highway' attitude of 'tough love' pits a chosen person against a chosen behaviour. The person will usually win. Seeing an unhealthy adjustment pattern early in a relationship can allow you to aid in the change or leave before it is too late. It's usually more difficult to get a partner to change once the relationship is established – because the power drive stops us from being coaxed to change our ways.

When you recognise unhealthy adjustment patterns in yourself or your partner, something should be done. Does his driving endanger you or the children? If so, it must be addressed. Is his or her behaviour becoming more aggressive or more withdrawing? If so, you should find out why. When the adjustments reach the neurotic or psychotic states, competent help must be brought in. It is not uncommon for a person who has been quite normal to develop severe adjustment patterns, which may include hearing voices, severe depression or other abnormal behaviours. It is difficult to realise that our loved one may have developed a severe mental problem, when they have always seemed so normal. And, just like alcoholics and drug abusers, we often deny that our mate has a problem. These mental adjustments will certainly hurt the romance – but reality must step in and save the relationship!

The psychological contract in marriage

The obvious and the hidden aspects of our relationships

Read this chapter if:

You wonder whether there are things you don't know
about your relationship

You want to get an idea as to why you and your mate
don't think alike

You want to get a glimpse of the deeper aspects of your
relationship

You want to see how you can develop a greater intimacy
by sharing unshared thoughts and ideas

You think a committed relationship is simple and can be
easily shared

It is a discomforting fact that many marriages are con-
ceived in neurosis. The need to be wanted, the need to
be independent of our parents and the need to feel that we
are adult are very poor reasons for marriage. Still, they are
quite common reasons for many marriages. We find the

Hydra-headed facets of the inferiority complex popping up again and again in the reasons for, and the problems of, marriage. Alcoholism and other drug-related problems, spousal and child beatings, and incestual molestations are the most negative of these manifestations of the inferiority complex. But control of the purse strings, sarcasm, passive aggressive behaviours and baseless jealousies are even more common. And many of the problems of sexual relations are rooted in the feelings of inferiority which have grown from our lack of control in our own lives.

Probably, no other culture has the idealised idiocy to believe that 'love conquers all' or that 'my marriage will be ecstasy'. While some people get lucky, most of us have to plan and work at it to produce the achievement of a perfect relationship. We are hampered to a large degree by not understanding how our unconscious needs are often more important than our conscious desires and understandings.

Possibly, the most important contribution of Sigmund Freud was that he popularised the idea that we have unconscious minds – that many of the essentials in our minds which direct our behaviour are unknown to us. They are below our conscious level. We therefore don't know what they are. But they are there!

Anyone with even a passing knowledge of psychology realises that many of the things we do are not done with intelligence – that is, for rational reasons. But, of course, we don't register the unconscious sources of many of our actions so we 'rationalise' our behaviours – giving reasons which sound good to us and which we believe to be true. The problem, of course, is that we cannot truly understand most of our underlying motivational forces. We just think that we do.

All of us do some things without honestly knowing why – in spite of our rationalisations. Some people behave *most* of the time without really knowing why. It is obvious that a psychotic who thinks he is Napoleon doesn't have all his marbles. It is a little less obvious when the neurotic blames others for his own faults. But it is even less obvious when one person continually 'puts down' a partner, or when that 'needed' drink is a must every night after work.

In our relationship understandings and agreements (i.e. our 'contracts'), we often deal with the needs and wants which are quite clear to us. We are guided by our career and recreational decisions our parenting decisions, and our finances. But additionally – we have psychological contracts. These are generally 'implied' contracts:

I drank more than I should have before we got married and I will continue to drink afterwards.

You were sweet before we got married so you should stay sweet.

But, sometimes, the 'contract' behaviours change. We had great sex before we got married, but not much sex now. Why? There are probably psychological reasons for the change. Those reasons are often deeply seated.

Another type of psychological problem develops when a person wants a parent figure who is like their father or mother or who will replace the father or mother whom they never had. Other times, a spouse wants to assume the parent role over their mate, always knowing 'what is good for him or her':

- he is a better cook than his homemaker wife, and he takes pride in showing her up and 'teaching' her how;
- she pampers and takes care of him continually when

Figure 14   When you look in the mirror, who do you see? A
friend or an enemy?

he is at home, because that's her job. Both of these
people may think they are 'loving' their mates, but,
actually, it is their power drives that are primary.
They are trying to reduce their own inferiority
complexes by showing that they are very good
(Figure 14).

The psychological contract

This is an essential, but seldom understood, aspect of
every relationship. Two psychotherapists (Clifford
Sager and Helen Singer Kaplan (eds), 'The marriage contract', *Progress in Group and Family Therapy*, Brunner/
Mazel, New York, 1972, pp. 483–497) have theorised
that there are three levels of psychological contract in
a marriage. They are: the conscious–verbalised; the

conscious–non-verbalised; and the unconscious, which, of course, cannot be verbalised. While marriage counsellors have traditionally recognised that the first two levels of understanding existed, they were not generally looking at the unconscious level of needs and drives. The levels are:

1 *The first level* is the contract that gets people into a marriage. They are aware (conscious) of their own desires and the desires of the other person. These understandings may be in the areas of religion, recreation, vocation, sex, family responsibilities, etc. The couple have talked about these, or have acted in such a way, so that the understanding for each person is clear.

2 *The second level* of contract is conscious (the person understands), but it has not been communicated to the other person (non-verbalised). This is an area which will lead to trouble and perhaps to divorce. The power drive, in any of its many manifestations, is often a major factor. It might be in the financial area – one spends too much money or is too stingy, and the other does not want to bring this up as a problem. It might be that one always gets his or her way without consulting the other – and the other won't say anything about it. It might be as simple as leaving on the lights when leaving a room, squeezing the toothpaste in the middle of the tube or leaving the toilet seat up or down – depending on which one irritates the spouse. Even such simple problems are often not discussed but continue to be irritants. But the person who is bothered by the action, or inaction, won't bring up the problem. It is common in marriage counselling for the counsellor to talk with both people for an hour

or two. This allows the first level of contract to be understood. Usually, the parties are seen separately for their second appointment. This gives the counsellor a chance to understand the problems which have developed at the second level – the 'conscious but non-verbalised' problems.

3   *The third level* of psychological contract, the 'unconscious non-verbalised' level, may never be addressed. It is extremely difficult to properly assess the unconscious mind – especially in the rather short time available for marriage counselling. The most common source of the problems at this level is the great inferiority feelings which many people have and their attempts to remedy them through their power drives. It is common in any counselling to believe what the troubled person says. The problem, however, is that what they say may not really indicate what is at the unconscious level of their minds. So, whether it is a friend or a trained therapist trying to help, there must be the realisation that what a person says is the problem, and the actual real problem, may be quite different. A person may blame a parent, employer, friend or mate for a problem when the real source of the problem may be deep in the unconscious mind of the troubled person.

Because of the essential nature of the needs found in the unconscious mind, developing a complete understanding of the relationship at the conscious level becomes an almost impossible task. However, if we can understand the many ramifications of the drive for power and can understand what we and our mate have experienced, we may have a bit more insight into understanding our real needs and how the relationship must develop to meet our needs and aid our growth. We have certainly already discussed some of our expectations in terms of economic priorities, children, hobbies, expected roles, affection and intimacy. This should give us a good start. But, as every book on marriage reiterates, we must be able to communicate both the good and the bad, the expectations and the realities. Consequently, a successful marriage requires two very mature people who are aware of their needs and the need to accept or compromise.

To aid us in understanding the various levels of expectations, or contracts, let us look at the classic case described by Sagar and Kaplan. While most of us will see the people in this case as a bit unusual, the insight developed may help to make us understand that we too may have hidden agendas.

This was a marriage between an English professor, who was also a writer and his wife, a former student who wanted to be a writer. Their original contract for marriage was an exchange between his need to learn to be sexual and her need to have help in developing her own writing career. Both of these relate to their inferiority complexes and their need for power in their lives. (These are not typical contract ideas for the average marriage. Thank God!!)

Their concerns which they had talked about and were aware of

The *conscious, verbalised* needs and understandings

WIFE

1   Men and women are equal. I will assume equal obligations and will take care of you when needed. I expect
equal rights and privileges.

2   You have the power to help me become a better writer
because you are a professor of English and a good
writer. I am insecure in my ability to write. I expect
you to assist me in being a better writer.

3   I am often depressed and moody. You should not
reject me when I am like that.

(In exchange for these things you do for me)

1   I am able to help you sexually and will be happy to do
it. I won't humiliate you because you are just learning
about sex.

HUSBAND

1 Men and women are equal. I will assume equal obligations and will take care of you when needed. I expect
equal rights and privileges.

2 I will help you to be a good writer and I won't compete
with you. But I will try to get you to write in a different
area than I do because your competitiveness makes me
uneasy.

(In exchange for these)

1 You will improve in your moods.

2 You will help me to become a sexually adequate man.

Not exactly your average 'gushing all over each other – life
will be ecstasy' feelings as the bride and groom walked
down the aisle!

The next level of the psychological contract is the 'conscious but not talked about' level. If you were to seek marriage counselling this would be uncovered at the first or second session. These are the things that 'bug' you but you don't say anything about or mention to your mate – however, you 'stew' about it, when your partner's behaviour doesn't change.

Conscious but not verbalised

Needs and understandings (not talked about)

WIFE

1 I am afraid that I will fail if I try to become a professional writer. I am not competitive. I am afraid I will fail. I am helpless. I am jealous of you because you are successful. I want and need your help so that I can be accepted by others.

2 I am afraid you will leave me because of my moodiness.

(In exchange for these)

1 You expect me to help you with sex. I will be happy to do that so that you feel that you are an adequately sexual man.

HUSBAND

1 I will help you to be a good writer and won't compete with you. But I will try to get you to write in a different area than I do because your competitiveness makes me uneasy.

2 I will keep trying to reassure you but it really bothers me. I hope that you mature quickly and become strong like my sister – who is really my ideal woman.

(In exchange for these)

1 I want many women but they will not want me unless I become better sexually. You are my only chance to become sexual.

Here, we see the inferiority complex recognised by both people in themselves, but they don't mention it to the other. Also, in the husband, we see that his sister is his ideal. We all have certain ideals in our minds – but we often don't know exactly what they are. I may want a woman who picks up after me, like my mother did. But I may also want a woman who is well educated and well travelled, like my Aunt Matilda. I would also like someone as sexy as Cher, as sweet as my high-school girlfriend and as rich as the Queen.

You can also imagine this scenario. A lower middle-class high-school girl has a best friend who is very rich. Both girls like to be with the poorer father because he has a great deal of time to spend with them. He takes them to the beach and camping. The rich girl's father is seldom home. But he has money and sends both girls to Hawaii for a graduation present. It is quite possible that each girl will want some of each father in a husband. It is nice to have money but it is also desirable to have someone home with whom to spend time.

We seldom sort out all the desirable and undesirable attributes we want in a mate – and, if we did, no one would fit our idealised dream. A number of years ago, before I entered the picture, my wife and a good friend were passing the time one weekend in my wife's cabin in the snow country. They came up with a list of ten 'criteria' for the perfect man. I came along some time later. (I trust that I fulfilled at least one criterion – but I haven't been shown the list.)

Just yesterday, the friend sent a greeting card with a list of ten 'requirements' in a man. The greeting-card writer saw it this way:

My top 10 requirements in a MAN (original list)

1 handsome;

2 charming;

3 financially secure;

4 a caring listener;

5 witty;

6 fit;

7 stylish dresser;

8 appreciates the finer things;

9 full of thoughtful little surprises;

10 an imaginative, romantic lover.

(Revised list – after no one was found to qualify for the original list.)

1 not too ugly;

2 doesn't belch or scratch in public;

3 has a job;

4 doesn't nod off while I'm talking;

5 usually remembers the punch lines of jokes;

6 sufficiently physically fit to carry the shopping bags;

7 usually wears matching socks;

8 knows not to buy wine with screw-top lids;

9 remembers to put the toilet seat down – sometimes;

10 shaves on weekends.

Probably nobody honestly feels that he or she is in total control. The president of the United States is the most powerful person in the world today. Does that mean that the president doesn't have inferiority feelings? Not on your life! Does Bill Clinton wish that his former girl-friends, or 'would be' girlfriends, had not negatively affected his image. You bet! Did he wish that Saddam Hussein had tripped over the side of the Hanging Gardens or that Fidel Castro had swallowed a large Havana cigar? I would assume so. Did Nixon wish that he had never been involved in Watergate? Did Reagan wish that he hadn't fallen asleep in his cabinet meetings? Does Jerry Ford wish that he didn't have the reputation as a clumsy golfer? Did Jimmy Carter wish that he hadn't said that he had 'lusted in his heart?' Hey! None of us are perfect.

So let's look at the unconscious level of our 'dream' couple for a moment. The inferiority feelings which were somewhat evident in the first level (conscious–verbalised) and became quite evident in the second level (conscious–non-verbalised) become much more explicit at the most basic levels of their minds (the unconscious–non-verbalised level). Their unexpressed needs can be seen to be fundamental to their motivations and the way they live their lives. For all of us, our deepest needs control our thinking and actions. Since we don't have a clear picture of what our deepest needs are, we certainly can't discuss them in developing a relationship contract.

The deepest level of psychological contract is the one which Sagar and Kaplan really 'discovered'. It is the unconscious level. At the unconscious level, we don't know what is in the deepest recesses of our minds. None of us know our unconscious thoughts. If we did, they would be 'conscious'.

To uncover even a small part of this area would require working with a trained and expert therapist for months or years. Even then, you might not tap into the roots of your motivations. As has been mentioned many times, the inferiority complex is a major controller of most people's behaviour. We don't like to think that it is there, but it is. For most of us, it is that lack of power to be what we want to be and do what we want to do.

Unconscious (so it can't be talked about)

WIFE

1   I am nothing – but I want to be everything. Only through your help can I achieve this?

2   You must be strong and powerful for me, so that I can use your power to control, dominate and compete. I will do whatever you want so that I can use your male power.

3   Females are passive – males are active. I want to destroy you for being a strong male. This makes me feel inferior. I will not leave you if you let me destroy you.

4   I am excited by the thought of your having sex with other women. I will let you go if you have other women for me.

5   I am afraid you will leave me if you have sex with other women because you will compare me with them. So you must not have other women because of that.

6   We must be close and intimate.

7   We must stay separate and not be intimate.

8   You must do all of these things. If you do I will stay with you.

HUSBAND

1 I want other men to envy me. They will only if I have other women and can brag about it.

2 But I am afraid to be sexually free. I can only do it if I have your permission. I expect you to approve of me being more sexual because of everything I do for you. If you give me the confidence and the ability to be sexually free and if I have your permission I will let you dominate me.

3 But women are inferior. I want to dominate you. If you dominate me I will be angry at you. I will hate myself for being so dependent I will not leave you if you let me dominate you and place you in an inferior position.

Our minds

If you say that these ideas don't make sense – you are absolutely right. But, we are not rational at our unconscious levels. So, we can have diametrically opposed demands at the unconscious level. Obviously, no one can satisfy a person with such unconscious ideas. We hope that the couple in the illustration is rather different from us. Still, we should recognise that both of us in a relationship may have some deep-seated needs which are unrecognised.

Box 4

You can imagine that, with all these differences in memories and values for each person, we start with more differences in our minds than those we have discussed – because we can only discuss what is in our conscious mind

The conscious mind Things of which we are aware	*Intellect* Independent thinking part of our mind	*Conscience* The values we practise *consciously*
Unconscious mind Things which we have forgotten from the conscious mind • Inherited drives (if they exist) • Experiences from our childhoods and from our later years which have bypassed our conscious minds		*Values which* we have forgotten or which are ingrained in us by our society or our religion – but which exist in our unconscious minds

If we are rational at all, it is only a small part of our conscious mind which would have that capacity. We might call this our intellect. It is that part of our mind that is reading this book and reacting to it.

Box 4 is a diagram of what our minds might be. The conscious mind contains everything that we can remember. It would also contain that part of our mind which can think and reason.

Box 4 is purposely made to show that the unconscious is much larger than the conscious. Freud said that the

Figure 15   A conscience is a small inner voice that gives you the odds.

conscious mind is only the tip of the iceberg. Our values (i.e. what we think is important) can also be both conscious and unconscious. What we value as good or hold as terrible can be held in our unconscious minds. For example, if you were sexually molested by a family member when you were two years old, you may have forgotten about it in your conscious mind, but your unconscious value may be that sex is terrible and an invasion of your privacy. If you were cuddled as an infant, you may value the physical contact. If you were not, your value of physical closeness would not be met (Figure 15).

The psychological side of the marriage contract is more important than the conscious questions such as finances. It is often basic to the problems which the couple says are the real problems. Financial problems are often a result of power drives – such as the husband holding the purse strings or the wife shopping excessively. Perhaps the husband spends too much money on his hobby, while the wife wants to save for a house. He may figure that, since he is the boss, he can show it by controlling the money and how it is spent. She may also want to show control by spending money or she may need the security of a house she can call her own to satisfy her own need to control.

There are some ways that you can tap into the unconscious mind and get a feeling of the most basic needs of your partner. Look, first, for any indication of inferiority feelings and how the power drive may be exhibited – or deadened.

Being argumentative, controlling, physically violent or being driven abnormally for success in some field are all possibilities. How does this person treat you, the children, people at work or friends? Is there a great deal of complaining about others who may have control over them or those whom they would like to control? Is your partner a fast driver or a reckless skier? These are some of the possible areas where power-drive frustrations can be seen.

Is the person withdrawing from the real world through alcohol or other drugs? Does the person withdraw into non-productive aloneness – listening to music or watching TV to a greater than normal extent? Even being overly involved in recreational pursuits can be an indication of masking those deep feelings of inferiority. And, of course, compulsive gambling is a common indication of deeply felt inferiorities (Figure 16).

Remember, we all have such feelings to some degree. It is how we handle them that can indicate how much we are controlled in a negative way by our unconscious minds. Wanting to be the leader of your country may be a very positive use of the drive for power. Being good in a sport is another. But just wanting to get married so that the world can see that you are desirable is neurotic.

This marriage business is more complicated than it first appeared, isn't it? No wonder we have misunderstandings as to what we want and where we are going.

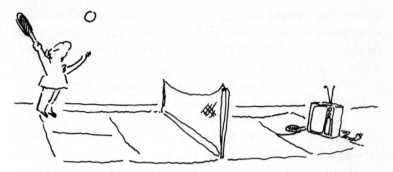

Figure 16   The television set is a poor participant in human
relationships.

Certainly, just having money doesn't answer our deep-
down needs. While money isn't an evil, it may not bring
all of the joys which we might like. Although it may be
surmised that, even if our most basic needs are not met
and we are not deeply happy, at least with money we can
suffer in comfort!!

Finding the realities

Obviously some of our partner's traits will be known to us
as we become serious in the relationship. But as the world
matures and changes us, as jobs and children excite or
stifle us, as new interests entice us – we become different
people. Our relationships will feel the tension or the attraction of these new influences on our lives. The positives
need to be appreciated while the tensions need to be minimised. As we change, our relationships change and we
need to be on the same wavelength as our partner.

  The growth and maturing of the relationship often
requires compromise – so while you may not get all you

want, you do get something – and your experience in a developing relationship deepens your appreciation for the uniqueness of the relationship and the depth of feeling, which is not experienced by enough partners in traditional or selfish relationships.

In our modern, often more self-centred, relationships, we are commonly looking for a relationship which will aid in our quest for self-fulfilment and happiness. Fulfilling our deepest desires and needs is essential. Happily, if we are mature and in a loving relationship, if we had negative experiences in our earlier life, the sources of inferiority and self-doubt can be minimised or eliminated. Love, in most cases, really can conquer all.

Our pasts are important for our futures

'The past is prologue' said Shakespeare. 'Those who do not remember the past are condemned to repeat it' is another truism. Over and over in our personal histories, just as in our social and cultural histories, we are reminded that our past is highly likely to influence, or even control, our future. To ignore this is to ignore the probabilities. I like to say that 1 in 10 will react against their past and, when that past was negative, to overcome it. That 1 in 10 ratio is not a scientific fact, but rather an indication of the probable effect of the past on our futures. By this, I mean that the majority of people who were abused as children will continue to abuse – but some will be repelled by their past and treat their own loved ones with the gentleness of a lamb. Alcoholism tends to reproduce itself. There are both genetic and social reasons for this.

But the past is influenced by the present. If your own parents' spousal abuse was caused by a poor mate-selection process but you have spent a great deal of time and energy selecting a person who is definitely gentle, your chances of being abused are greatly reduced. And while children of divorced parents are 10% more likely to get a divorce, many take extra care to both select a stable mate and to keep the relationship going in a positive way.

Our situations, past and present, influence where we are today. As an outsider observing another person's outward expression of a personality trait, we are likely to judge that person based only on what we have just seen. We may not know that the person has just lost his job or that her child has just been found dead from an overdose. It reminds me of a Buddhist story about a man who knocked on the door, of his friend. When the friend opened the door he yelled at him to go away. The man left, but was upset by his friend. What he did not find out until later was that his friend's mother had just died violently. So the expected warm welcome was not forth-coming, but rather was replaced by a reaction of anger or anguish. Once we understand the whole picture, we can understand that the friend's hostility could be understood.

Study after study indicate that discovering real love and experiencing a high level of family life are on the top of most wish lists. A good relationship is far more of an aid than a hindrance in self-fulfilment. It is, therefore, intel-ligent to look deeply at ourselves, our partner and our relationship to see how we can more intelligently and lovingly chart our course through life by understanding, caring, accepting and changing. Modern marriage demands such intelligent dynamism.

What do you want from your relationship?

Are my needs being met?

Read this chapter if:

You think your relationship isn't as satisfying as you thought it would be

You are concerned with the intimacy of your relationship

You wonder if you are both mature enough for a modern marriage

You think your mate isn't helping you toward your goals or satisfying your needs

You are wondering whether you and your mate are on the same wavelengths (take the self-test)

You wonder where your real interests lie (take the self-test)

You are contemplating marriage and wonder what the major issues should be

We have taken a brief look at what might motivate us and our partners and how we might react to stresses. Understanding these chapters should give us some insight into why we act as we do, how others may act and how we might mesh or conflict in a relationship. We also looked at the nature of being able to maturely love unselfishly. While we need to look at the realities of our own and our partner's approaches to the world – the power of honestly and unselfishly loving can eliminate or minimise those potential negatives which were illustrated.

To see the psychological realities which influence each of us and which influence our relationship is essential, if we are to help each of us to grow and our relationship to mature. If we can understand where we are, it will be easier to plan for our future. If we can understand our own deeper motivations, it will be easier to effectively communicate with the idea of realistic growth rather than petty self-righteousness. The reality of the relationship is the whole – not the surface. It includes our unconscious beliefs and our subconscious reactions, not just our conscious statements and our obvious style of behaving.

Finding our dream

More people are living as single adults today than in the past. While, in 1970, 28% were living as singles, today there are 39%. Is that because they believe they can be happier alone or is it that it is more difficult to find that dream mate? For those out there looking, there are over 3,000 dating services earning over a billion dollars a year. (Dating is the surveying of the field of eligible people to find out with whom you would like to be incompatible in a committed relationship!!) Advertising in the classifieds of newspapers and magazines brings in about 500 million dollars a year. And now the Internet has several match-making services. In the UK, there is a satellite channel devoted to dating. We certainly seem to want companion-ship – if not a life-long commitment! Solitaire may be an enjoyable card game, but playing the game of life alone it is not an ideal lifestyle for most of us. What is it that you want?

Whether you are searching for your dream or are living with it – there are realities to consider.

'It's a funny thing about life; if you refuse to accept anything but the best, you very often get it,' said Somerset Maugham. And if we want the best, we had better make some plans. The 'good luck bug' just doesn't jump into your soup without being enticed there. We often hear that, 'luck favours the prepared mind', or 'luck is the result of hard work'. So, if we want to be lucky in our relationships, we had better know what we expect to find in that pot at the end of the rainbow. One acquain-tance was quite clear in her expectations. She told me that all she wanted was a man who would respect her and love her. She didn't think that was too much to expect from a multimillionaire.

Both in business and marriage, problems are likely to occur when there is a difference between what we expect to happen (our ideal) and what really happens. It makes sense to think through our expectations and plan for them – if they are realistic. We can then adjust our 'ideal' and make it more realistic.

Just because a person is good looking, has an outgoing personality and has a good job is not a guarantee that our needs will be met nor that we can meet that person's needs. And more than needs, we both have our potentials which need developing as we move through life's challenges and opportunities. As psychologist Abraham Maslow said, if we are to fully develop ourselves we must be moving toward 'self-actualisations' – that truly human achievement which is the highest level at which a human being can operate.

Additionally, we have expectations for our marriages and other close relationships. Our expectations come from our own families, from our parents, from our culture, from the media, from our successful or failed relationships, from our religions and from fairy tales. These fantasies of a happy marriage are often fuzzy and unrealistic. Most people expect a marriage to be a pot of gold with them taking the riches. But marriage is a contract between two people who are supposed to be mature adults. If we are to be intelligent about our relationship, we must have some clear expectations and goals so that our relationship 'contracts' or understandings can be understood.

'*I want to live in a big house with a view of the city*.' But what if that house is emotionally cold because the occupants are working so hard to make the payments that they can't enjoy the warmth of the fireplace or the joy of the passion that had once kindled the relationship.

What do you honestly want most from life? Most people find that their major concerns in life involve a job, a relationship, children, reaching their highest potentials (self-actualisation) and recreation. If children pop into the relationship before the career goals are achieved, there may be dissatisfaction. The same could be true for the person who puts recreation ahead of the relationship. All five areas must be seen in perspective. Each should be considered in terms of: whether to, when, why, where and how. Should one interest take precedence at a certain time in your life? Exactly what do you want now in each of these interest areas? Will this change in your future?

Must something be given up to have the best chance of achieving those goals? What if I say '*I want to be successful in my profession and I want a great deal of time with my family*.' Is there really enough time in your week to do both? Probably – if you give up sleeping! This is an important subject to discuss when you are entering a relationship which has some long-term potential.

If you can't do two or three things at the same time, perhaps you can do one after the other. Gro Harlem Brundtland, former prime minister of Norway, now head of the World Health Organization and one of the most respected world leaders, was a medical doctor and the mother of children. Later in life, she decided on a career in national politics, where she rapidly rose to the top. Now she is a world leader.

Think deeply. What is it that you really want in a relationship? Is it financial security? Children? A playmate? Sex? A mother or father substitute? Do you really need someone to do this for you or can you do it yourself? Can you get the education you need to procure the job you want? Or, must you marry someone who has already done that, so that you can be secure? Would you be happier living alone, doing what you want, when you want to – and perhaps having a playmate only part-time? If you are a thinking person, you must answer questions such as these.

Your mate

Many women marry men with the idea that they can shape them up. Get him to stop drinking so much. Get him to give up smoking or gambling. Get him to lose 30 pounds. And get him away from the TV on the weekends. Ooops!! (We're tramping on sacred ground here.) You've heard the story of what a bride experiences as she enters the church. She sees the *aisle*, then the *altar*, then hears the *hymn*. But she is thinking 'I'll alter him.' Of course, we men all need some shaping up!

While making positive changes are worthwhile goals, unless it was in your marriage agreement *'you're gonna have trouble!'* First, his well-settled habits, which have developed as he took the easy path through life, will be difficult to change. You have to fight his power drive (he doesn't want to be told what to do) and you will have to get him to discipline himself. It was his lack of discipline which got him into this mess in the first place.

Far better to settle down with someone who is already perfect. So, seriously think about perfecting *your* golf swing, *your* knitting or *your* education. It will be a lot easier and a lot more fun. The frequent plea on Oprah is that 'I am good – so I deserve to be in a happy relationship.' But, it is not enough to be deserving, you must do something to make yourself more attractive as a person. While you must begin, as Socrates said, by knowing yourself, you need to make yourself happy by becoming the most that you can be. The next part is more difficult – finding someone equally self-actualised.

The poet Ovid tells the story of the ancient Greek, Pygmalion, who had made a beautiful marble statue and wanted it turned into a woman. The goddess Aphrodite obliged, and Pygmalion married the beautiful woman. George Bernard Shaw took the same story and wrote the play *Pygmalion* in which Professor Higgins changed Eliza Doolittle from a Cockney street waif into a cultured lady. (You saw the musical version in *My Fair Lady*.) Let me tell you – it's a lot easier to do this with a pen and paper than with a whip and chain.

Aging and changing

A number of psychologists and educators have observed stages that we must go through as we progress through

life. The needs that we have at 18 are not the needs we
should have at 40 or 50. For example, an 18-year-old
might marry as a way of becoming independent from his
or her parents. But 40-year-olds should be pretty well
independent by that time. If not, maybe they should
marry an 18-year-old!!

Psychologist Erik Erikson has developed the most
commonly accepted series of life stages and crises which
he says we must solve as we mature. There are several such
crises prior to becoming a young adult – but let's just look
at those most appropriate to our ages during marriage.

Erikson believes that the young adult (ages 18–30)
must come to grips with the realities which the teenager
should have planned for, such as: choosing a mate; learning to live with a life partner; possibly starting a family;
moving forward in a career; taking civic responsibility and
finding congenial adult companions.

From the age of 18, most of us must: work at jobs –
often unchallenging; socialise with others – often rewarding; study and learn – sometimes exciting, sometimes not;
and plan for the future. While we may have the desire to
travel and learn, we seldom have the necessary finances.
While we would like to become more independent of our
parents, we often cannot. And while we frequently would
prefer to spend our time in recreational pursuits and with
friends, we cannot, because the financial duties of adulthood call. There are sacrifices to be made in order to
achieve the independence and competencies which maturity requires.

During these years, we may develop intense relationships. We may marry and become parents. We may find
ourselves being punished by the law for immature and
antisocial behaviour. We may be unsatisfied in our
careers because we are not yet sufficiently experienced
to take hold of the tiller and steer our ship. We are
walking, while yearning to fly.

Erikson sees this period of *young adulthood* as the time when we must decide on the solution to the crisis of 'intimacy versus isolation'. If we have successfully met the earlier life crises and developed a sense of identity, it is now time to determine whether or not our lives can or should be shared with another. Being able to develop real relationships with others as well as developing a feeling of competency about our sexual abilities are part of the crisis which needs to be solved from the ages of about 18–25.

Erikson then sees the next period as *adulthood*. It brings the crisis of 'generativity versus stagnation'. Erikson believes that individuals must be productive in their society and helpful to other people. Being a good parent, being successful in our occupations or doing some kind of social work are all situations which might indicate at least partial productiveness (generativity). But many people meet this crisis by remaining self-centred or by withdrawing from the reality of the world. The ease of withdrawing into the television set, while letting Hollywood entertain you, stops the possibility of generating a productive and meaningful life. If a person has not met this psychological need to be productive in some area of life, the resultant problems may find their way into the relationship as a general dissatisfaction. But the problem is usually in the person, not in the relationship. If you have not been productive it is never too late to start.

The next crisis comes during middle-age. The middle aged person (ages 30–50) must develop more fully the tasks of early adulthood. There is more of a need to participate in the development of the society by active interest in civic and political groups. An acceptable standard of living should be achieved. If you are a parent, there must be time spent with children to aid them in satisfactorily achieving their own developmental tasks. Further growth as a person can be achieved by using recreational time wisely – for play, study or sharing your life. The primary relationship, such as husband or wife, requires continuous attention and time so that the relationship grows stronger.

So we can expect that each period of our lives will present us with challenges which we must meet. We not only need to meet our own 'crises' but we must help our mates to meet theirs. And it is quite unlikely that we will go through the identical stages of each crisis at the same time. Furthermore, as we meet these challenges of maturing, we become different – and hopefully better. But each change is going to require a change in our relationship contracts. We just do not remain the same people we were when we first got together.

We bring our expectations with us

It has been said that we spend our whole lives looking for the perfect mate – and then we die. While this may be true for many people, most of us are quite willing to find somebody who is close to what we think we want, then start from there.

Most of us grew up in families – usually two biological parents, sometimes one parent, often step-parents, sometimes in orphanages or in foster families. Because of, or in spite of, our upbringing, we have some ideas on what an ideal marriage will be. Our ideas may be based on the fact that our upbringing was nearly ideal and that our parents had a great relationship with each other and with their children. Other times, our upbringing was not so happy and we vow never to experience, or have our children experience, what we had gone through – physical and sexual abuse, alcoholic parents, parents who were absent either physically or in their lack of attention toward us.

If mother always picked up her son's clothes from the foot of the bed, he probably expects his wife to follow suit. If father doted on daughter's every word, she will expect the same attention from her husband. In today's busy life, with marriages becoming more egalitarian, probably both people will be a wee bit disappointed after the wedding chimes have faded.

Even people who have lived together in an egalitarian relationship will often revert to what they expected from a marriage after they have formally said 'I do'. That strong egalitarian man may revert to being mama's little boy and need to be picked up after. Some very serious thinking about what you honestly want and need from a relationship should be part of that well-thought-out relationship contract which you should, or can, develop.

If you have been divorced, you probably have some ideas of what you want and what you don't want. Divorce often makes people a bit more realistic – if they are intelligent and mature. If they are not too smart or immature, they are likely to make the same mistakes again and again because they don't know what to look for and they are marrying out of a need for security.

With or without children, there are a couple of areas which continue to emerge as primary concerns or problems. A lack of sexual intimacy is one. This will be discussed in Chapter 7. Financial considerations will be discussed in Chapter 8. But a major problem in dual-career marriages is the lack of equity in handling household chores. It is discussed in Chapter 9 on communication, but must be mentioned here. With most working women doing 70 to 90+ % of the home tasks (shopping, cooking, cleaning, childcare). it isn't fair. The equal division of labour should be discussed before marriage but, if not then, as soon as it is recognised as a problem.

These three areas must be considered when you are thinking of 'what you want' in your relationship – and the earlier the discussion, the better.

Intimacy

Intimacy is an essential ingredient in close relationships. We often focus on sexual intimacy, but real intimacy requires more than the sharing of bodies, it requires a sharing of minds. It requires the sharing of feelings and thoughts, of work and play, of goals and values. It does not mean that we must do everything together or think exactly alike, but it means that we must share our thoughts. We must bare ourselves so that our partner can understand – and hopefully appreciate us more. It is easy to share the good things, the successes and goals. It is much more difficult to share our fears and weaknesses because they show our vulnerability and insecurity.

Women have been acculturated to be able to be open and intimate. Men have often not learned the ability to be open. Cultural differences often make it even more difficult for men, because most of the cultures in the developed world have required that they be 'in control' and 'all powerful'. The fears of being judged, rejected or hurt can separate many people from the most satisfying aspects of a truly committed relationship. College-educated men in America and Scandinavian men seem to be ahead of the pack in developing the capabilities of being emotionally and intellectually intimate.

Former US President Jimmy Carter, in an interview (*US News and World Report*, 9 December 1996, p. 86), said that in the early years of his marriage he had difficulty in talking to his wife when he had an unresolved problem or was in trouble. 'I didn't want her to know I was vulnerable to doubt and failure, and I didn't share everything with her.' Such an attitude might have ruined his marriage, he said. 'One of the most difficult challenges for me has been questioning my dominant role.' This inability to become honestly intimate is common in men. But real closeness cannot be gained if people cannot honestly share – and become truly intimate.

Should all close relationships be marriages?

Some heterosexual couples want to live together without taking the traditional marriage vows. At the same time, some homosexual couples want to take those same marriage vows to sanctify and secularise their commitments.

A permanent heterosexual relationship

This is a nearly universal goal in the Western world. Relationship is the key word. Most of us need relationships to live as happy human beings. If Erich Fromm is right (see Chapter 2, p. 48), we need deep, loving relationships to help us overcome our feelings of aloneness which have become even more important because of our impersonal societies. And what could be more ideal than a close friendship between equal partners who can express their friendship in every way – including sexual expression?

Our romantic notions of marriage seem to have emphasised the sexual aspect to a degree which far exceeds reality. There is no doubt that sexual expression between good friends is a rewarding type of experience. But when the sex act becomes more important than the friendship, perhaps the relationship is less than it could be.

While we are looking at the idea of 'relationship', we must be aware that the reasons for a relationship of marriage have changed drastically over the centuries and are changing very rapidly now. The official reasons for marriages in earlier times were primarily economic. A man needed a woman to produce children to work on the farm or herd the sheep. Certainly from these economic urges loving relationships often developed. And, as today, sometimes the attraction came before the marriage. David and Bathsheba, Dante and Beatrice and even the fictional Romeo and Juliet illustrate the eternal reality – that men and women are often attracted to each other. Given the facts of the nearly universal need for a deep relationship and the attraction of people for each other, there will undoubtedly continue to be the recognition of such a relationship.

Do I want a long-term commitment for the right reasons?

The purpose of life is not to get married, but rather, to live within the right relationships and to be happy with ourselves – to become authentic persons. In a good marriage, both personalities will probably be strengthened, but such strength must come from somebody on our own level. So, while a good marriage may make each person stronger, we shouldn't get married just to make up for our weaknesses.

Quite often, people, especially young people, try to find shortcuts to adulthood by picking up the outward signs of it – such as having a full-time job, entering into a marriage or having children. But when we move from a home in which the parents provided the security to a home where a mate provides the security, we have not demonstrated the necessary ingredient of maturity – that we are able to live alone. Young marriages so often are entered into to meet the needs for security and independence of the adolescents getting married. These are not mature reasons for such a commitment. Real romance can't flower, if the seeds are immature!

A person does not mature all at once. Sexual maturity comes before emotional maturity. For this reason, many marriages have resulted from a sexual drive rather than from emotional stability. Great numbers of people of both sexes have not reconciled the conflicts within their own personalities before they get married. It is important that we understand 'who we are' before we take on somebody else in a relationship as intense and as close as a marriage. If we don't have a positive self-identity, a true feeling of self-esteem and the unselfish ability to love, we cannot enter a positive adult relationship.

Another problem which people encounter when considering marriage is that they may not know what love is. Many people say 'I love', but mean 'I want' or 'I need'. Hopefully, as we become more aware of the potential problems and joys of marriage, we will look more critically at ourselves and at the type of person we might marry or have already married.

Other questions are: What do we need from each other? Do we marry to make up for everything we have missed in our lives? Are we in the relationship to make up for qualities we lack, hoping that our partner will complement our weaknesses and make up for them? What if the spouse begins to change that quality which we admired? The change can be enormously threatening. A woman who was a 'clinging vine' type but becomes more power driven, as she progresses through college or moves upward in her job, can threaten an insecure husband – leading to a possible break-up of the marriage.

The fact that people marry to find happiness makes the marriage unstable. If we become unhappy, the reason for marrying is no longer present, and the marriage breaks up.

Because people *do* change, expectations in a marriage may also change. As women become more aware that they can break from the traditional gender roles, they may look for self-fulfilment in ways other than being a wife and mother. This often happens after being in a traditional marriage relationship for a number of years. Such a recognition of our potentials can change the whole reason for being in a relationship.

Not all of our behaviour patterns are fixed early in life. People are often cowards. A man may choose a wife just because she's pretty, or she is somebody who doesn't challenge his intellect, or who's immaturity matches his own. What are the chances that such a girl will grow into a woman who can be loved for whom she is? Bodies and faces change – as do minds. What will be left when the hands and face of the beautiful body have aged? Then a person's virtues, or lack of them, become primary.

While appearance isn't everything, it isn't 'nothing' either. For example, a man does not insist on physical beauty in a woman who is honestly a friend, who shows she cares and who builds up his morale. After a while, he realises that she is beautiful – he just hadn't noticed it at first. Women are much smarter about appearance. They tend to look deeper into personal traits and to the ability of a man to be a source of mental and physical security.

In a survey of more than 10,000 people in 37 cultures on six continents, it was found that men consistently valued youth and physical beauty more than women did. Women were consistently interested in a man's status, ambition, money and property (study by David Buss [University of Michigan] cited in *US News and World Report*, 19 July 1993, p. 58).

The conclusion was that, because the findings were uniform throughout the cultures, these preferences might be linked to a fundamental aspect of personality. Such ideas might be genetic rather than learned. However, it might also be that, since women use more time in child bearing and rearing, they might have learned throughout the ages that it is best to have a husband who can provide security for them. Men, throughout the ages, have been primarily interested in having children to help with the family work. A woman's reproductive potential was therefore of primary concern. Youth, it is believed, would be more likely to be successful in bearing more children.

Roles in marriage

The rapid changes in the objectives of male and female relationships in marriage are mind-boggling. From an economic relationship of general permanence during earlier days, marriage has rapidly changed to a potentially less permanent relationship – due to easier divorces, more free time and longer lives. It has the potential of being a childless relationship due to contraceptives and abortions, or it can be a traditional family.

Some people believe, with Freud, that 'biology is destiny'. This approach holds that our traditions are bio-logically based. The late psychiatrist, Theodor Reik, in his book *Sex in Man and Woman: Its Emotional Variations* (Greenwood Press, Westport, CN, 1975), took such a traditional position. He concluded that, in general, our biological heredity gives us very different outlooks as to our roles in marriage. In short, he states that 'women love men but men love work'. Let us look at this traditional approach to see where we have been – then decide whether we want to stay there or move on.

Reik held that the vast majority of men place women, love, sex, etc. in a wholly separate category from their work. They rarely think of their wives at work. Women, on the other hand, are rarely separated from their husbands in their thoughts. While at work, married men seldom mention their families. Their conversations usually revolve around sports, their jobs and other non-family subjects. Married women at their jobs generally have conversations which revolve around their families.

Reik found that men are not basically at home in the universe, so they seek to explore it and to change it. Women form the chain of humanity and are therefore at home in the world and not likely to want to change it. It was Reik's belief that a man tends to evaluate himself by how successful he is at his work. A woman tends to evaluate herself by the man who chooses to marry her. The desire in women to work is not as authentic as it is in men. For most women, the nicest thing that she can hear from the man she loves is 'I love you'. For a man, the nicest thing he can hear is for a woman to say 'I'm so proud of you'. Reik also believed that the women's liberation movement would not go far because the biological and emotional differences between the sexes are basically unchangeable. No variation in society's laws or cultural pattern would change them. I think he missed the mark, here!

Reik has also stated that there are four areas of importance which a married man can fulfil. He can be a good husband, a good father, a good provider or should accomplish something remarkable in his field. If a man does any two of these, he can be considered a socially valuable person. A married woman should be a good housewife, a good mistress and a good mother. If she fulfils any two of these, she can be considered a socially valuable person. Reik, of course, was looking at the traditional roles. Did he see them clearly? Are these historical roles the ideal? For some people the answer seems to be 'yes'. For others, it is a loud 'NO'.

A more common set of typical roles expected of a woman is that she be a wife–mother, a companion or an economic partner. Problems occur when a woman expects to fulfil two, but her husband expects her to fulfil another one. If the husband expects his wife to be a companion and a wife–mother, but she expects to be a companion and an economic partner, problems will probably result. Today, with so many female college graduates, more women are looking at the companion–economic partner roles in marriage. This is especially true of the younger women. Quite often, however, before their child-bearing years are over, they opt for a child and the wife–mother role becomes an option. Or, more commonly, she becomes a mother, then soon returns to work as an economic partner. She now often has problems because of insufficient time to be an effective mother, a worker and a companion. There is seldom enough time in a week to do all three effectively.

Many traditional women really believe that they can be fulfilled by serving their husbands. A wife might say 'This is my real fulfilment as a woman – to cook, to keep a nice home, to raise wonderful children and to keep my husband happy.' For many women, this is an illusion which is shattered within a few years. During the early years of marriage, a great deal of satisfaction seems to come from playing roles that the partner feels are desirable – and in having a good sexual relationship. Many times, this is little more than the wife bolstering the ego needs of the husband. But when they get a little older, dissatisfaction may set in (Box 5).

A study done at the University of Connecticut

Box 5

Some very common disagreements should be discussed. They include:

- How should the money be spent and who has control of the money?
- How often shall we have sex?
- Who does what housework?
- Should we have children? How many? And how will child-raising responsibilities be divided?
- What ground rules should we have for discussions of disagreements?
- What role should our jobs play in terms of time and the relationship?

---

attempted to measure the effect of male dominance and other gender relationships. The researchers expected a more traditional type of answer to females being submissive and more open to sacrifice. However, the results of the study showed that the college women tested expected more equality in their relationships. This was attributed to the development of more feminist attitudes and the expectation of equal treatment in their relationships (Jerold Heiss, 'Gender and romantic love roles', *Sociological Quarterly*, **32**(4), 1991, 575–591) (Figure 17).

It is more commonly found, today, that couples favour a marriage in which both spouses work, share the household chores and raise the children. Some couples have adopted roles in which they have an exact 50–50 split in the household chores and child raising. The husband does

Figure 17   Chauvinist pigs of both sexes describe their ideal
mates as 'angels at home' and 'devils in bed'.

the job on Monday, Wednesday and Friday, and the wife
does the job on Tuesday, Thursday and Saturday. In
other marriages, the husband has adopted the typical
wife's role as the homemaker and does all or most of the
household chores while the wife is the economic provider
for the couple.

In a modern marriage, the traditional roles need to be
shared in some way. The husband may be the economic
provider only and the wife be a domestic worker, or the
husband can be the domestic worker and the wife the
provider, or they can both be providers *and* domestic
workers. There are many types of workable combinations.
A man may love to cook and a woman may hate to cook, or
perhaps both partners hate housework, but they can split
it up and at least share the chores – or hire a housekeeper.

The worst thing that a woman can do is to depend too
much on her husband for protection and security. The
woman who does this will have such security only as
long as the husband is willing to give it to her. Such
women are in a position to be badly frustrated and depressed, if their security is withdrawn.

Quite often, a woman learns to play 'helpless', making her subject to her husband's dominance. But a woman in a traditional role may actually be quite dominant and very aggressive. Their power drive is likely to be directed against safe targets such as children and other women. Career women, on the other hand, tend to be less aggressive – probably because their power drives are more fulfilled in their careers.

One of life's anachronisms is that the abilities that make a man a good husband often disqualify him for executive success. If a man spends much of his time at his job and is successful in fulfilling his power drive, he will probably be a successful executive. But the love ability, necessary to be a successful husband and father, also takes a great deal of time. If a man can honestly say that love is not that important to him, he should question whether or not he should marry. And he should definitely consider the consequences to any children he might sire, if he's not willing to give them his time.

Serious thoughts need to be given to the roles which we expect to play after marriage. Misty, romantic notions often cloud our thinking. How many broken marriages might never have been contracted, if the people really understood themselves and the ideas of their mutual roles in their coming marriage?

When a man is expecting his wife to stay home, raise the kids and perhaps join a bridge group, many problems may develop if she decides to go to school or seek a job. Does his psychological insecurity make it difficult or impossible for him to lose his place as the sole provider? What if her pay exceeds his? Who will take care of the home? Will they share duties, hire a maid, will she meet a more attractive man on the job?

Today's university-educated couples are very likely to have dual-career marriages. In a recent study, it was found that in marriages in which both partners had high-level careers, such as management or professional jobs, both the husband and the wife had similar experiences in both the positive and the negative aspects of the pressures. Women, however, showed a somewhat higher level of stress, probably due to the fact that they did more of the domestic jobs than did their husbands. In an unexpected finding, those couples with children actually had less total stress. Another study indicated that the wives generally did more compromising than did their husbands and that the time available for personal activities outside of the home was less for the women than the men ('Working couples need personal time', *The Menninger Letter*, October 1994, pp. 6–7).

Even in traditional Japan, where women of the past were quite subservient to their husbands, the picture is rapidly changing. With 2,000,000 fewer men than women in the country, with women having an edge in higher education and with more women working in high-profile jobs, these women have become quite demanding. If they even choose to marry, they usually want egalitarian marriages which will not affect their careers.

With dual careers, money is not the problem that it once was. The problems relate far more often to the husband not doing his fair share of the housework and, child raising, and, equally, his not providing the emotional support that his wife needs. Women have been raised with the idea of doing housework, raising the children and giving their husbands emotional support. Men have been raised with the idea of providing financial security and having regular sex. Consequently, when men have a good job and get enough sex, they are often happy. But women have become increasingly unhappy when they are not married to an emotionally supportive man and/or one who isn't doing his share of the domestic duties. You may have noticed that being unhappy takes the romance out of the relationship!

Commonly, the lack of fulfilment of the wife's needs leads her to the divorce attorney. She is ready to go it alone. She believes that she can get just as much emotional warmth alone as she got married – none. And she doesn't have to pick up after somebody else. Often the husband is astounded at his wife's rejection, because he was happy in the relationship. On the other hand, when men head for the divorce court, they commonly do it to move in with somebody else. Often, they did not get the sexual warmth which they craved and found somebody else more 'understanding'.

When the marriage expectations include a mutual need for a best friend and a fair division of labour in housework and child raising, men generally have a lot more to learn and much more to do to hold up their end of the bargain. But if this is not to be part of the deal, those men need to find women who expect the same roles as they expect. Understanding what roles you honestly want for your relationship is a critical issue for a modern marriage. This must be a major area of discussion and planning.

The dynamics of a marriage relationship

A man who is really concerned with his wife's happiness must accept what is best for her. Is she achievement (power) oriented rather than home and children (caretaking) oriented? Can he see the essential nature of the financial security she brings to the marriage and her own (financial) independence, which could be a necessity, should he die or become incapacitated. With growing inflation, it may well be that her income becomes an essential part of the family's economic survival. Can a couple make their two careers an asset rather than a liability? Can they now hire a gardener, a housekeeper, a laundress, a shopper or will they continue to assume the traditional roles while holding two jobs?

As the roles change, if we can understand them and adapt to them, we may be able to have more dynamic marriages. Marriage takes two people – each living a separate life – and puts them together. In the past, it was moulding two people into one life, the husband's.

Marriage styles have become important because many people are questioning the values which Western society has developed. Among the values being questioned are that:

- marriage requires life-long commitment;
- married couples should have children; and
- men and women have distinct roles to play in marriages.

The advantages and disadvantages of the various roles people may play in a marriage depend on the aptitudes, desires and expectations of the people involved. Just as not everyone likes chocolate ice cream, not everyone will enjoy marriage. And the flavours of marriages that people may enjoy range from vanilla to chocolate–almond–cappuccino. The roles that people expect to play can be affected by several factors including: the gender expectations of society, the relationships and expectations which we learned in our families and our unsatisfied psychological needs (particularly power) (Otto Kernberg, 'Aggression und Liebe in Zweierbeziehungen' [Aggression and love in the relationship of the couple], *Psyche-Zeitschrift für Psychoanalysis und ihre Anwendungen*, **45**(9), September 1992, 797–820).

Research is now being started to look at the stages that marriages may go through. Just as psychologists have charted the 'developmental tasks' of the individual in a society, it is now thought that relationships may go through stages also. There may be shifting needs of closeness and distance between the partners.

An example of a few of the stages could be:

- the courtship period where both people are on their best behaviour and are excited by the 'chemistry' and romance of the situation which makes everything appear to be perfect;
- the period of recognition that the other person has some faults will probably follow the courtship period;
- any period of change, such as: moving or increased education;
- the period when the first child arrives;
- the period when the last child leaves;
- mid-life changes such as menopause and 'midlife crisis',
- the time after retirement;
- the period after the death of one of the partners.

Does this mean that you married the wrong person, or is it really the opportunity to recognise that the two of you are really more different that it seemed during the courtship period. This may be the time for marriage counselling to help the couple see how they will need to accept and adjust – and where the positives can lie because of the differences.

The last few decades have seen a great rise in selfishness – the 'me generation'. We have often lost the discipline for working for the long haul and look only at the present time. If my car doesn't work, I get a new one. If my husband doesn't fit my needs, I throw him out and get a new one. In a modern marriage, because of the complexity, there is more opportunity for both frustration and growth. We need to keep our eyes on the 'growth' aspects. Our relationships should help both of us to grow. That's where the romance lies!

Self-test on seeing things the same way

Take the test then have your partner take the test.
Do you see things the same way?

	Always	Often	Usually	Seldom	Never
1 (a) I interrupt during discussions	☐	☐	☐	☐	☐
(b) My partner interrupts during discussions	☐	☐	☐	☐	☐
2 (a) I can communicate my deepest thoughts	☐	☐	☐	☐	☐
(b) My partner can communicate his or her deepest thoughts	☐	☐	☐	☐	☐
3 (a) I believe that my partner knows what I am feeling	☐	☐	☐	☐	☐
(b) I believe that I know what my partner is feeling	☐	☐	☐	☐	☐
4 (a) I try to compromise	☐	☐	☐	☐	☐
(b) My partner tries to compromise	☐	☐	☐	☐	☐
5 (a) When we argue, I stick to the issues	☐	☐	☐	☐	☐
(b) When we argue, my partner sticks to the issues	☐	☐	☐	☐	☐
6 (a) I am willing to give up my position in order to have an effective compromise	☐	☐	☐	☐	☐
(b) My partner is willing to give up his or her position in order to have an effective compromise	☐	☐	☐	☐	☐
7 (a) I can express my anger or hurt	☐	☐	☐	☐	☐
(b) My partner can express anger or hurt	☐	☐	☐	☐	☐

8 (a) While I can give hints about   ☐   ☐   ☐   ☐   ☐
          what is bothering me, I have
          trouble expressing it clearly

   (b) My partner can give hints about   ☐   ☐   ☐   ☐   ☐
        concerns, but has trouble
        expressing it clearly

9 (a) I am willing to ask questions   ☐   ☐   ☐   ☐   ☐
          about my partner's beliefs,
          values, and ideas

   (b) My partner is willing to ask   ☐   ☐   ☐   ☐   ☐
        questions about my beliefs,
        values, and ideas.

What qualities do you desire in a mate?
_____

What qualities can you offer to a mate?
_____

What are your shortcomings?
_____

What role do you want to play in a relationship?
_____

What role would you desire that your mate play in
a marriage?
_____

What do you really want out of marriage?
_____

How much money will satisfy you?
_____

Are children important?

What qualities do you see as essential to a happy committed relationship?

If you marry, what makes you think that you will be in among those who are successful?

Self-test on personality style

1 I feel that
  (a) my mate is more in control of the relation-
      ship than I am
  (b) that we are equally in control
  (c) that I am more in control
  (d) that neither of us seems to show any
      controlling influence

      _____

2 We have
  (a) few things in common
  (b) some things in common
  (c) many common interests

      _____

3 I have
  (a) some doubts about marriage
  (b) few doubts about our future
  (c) no doubts about the success of our
      marriage

      _____

4 I am looking primarily for
  (a) security
  (b) adventure – such as travelling, challenging
      career, etc.

      _____

5 I don't worry about things until they have
  happened   _____

Self-test on my desires within the marriage (true or false)

1 My marriage is more important than my career, my friends or anything else

_____

2 I can have both an exciting career and a happy marriage

_____

3 My mate (or potential mate) has no goals or desires which would interfere with our marriage

_____

4 My career is more important than my marriage

_____

5 My family is more important to me than my marriage

_____

6 My mate (or intended mate) has career goals which I don't fully approve of

_____

7 I have some doubts whether I can handle it, if my spouse becomes more successful than me

_____

8 How many hours a week do you expect to spend on your career (including further education towards that career)?

_____

9 How many hours a week do you expect to pursue recreational interests (cards, golf, theatre, politics, etc.) alone or with others than your spouse?   _____

10 How many hours a week do you expect to spend doing things with only your spouse (such as dinners out, golf, movies, just talking)?   _____

11 How many hours a week do you expect to do things with your spouse along with other people (such as parties, church groups, political groups, sports)?

_____

Self-test on interests

On a scale of 1–10, with 0 being 'no interest' and 10 being a 'life-consuming interest', how do you rate yourself and your spouse (potential spouse) in terms of each of these:

	Self	Spouse
Participating in sports	☐	☐
Watching sports on TV or in person	☐	☐
Reading	☐	☐
Watching television	☐	☐
Listening to music	☐	☐
Dancing	☐	☐
Being outdoors (walking, riding a bike, riding a horse)	☐	☐
Business-related activities	☐	☐
Attending classes to obtain a degree	☐	☐
Attending classes to obtain more general knowledge	☐	☐

Going to nightclubs ☐ ☐

Going to the racetrack ☐ ☐

Gambling ☐ ☐

Playing cards for fun ☐ ☐

Doing artistic or craft work ☐ ☐
(playing an instrument,
painting or drawing,
sculpting, acting, singing,
writing)

Being in discussion groups ☐ ☐

Doing church work ☐ ☐

Doing charity work ☐ ☐

Going to museums, art ☐ ☐
exhibitions, etc.

Attending movies ☐ ☐

Being with friends or family ☐ ☐

Working for political or ☐ ☐
environmental causes

Attending service-club meetings ☐ ☐
and activities (Rotary, Lions, etc.)

Working on solitary hobbies ☐ ☐
(stamp collecting, model
building, sewing, knitting,
quilting, woodworking, etc.)

Driving (automobile or ☐ ☐
   motorcycle)

Understanding the sexual contract

Have things changed sexually for you?

Read this chapter if:

You are having a sex problem

Your reduction of sexual activity seems to be causing problems

Your sexual activity has reduced since your marriage

You don't know why your sexual activity has become less frequent or less fun

Your sex life needs some spicing up

You wonder how you and your partner differ in your thinking about sex (take the self-test)

The understandings, or contracts, which we form in our relationships often change. When we are the ones changing a term of the relationship understanding, we think nothing of it. But when the other person changes the understanding without our permission, we often take unkindly to that new behaviour. A change in the 'sexual contract' is quite common. Let's use this area of behaviour to illustrate how our behaviour, can change in any relationship understanding. While a change in sexual activity is not the only area in which we may adopt new behaviour, it gives us a concrete example of how an important area of our behaviour can affect our relationships. And since cuddling and sexual intercourse are usually thought of as being rather romantic ways to spend our time, applying reality to our romantic expectations is a particularly important area to investigate.

There are a number of things we may do, while dating or engaged, which are done to show our partners how much we like them and want to share their interests. He goes to the ballet or visits Aunt Minnie – but doesn't like it. She goes to a soccer match or joins him for an early morning fishing expedition – and doesn't like it. These are relatively minor, and, thankfully, occasional activities. They may not continue after the marriage. But sexual intimacy is rather major for most people and it is not expected to be an occasional activity. When the premarital sexual activity is greatly reduced sometime after the marriage, it may be a cause for concern. An important part of the 'marriage contract' has been abrogated.

When the terms of the original sexual contract are changed, sex every night or once a week, whatever it was, the person who is pressured into adjusting to the partner's new interest, or lack of interest, will generally feel negative about it. We are, after all, primarily interested in our own feelings and interests. If problems develop, either because of an increased or a decreased interest in sexual intimacy, feelings of rejection will normally be felt by the person who wants more sex. If the other person gives in, there will be more of a feeling of being coerced and not considered in the relationship. This creates strong negative feelings on the other side. You've

probably noticed that sex is rather intimate. When conflicts in the expression of intimacy emerge, it can create a
negative fog over the whole relationship.

When looking at sexual activity, or inactivity, we have
to be strongly aware that when sex becomes infrequent or
absent, it is sending a signal that we are not being fully
accepted. When sex is withheld, so is acceptance. In most
cases, it is that conscious or unconscious need to be accepted which is critical to our psychological well-being –
to our feeling of self-worth. And, of course, it is not the sex
act itself but that feeling of intimacy which is conveyed
during intercourse. Does he treat her as a masturbation
machine? Does she just lie there? While we can argue
that sexual intercourse, intimacy and acceptance are quite
different, in the minds of many – they are inseparable. So
while an orgasm is good, it is not critical to our psychological health – but feeling completely accepted is essential.

There is an often-quoted observation among marriage
therapists that in a good relationship sex is 10% but in a
bad relationship it is 90%. A lack of mental intimacy is
most likely to be shown by a physical withdrawing and a
lack of physical intimacy. This will then often begin the
downward spiral of one person negatively reacting to the
situation, then the other responding in kind. No good can
come from this 'tit for tat' series of retaliations. The increase in the dissatisfaction leads to disillusionment which
may then lead to anger, which can lead to a break-up.

Negative changes in our relationship contracts

A major factor in relationship problems is that we often
see things quite differently. Of course, we both think we

are right – and we are, from our own points of view. She may think he watches too much television, he thinks he doesn't. She thinks the house is dirty and needs cleaning, he doesn't see it. She thinks she does not get enough sexual intimacy, he thinks their sexual relationship is just fine.

Let's use sex as an example of the kind of changes which can occur after marriage. Interests *can* change. Just as people can become neurotic or psychotic after marriage, they can become alcoholics, compulsive gamblers or criminals after marriage. They can also become sexually omnivorous or celibate after marriage. And they can develop mental illnesses which manifest themselves in their approach to their sexuality.

A major cause of divorce for a large number of people is that the sexual intimacy has been severely reduced since the marriage. An old college teacher of mine said that if you put a bean into a jar every time you had sex during the first year of marriage, then took one out every time you had sex after that first year, you'd never get them all out of the jar. That is a little extreme, and it was said some years prior to the 'sexual revolution', but it illustrates a point. The desire for sexual relations often dwindles for one or both of the partners in a marriage.

This isn't always true, of course. One woman I know has bragged that she and her husband have had sex every day of their 40-year marriage – and it has always been great. (No problems with the sexual contract in that relationship!) But many people are not quite so amorous – or lucky!!

One client divorced three times – each time after the sexual activity left the relationship. The first marriage lasted three years. The sex dwindled from daily to once every week or two. He therefore strayed and married his new love. The second marriage lasted ten years until she became celibate. Again he strayed and again married his new love. That lasted 20 years but when the sex reduced to about once a week that marriage also bit the dust. He told me that 'when the sex and physical intimacy goes out of the marriage – so do I'. While some people can be tolerant for a while of: headaches, backache, fatigue, genital soreness and the raft of other real or feigned excuses, the point is that the person wanting to make love is frustrated by the partner's lack of interest. The partner who doesn't want sex, for whatever reason, gets what he or she wants. The person wanting the physical intimacy of sex does not get what is desired. This registers on the mind as rejection – and anger or frustration results. She sees that he has time for work, for golf, for playing cards, but not for intense cuddling. He sees she has time for the children, her job, clothes shopping and meditation – but not for sexual intimacy. So, when that intimacy is reduced, and rejection is felt, an emotional distance is usually created. For many people, this is the most serious rejection which can be felt.

To have 'happy sex', both people must want it. If one wants it and the other doesn't, one has to give in totally – either to get what is wanted or to be content without it. There is no *compromise* in that situation. You might say 'well let's do it for five minutes then stop'. But that would be even more frustrating!! The point is that for each time there is a 'desire disagreement' in the sexual moment, one person wins 100% and the other loses 100%. On the opposite end of the 'sexual-desire spectrum' was a California woman who related, during a marriage-counselling session, that she had never been sexually attracted to her husband. After the divorce, he sued her for fraud because before the marriage he had asked her if she had any secrets, any things she was covering up, relative to her feelings. She said no. The jury found that her behaviour constituted fraud and awarded her ex-husband nearly $250,000 in damages. Only in California!!!

But, along that line, a survey done a few years ago asked men and women to rank the top ten romantic things that can happen in a relationship. They agreed on seven of the ten areas. However, men put sex in the top ten, women didn't. Throughout the millennia, most men seem to have had an obsession with sex which the average woman has not shared. Recently, women's sexual appetites have often increased while, strangely, many men's have receded. Nevertheless, the bubbling cauldron of testosterone seems to boil stronger in the loins of the male than in those of the female.

It seems strange to many of us that women, who seem to have much more orgasmic potential, both in total excitement and the possibility of multiple orgasms, are more likely to back off from the earlier sexual relationship. If the Greek legend of the mythical Tiresias is anywhere near true, women can have far more enjoyment from sexual relationships than do men.

The myth of Tiresias is that, one day while walking, he came upon two snakes which were mating. He separated them from their conjugal activity. As a punishment, he was turned into a woman. Seven years later, she again saw two snakes copulating and separated them. Her punishment now was that she was changed back to her original sex. Sometime thereafter, Zeus, the head of the Greek gods, and his wife Hera were arguing about whether men or women got the most pleasure from sex. Since only Tiresias had lived both as a man and a woman, he was asked to settle their argument. He replied that if pleasure has ten levels, women reach the ninth in orgasm while men only reach the first level. But Hera was enraged for his having revealed the secret of her sex so she blinded him (Figure 18).

It is quite common today for a couple to have sex nearly every time they see each other from early in the relationship. (It appears that both sexes enjoy this activ-

Figure 18 High heels were invented by a woman who was kissed
on the forehead (Christopher Morley).

ity!) Commonly it has been the woman who has backed
off, but sometimes it is the man. Whoever it was – the
contract has been changed. That *implied contract* 'that
there would be sex every day' has now been reduced to
the national average two or three times a week, or less.
Sometimes, it is stopped completely. Now we have a
major contract change.

In the previously mentioned contract of Rex and
Teresa LeGalley, one of the provisions is how often
they will have 'healthy sex'. For them, the contract calls
for three to five times a week. This may sound crass, but it
may be an intelligent approach to a very real problem.

Why we have sex

In looking at the motivation for sex, we can understand
that people can have sex for any or all of the following
three reasons: for physical intimacy, to become parents,
or for recreation – and the excitement of an orgasm. (But
whatever the reason, we should be reminded of what

author D. H. Lawrence said 'Sex should be friendly, otherwise stick to more sanitary toys'.) Whatever your reasons, when problems occur they are either the result of a change in one of these three areas or they are results of deeper seated psychological problems, which may or may not have been evident at the time of the marriage. It has often been said that women have sex because of love and men have love because of sex. Men often need the physical intimacy of sex in order to feel accepted.

For many people, especially men, mental intimacy is closely connected to physical intimacy. When this is true, a reduction in sexual activity indicates, rightly or wrongly, a reduction in mental closeness. Naturally, when we feel that the mental closeness has been reduced, there is a good chance that we will look for another partner who will be mentally close. And there you have a major impulse for infidelity.

While it would be ideal if the 'wronged' person could talk about it, sex is too often a taboo subject. Moreover, if someone is no longer mentally intimate, isn't it possible that they have thought their way into their behaviour? Well, sometimes they have and sometimes they haven't. Sometimes, they don't realise that they have created an emotional distance between themselves and their mates. Other 'important' activities have gotten in the way – work, recreation, childcare and the social schedule can each work against continuing the closeness which all relationships need.

Communication is important. The air really needs to be cleared. If you are having sexual problems, it is essential to find out if your mate *realises* that he or she has backed off of sex. Also, has your mate backed off from you emotionally. And if so, why? Once this is cleared up, you must find out: whether the problems can be solved with or without professional help, or do we head for the divorce court? (Communication and problem solving are discussed in the Chapters 9 and 10.)

There are a couple of negative reasons for having, or not having, sex. Some people, both men and women, will use it as a means of power and control over the other. It may be used in a political way, as a way of getting what we want. Sometimes, withholding sex is also a way of showing power in the relationship – being in the controlling position. Often, our sexual perspective and behaviour, whether indulging or withholding sex, is an indication of power – power over women by men and power over men by women.

One husband revealed in counselling that his very good-looking wife, who was great in bed, informed him shortly after the wedding that she 'didn't have to do THAT anymore.' Her sexual activity and apparent interest in him, which was a major reason for his marrying her, was used as a tool to accomplish her goal of marrying a rather well-off lawyer. This was definitely a use of sex to accomplish an objective. Of course, this is nothing new, just look at what Delilah did to Samson!

How important is sex anyway?

You remember Eliza Doolittle, in the musical *My Fair Lady*, singing to her sexually unaggressive suitor the song *Show Me*. She reminded him that there is a time for body language rather than the spoken language, for cuddling rather than conversation, for sex not for soliloquy. Eliza summed up our romantic inclinations and expectations about being loved and having intimate, and hopefully frequent, sexual communication.

One well-known therapist once said that you don't have to know someone to play tennis with them, why do you have to know someone to have sex with them. That

may have been a point of view of the wild 1960s, but for
many it has changed today. As I remember, playing tennis
is not a high-risk activity for contacting AIDS or any of
the other sexually transmitted diseases. And even though
'love' is part of the tennis scoring system, pregnancy never
follows a 'love' game due to the tennis score. However,
pregnancy *can* result from 'scoring' after the match!

But sex may not be all-important in a marriage. The
partners in one marriage I know have an agreement. The
wife doesn't like sex, so the husband can have sex with
anybody he wants as long as he doesn't bother his wife.
The rest of their marriage is more traditional. So, not
everyone sees sexual activity as being primary in their
marriage. Still, most do. Then, why do we find these
changes in desires?

Common reasons for changes in the desire for physical intimacy

There can be many reasons for people to want less sex.
Sometimes, it is a physical problem and help must be
sought from a medical doctor. But, more often, it is pre-
occupation with the job, child-rearing fatigue, late-night
TV or some other 'important' reasons which create stresses. One major reason, and a concern for marriage counselling, is that when other problems develop which
separate the minds of the people – their bodies are not
too interested in getting close. So, other areas of our
relationship contracts can affect our sexual contract.

Any number of factors can create this separation of the
minds. Very often, it is a power drive–control issue.
Often, it is related to financial problems. Sometimes, the

problems of child raising are the cause. And the rivalry for attention in step-families is a common factor. Not too many step families mimic the Brady Bunch. So when the bodies separate, people need to look quickly at the underlying causes of the problems. Anger at our partner is certainly going to eliminate any feeling for intimacy – so, sex is probably out of the question.

Many people react to problems in a passive–aggressive way. They are aggressive against their mates by being passive. Such people may make certain that they don't touch the partner, they may be quite silent and, of course, the *coup de grâce* is to cut off the sexual relationship. Claiming to have a headache or other physical problem is a common method of avoidance. Feigning fatigue is another method of separation. Turning our backs to the other when getting into bed – or going to bed earlier or later, are common methods of avoiding sexual intimacy.

For some devoutly religious people, particularly for some Roman Catholics, problems may develop when sex is seen primarily as a means for procreation and contraception is considered to be immoral. Once there is no longer a desire to reproduce, sex may be stopped. One man, whom I had known for years, had a wife who refused sex after their last child was born. She said that she didn't want any more babies. Both being very devout Catholics, there was no more sex. He threw his energies into his job as a teacher, a coach and later a school administrator. Fifteen years after her vow of celibacy his wife died. He married an ex-nun – and they have lived happily ever after.

A patient, who was severely neurotic, probably as a result of an unfulfilling marriage and a psychotic mother, became extremely religious. In her earlier life, she had been a Catholic. In her early 20s, she became atheistic. But, as life's problems forced her to seek satisfaction for her *power drive* (what better way to become powerful than to become holier than everyone else), she combined Judaeo-Christianity with Buddhism and Hinduism. She tried Christian Science and Rosicrucianism. Eventually, she settled on founding her own religion. She was its only member. Along the way, as a means of spending time with her quest for the supernatural, she gave up sex and took a vow of chastity. This was more than her husband could take. He filed for divorce. She didn't want a divorce and said that she would have sex with him once a week. That wasn't enough of a contract change for him. And, besides, he had already found a more sexually eager companion.

Being better in bed

While the legendary Don Juan had a reputation as a pretty good seducer of the fairer sex, he didn't have the information on technical expertise which we have today to make us more effective in pleasing our lover in foreplay, multiple orgasms and afterplay. (Isn't it just like scientists to analyse something until we forget the joy of the whole.) Anyway, we have the physiological and psychological knowledge to make sex even more fun.

Men need to realise that there are two people there in the sack. Both should be satisfied. Most men can have an orgasm through simple intercourse. Most women need more. The stimulation of the penis by the vagina can get him hot, but the clitoris may not be adequately stimulated by his simple in and out 'pelvic thrusts'.

Oral sex, once frowned upon, has become more common. The tongue is a much better stimulator of the clitoris than is the penis – and a better stimulator of the

Figure 19 People are the only animals that blush – or need to (Mark Twain).

penis than the vagina. But the movement of the tongue may not be enough. You may need to say 'higher', or 'lower', or 'harder', or 'softer'. The typical man, with his inferiority complex out front, may not like his partner's directions because it indicates that he isn't as good at this important carnal activity as he thinks he is. The more a man's inferiority complex is hidden in his *macho* aura, the harder it is to realise that he is not perfect in everything he does. Here again, women generally are more mature in their abilities to verbalise and to accept suggestions (Figure 19).

Not finished with you yet, guys! Many a man thinks that it is enough to have his orgasm, then he can roll over and go to sleep. He's satisfied. She wants more cuddling. These are things that must be talked about. Just because you said 'I do' doesn't mean that the hands of Cupid will grip your genitals and make you a Lothario-like lover. We've got to realise that none of us are perfect at anything – but we can get better.

It is, therefore, important to be able to talk about how good our sexual intimacy is – and where it might be lacking. If we have talked about this in developing a relationship agreement, we are prepared to hear that we aren't perfect. Then, with a little help from our partner, we may be able to get just a little closer to the classic charms of Casanova.

Good sex

Good sex is more than just technique. The best sex is a union of two caring people who have high self-esteem. People who feel good about themselves can let themselves go. Women who are financially successful generally have high self-esteem. This combination allows them to meet and mate with men with similar attributes. When you honestly feel good about yourself, you can fully enjoy sex – and not use it as a tool for manipulation or control. You are able to be open, trusting and loving.

Straying from the contract

The understandings which we develop, before we are married and after we have lived together, may need to be adjusted because of psychological, physical or social changes in our lives. Examples of physical changes might be if one partner developed Alzheimer's disease or was crippled in an accident. A social change could be losing our job. A psychological change might be the types of behaviours which men or women might undergo when 'going through the change of life' or 'midlife crisis'.

When stresses affect us, we make adjustments in the physical, psychological or social areas of our lives. Sometimes, these adjustments are made in our sexual activity – or inactivity. Let us take a few minutes to look at how some people change in sexual areas. You should be aware of such changes because one or more of them could happen in your life. Remember that these are examples of behaviours in only the sexual area of our lives, but changes equally or even more severe can develop in other areas of our lives, and thereby affect our relationships – as we saw in Chapter 4.

What about extramarital sex (adultery)?

One reason for adultery is that sex is sensitive – and, unless you are using your mate as a 'thing', you will back off when he or she backs off. But you fume – and perhaps you will find another body to share your physical intimacy with (Box 6).

Another reason for adultery is satisfying our power drives. When we make a 'conquest', male or female, we feel good about ourselves. (We may hate ourselves in the morning – but it feels good at the time!) Whether our inferiority feelings are deep and rooted in our childhoods, or more shallow but fuelled by the rejection by our mates, becoming intimate with somebody new is psychologically a very good way to make us minimise our self-doubts and think that we are OK. Of course, the temporary joy which the 'fling' gives us may not balance the scales, when the resultant outcome is an expensive and unwanted divorce.

Box 6   Adultery

For those who have had sex outside of marriage:

When married	Years of marriage before extramarital affair
Men:	
Before 1960	11
During the 1960s	7
After 1970	5
Women:	
Before 1960	$14\frac{1}{2}$
During 1960s	8
After 1970	$4\frac{1}{2}$

Many were always faithful.
(Annette Lawson, *Adultery: An Analysis of Love and Betrayal*, Basic Books, New York.)

We have typically said that men's sex drives are more likely to get them into extramarital affairs. However, recent studies of women in the workforce show that they are just as likely to enter into affairs as are men. So, it may be the sociological opportunity, along with the psychological need, rather than the biological drive which is the proximate cause of sexual infidelity. Again, we find the necessity to be accepted, by both men and women, as a major need for our psychological selves.

People who do not feel that they are important to their partners can become jealous of whatever or whoever is taking up the time of their spouse. Of course, jealousy can be caused by any time spent away from a loved one. Bar-hopping after work with friends, spending time in recreational pursuits or in helping with youth sports, spending the evenings in college classes or even over-devotion to work can make the spouse feel insecure or jealous. Some of these 'jealousies of time' can be understood and tolerated, but others cannot. It is often possible to reduce the feeling of loneliness by finding another human being who is willing to give time and intimacy.

An affair can also be sought by people whose marriages are not intellectually or emotionally fulfilling and who are seeking a deeper relationship outside of the marriage. It is also practised by people who see sex only as fun and by people who are sexually curious.

A study by Shirley Glass surveyed over 300 married people and found that men's reasons for extramarital sex was more often sexual deprivation. They were able to separate the sex from a feeling of love. Women, on the other hand, were more likely to indulge in extramarital sex if they felt that they were in love. Women tend to think that love and sex go together. Men don't always see it that way (Shirley Glass and Thomas Wright 'Justifications for extramarital relationships: The association between attitudes, behaviours, and gender', *Journal of Sex Research*, **29**(3), August 1992, 361–387.) When we talk to people whose spouses have had affairs, we see the same kinds of view. Men were more interested in what happened physically. Was there oral sex? Was there sado-masochistic sex? But women are more interested in how their husbands *felt* about the lover.

The peoples of the UK and the USA have typically held to the idea that sex outside of marriage is a gross violation of the marriage contract. Many other countries in the world, the most notable being France, have long recognised that a lover on the side makes life a bit more spicy. However, at the funeral of former Prime Minister François Mitterand, when both his wife and his mistress showed up at the graveside with their (read 'his') children, even some of the French were surprised.

Often, a person seeking sex outside of the marriage is seeking it because the spouse has broken the 'implied contract' of sufficient sex within the marriage. Then, when that person succeeds in finding sex, he or she has broken another 'term' of the marriage contract, that there will only be sex inside the marriage relationship. So, often, we have both people breaking their sexual contracts – one withdrawing from sex, the other finding it outside the relationship. Which one is the most at fault?

The idea of monogamy is not a universal custom. Even in the Bible, we have David sleeping with Bathsheba, the wife of Uriah, and conceiving Solomon who eventually had 700 wives and 300 concubines. The Muslim religion, of course, allows for multiple marriage. The Mormons in the USA began their religion using the Biblical allowance for multiple wives, but abandoned the practice after the US government frowned on the idea.

How important should sexual exclusivity really be? The greater danger for a marriage is when the new-found intimacy is 'mind to mind' and *mental intimacy*, rather than when it is 'body to body' and *physical intimacy*. In many cultures, sexual exclusivity is not really 'all important' as it is in America and much of Europe. According to Eskimo tradition, a wife is able to offer sex to her husband's companions or friends as a gesture of welcome and friendship. Among the Kurkuru Indians, who live in the Amazon area, everyone in the village has four to twelve lovers (Helen Fisher, *The Sex Contract: The Evolution of Human Behavior*, William Morrow, New York). And, of course, the French tradition of Mardi Gras often allows people to be sexually free, at least for a few days.

Adultery can also be seen among many animals – beavers, ducks and others. Nearly 40% of cultures permit adultery, at least sometimes. Some societies allow sexual freedom during puberty initiation. Some societies allow a man to have sex with his wife's sister, because if his wife dies his sister-in-law could become his wife. In the Bible, many people think that the 'sin of Onan' (Genesis 38:8) was that he would not procreate children with his dead brother's wife. Whenever they had sex, 'he spilled his seed on the ground' and God killed him for that sin.

For those who have high biological and psychosocial drives – adultery is often difficult to avoid. But what about that marriage agreement – and the implied contract?

Back in the 1960s, many middle-class couples discovered the 'joy' of adultery. 'Wife swapping', as it was often called, had couples going to parties then swapping mates for the evening. Usually, it was the men who had to talk their wives into doing it. But, often, it was the wives who wanted to continue the game. A group of six couples, all my neighbours, enjoyed playing the game. All the marriages ended in divorce.

About that time, a couple wrote a book about 'open' marriages. It stated that sex outside of marriage is OK, if both partners understand what was happening. What a great idea! But they too ended their long-term marriage with divorce.

Real monogamy may not lie in the erogenous zones between the legs – but in our minds. A deeply felt love of one's mate may not need total sexual commitment. The bodies having sex would not be so important – as long as the minds were faithful. Many men take this view. Their wives are really more important, but they need that extra-curricular sex either because they don't get enough at home or they like the thrill of the chase and the feeling of conquest.

We are a bit more accepting of adultery today. No longer are scarlet letters branded into your head as in old Salem. And, in the divorce court, adulterous women can usually get alimony and keep the kids. Older laws usually disallowed an adulterer from profiting.

It seems that, typically, men are more upset by adultery than are women. In the USA, three times as many men as women were greatly upset by adultery. In Germany, it was only a 50% margin of men over women. Clearly, it is a cultural attribute as to whether or not adultery is evil. It really depends on how important monogamous sex is in that culture.

Marriage requires commitment, but does that commitment have to be sexual? Is sex a basis for marriage? The answer to this should be 'no'. Is it a fundamental part of marriage? Is it an activity of marriage in which the minds and the bodies of the partners can be extremely intimate? Here, the answers are 'yes', or at least they should be 'yes'. Is it possible in some marriages to minimise the intimacy of sexual communication yet find the necessary intimacies in areas other than sexual? Some people say 'yes', but most of us still view the idea of sexual fidelity as being of major importance.

It seems that there are few marriages or male–female relationships in which sex does not carry at least some importance as a means of showing that the people feel close and intimate. But there do seem to be relationships in which sex is viewed to be primarily entertainment or where it is viewed to be both entertainment and a means of expressing closeness, depending on the social situation.

It is far easier to state a belief in these freer ideas of sex than it is to live by it. Years ago, one of the major advocates of free sex, Havelock Ellis, had a group of followers who engaged freely in sex with others in the group. By doing this, they were attempting to show their freedom from, and their disdain for, traditional morality. At one

Figure 20   The love bug got me.

time, Havelock became especially enamoured with one of the women in his flock. When he found that she was also enjoying sex with another man, he became enraged and banned them both from his group. He eventually allowed them to return, but the understanding was that Havelock's special person would not have sex with anyone but him. It was a case of 'what's yours is mine and what's mine is my own' (Figure 20).

Marriage fidelity (faith and trust) is made up of mutual belonging, affection and selflessness. This allows us to enter deeply into a friendship with our mate. When this is counteracted by a sexual liaison with someone other than the mate, negative feelings can run very deep.

For people whose marriages are fulfilling, there is probably no need to look elsewhere, since a great part of the joy of sex is found in sharing it with your best friend. And no matter what techniques are used, an orgasm is an orgasm. So for happily married people, extramarital sex seems to have far more disadvantages than advantages.

On a scale of 1–10, how would you rate your partner's straying? Is an affair the one type of behaviour which you cannot tolerate, the one type of behaviour which will send you to the divorce lawyer? Or could you see it as merely an indiscretion – a brief admission of human frailty?

So what can we do?

First, you have to know what you need and what you want. You must be able to talk about it – when it is good or bad. Sex is such a complicated thing. Our bodies are controlled by our hormones and brains in directing our genitals. Then, our brains signal our bodies to do, or not to do, something which is the most intimate activity which can be performed. Add to this that your partner is involved with his or her own set of mind–body accelerators and brakes – and you have one heck of a complicated system.

If sex is important to you, it should be discussed before you exchange rings and say 'I do'. Because, maybe, he or she 'won't' after a few months or years. When problems develop, you MUST talk about it. It is too important to ignore. If you can't come to an agreement, get to a competent therapist. And, if necessary, see a qualified sex therapist.

While it may be enough to roll over in bed and fondle some erogenous zones, a little out-of-bedroom romance is always a good idea. When you were dating, there were undoubtedly dinners out, picnics, walks and other wonderful ways to spend time together. These made you close. What about now? What are you doing to keep your imaginations tingling? Most of us need touching, hugs, compliments and other signs of affection to keep our emotional batteries charged.

Sex should be fun and it should be often. So don't cheat yourself – make sure that it is great. If not GREAT, at least let's hope is was 'good' for you!!

Self-test on sexuality and sexual preferences

Each partner can answer these questions alone, then talk about those which show some differences:

TRUE or FALSE

1 An orgasm is the greatest feeling
I have ever had   ☐   ☐

2 I've never had an orgasm   ☐   ☐

3 I can only have an orgasm through
oral sex   ☐   ☐

4 I can only have an orgasm through
masturbation   ☐   ☐

5 I can have an orgasm during sexual
intercourse   ☐   ☐

6 Having an orgasm isn't really very
important to me   ☐   ☐

7 I worry about my mate (potential
mate) having an affair at some time   ☐   ☐

8 My reaction to his or her having
an affair would be to break up the
relationship   ☐   ☐

TRUE or FALSE

9 My reaction to my partner having
an affair would be to seek
counselling   ☐   ☐

10 I am more experienced sexually than
my mate   ☐   ☐

11 I would prefer to never have sex ☐   ☐

For the following three questions put in the appropriate number:

I would like to have sex _____ times a day.

I would like to have sex _____ times a week.

I would like to have sex _____ time a month.

I prefer sex in the morning ☐   at night ☐
no preference ☐

Biological forces and your sexuality

What controls and stimulates your body and mind?

Read this chapter if:

You wonder why you want more sex

You wonder why you want less sex

You wonder why you ejaculate too quickly

You wonder how to reduce your ejaculation problems

You wonder what happens chemically in your body
when you are touched tenderly

You wonder why your body chemicals affect your sex life
for better or worse

You wonder what happens in your brain to create
your orgasm

You wonder why your sexual desires fluctuate during
your menstrual cycle

You wonder how smoking reduces your potential to
have an orgasm

Your mate has taken an approach to sexuality which you
don't think is normal

Our gendered genetic make-ups can increase or decrease our sexual desires and performances. We must understand that all sexual behaviour is not a product of our conscious minds. Naturally occurring substances in the body can affect us while being beyond our conscious control. Consequently, much of our behaviour cannot be changed by discussion, argument or psychotherapy. While, again, the focus here is on sex, biology is being found to influence much of our behaviour. Current estimates are that about 50% of behaviour is biologically oriented and 75% of our intelligence is genetically based. Consequently, understanding the 'reality' of our romance must include some hidden realities.

Much of what we hear about sexual response deals with either not wanting it because of 'having a headache' or 'being too tired', or of wanting it 'too much' because of being 'oversexed'. Usually, we ascribe the reasons to psychological or social causes – the stress of the job or the children, not feeling close to our 'loved one' or some other more psychologically obvious explanation from the worlds of Freud, Kinsey or Masters and Johnson. However, the hidden effects of hormones and other body chemicals, inadequate nutrition or even the process of disease can strongly affect our sexual interest and performance.

In this chapter, we will look at both the normal and the abnormal in terms of our physiology and our psychology – our bodies and our minds. If you understand the many possible causes for sexual problems, you should realise that if any such problems affect your relationship – there is help available. If we are to use reality to foster our romance, we must understand a bit more about reality. And the more we know, the more complex it is to understand each of us as individuals and the more problematical our relationship puzzle becomes.

Some physiological influences on our sexual interests and abilities

While psychological obstacles are often the cause of sexual difficulties, in recent years we have found that our genes generate or reduce many of our drives and desires. Our genetic make-ups and hormones go a long way in determining our aggressiveness, intelligence, obesity and even honesty. Today, we know that our genes and hormones also significantly affect our sex drives and the enjoyment of their satisfaction. While our genes can be praised or blamed for nearly 50% of our actions, they do it by affecting our nervous systems and our brains through neurotransmitters, hormones and peptides (small amino-acid molecules).

Nutrition, or the way our bodies process nutrients, can also be a factor. An example of a nutritional or metabolic problem is indicated by a study that showed that there is more magnesium in semen than in the blood. But men who ejaculated early had a lower than normal amount of magnesium in their semen, even though the magnesium in their blood was normal (A. E. Omu, A. A. Al-Bader, H. Dashti and M. A. Oriowo, 'Magnesium in human semen: Possible role in premature ejaculation', *Arch. Androl.*, **46**(1), January–February 2001, 59–66). While this is only one study and more studies are needed, it does give us some food for thought. Is it possible that premature ejaculation may sometimes be related to our nutrition?

As intelligent partners in a relationship, we must be aware that every sexual advance or retreat is not necessarily a conscious decision. We are often pulled or pushed by our biochemistry. But also, often our biochemistry is nudged by what is happening to our senses. The caresses of the skin, the scent of the other's body or the visual excitement created by looking at our loved one can all play a part in agitating our 'innards' and 'hopping up' our hormones. So, our 'sexual contract' can be changed, or at least influenced, by factors which we can't talk about – because we don't know what's happening to us. We may need the input or the help of an endocrinologist or a psychiatrist, rather than a psychologist or lawyer, to help us to understand ourselves and to discuss our approach to a more 'liveable' sexual contract.

As with other areas of biological and psychological research, animals are usually the 'volunteer' subjects for research. From animal studies, we can generally, but not always, project how humans might react. As the research matures, we do more studies on people. In the following sections, we discuss our nervous systems, skin scents and hormones. Some areas, like the sex (steroid) hormones testosterone and oestrogen, have been researched extensively with humans. Others, such as the hormones oxytocin and vasopressin, have been researched in some areas with humans, but the potential sexual effects have been done with animals. And their effects on animals can vary from species to species (T. R. Insel *et al.* 'Gonadal steroids have paradoxical effects on brain oxytocin receptors'. *J. Neuroendocrinology*, **5**(6), December 1993, 619–628). Consequently, some of the potential actions of many of the body's chemicals are only hypothetical. But, they are still fun to wonder about. For those of you who want to investigate further either through library research of through the Internet (through Medline), we have noted several bibliographical references throughout the text of this chapter. The research seems to multiply daily in so many scientific disciplines.

Neurotransmitters

There are several dozen neurotransmitters in our nervous system. They are the chemicals which transmit an electrical impulse from one nerve to the next. The electrical impulse travels down a nerve until it reaches the gap at the end of the nerve (called the *synapse*). As it cannot jump over the synapse like an electrical spark, the electrical impulse stimulates the release of a chemical (neurotransmitter) which crosses the synapse then initiates a new electrical impulse in the next nerve (Figure 21).

Nerve endings may be stimulated by different neurotransmitters. So one nerve which stimulates excitement may be triggered by noradrenaline, another may be stimulated by dopamine. Another nerve which acts to calm you down may be controlled by acetylcholine while another calming nerve may be controlled by serotonin.

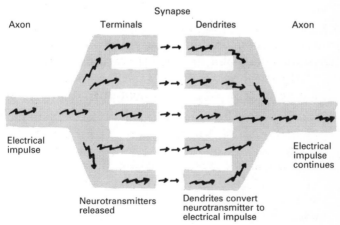

Figure 21   Functioning of the nerve and synapse.

To give you some ideas as to how these neurotransmitters work, let's look for a moment at illegal drugs. A downer such as a barbiturate sleeping pill stops the neurotransmitters from being released by the nerve so they cannot go across the synapse and stimulate the next nerve. The person taking the barbiturate will then go to sleep. But you can also increase your ability to sleep by increasing the release of the 'calming' neurotransmitter serotonin. This can be done by proper protein intake or by certain prescription drugs.

With the exception of alcohol, which affects the nerve cell and reduces its ability to allow an electrical impulse to travel its length, nearly all illegal drugs work by changing the effect of the various neurotransmitters in different parts of the brain. (Alcohol may also affect some neurotransmitters, such as increasing GABA and decreasing glutamine – both of which calm the person and make him sluggish.) By decreasing the ability of the nerves to function effectively, our thinking and reacting are slowed down. For example, in the pituitary gland, the hypothalamus and other sections of the brain, any of which affect our sexual appetites and abilities, alcohol reduces our discrimination and our ability to say 'no' while it also reduces our sexual abilities. At least as long ago as Shakespeare (Macbeth Act 2, scene 3), it was recognised that alcohol may stir our passions while it dulls our potentials:

Macduff: *What three things does drink especially promote?*

Porter: *Marry sir, nose-painting, sleep, and urine. Lechery, sir it provokes, and unprovokes; it provokes the desire, but it takes away the performance ...*

The psychoactive drugs do this by either increasing the normal amount of neurotransmitter which is in the synapse or by decreasing it. In some cases, the drug mimics a neurotransmitter. For example, nicotine acts as if it is acetylcholine so it has a calming affect. Of course, it also stimulates the adrenal glands to produce more adrenaline so it also has an upper effect. Because of these opposite effects, tobacco is the only drug that has noticeable upper and downer effects at the same time.

Cocaine stimulates the neurotransmitter dopamine in specific parts of the brain – in the areas similar to where orgasm occurs. Heroin has stimulating effects on some neurotransmitters but its major effect is on the calming neurotransmitters. Each drug, whether marijuana, ecstasy, LSD or tobacco has its effect on various neurotransmitters in different parts of the brain. Similarly, our sexual urges or inhibitions are often the result of too much or too little of a neurotransmitter in a certain part of the brain (Figure 22 and Box 7).

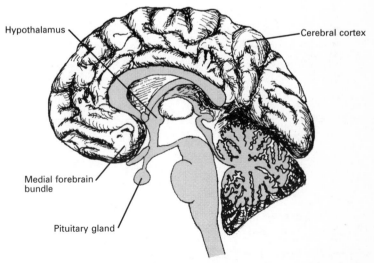

Figure 22   Some areas of the brain that are influenced by drugs.

Box 7 Effects of drugs on neurotransmitters and the nervous system

	Acetylcholine	Norepinephrine (noradrenalin)	Dopamine	Serotonin	Brain	Other
Downers						
Alcohol					Acts on nerves (slows transmission); disrupts reticular activating system making behaviour prediction impossible	
Opiates	Decrease output	Increase (results in euphoria)	Increase	Increase synthesis (so analgesic) results in tolerance	Reduce response of hypothalamus	Depress pituitary
Barbiturates	Decrease release	Decrease release	Decrease release			
Tranquillisers:						
Phenothiazines	Occupy synapse and block action (therefore antipsychotic)	Occupy synapse and block action (therefore antipsychotic)	Occupy synapse and block action (therefore antipsychotic)	Occupy synapse and block action (therefore antipsychotic)	Depress reticular activating system, hypothalamus and periventricular system	
Valium		Reduces		Reduces	Depresses through the limbic system	

Uppers						
Nicotine	Blocks and excites the dendrites – mimics acetylcholine				Stimulates central nervous system	Increases adrenalin
Amphetamines	Stimulate production	Cause slow continuous release and block re-uptake	Block re-uptake		Stimulate medial forebrain bundle (flash of pleasure) and reticular activating system	Increase adrenalin
Cocaine	Prevents re-uptake	Increases release and prevents re-uptake			Anaesthetic	
Xanthines (caffeine, etc.)		Stimulate release in medulla and brain			Stimulate cerebral cortex	Increase pulse, usually dilates (but can constrict) blood vessels
MDMA (ecstasy)			Increases release	Increases release	Destruction of dopamine and serotonin producing cells, possible brain damage	Similar effects to methamphetamine and mescaline, possible symptoms of Parkinson's disease, possible brain damage
Hallucinogenics						
LSD	Increases	Increases		Stimulates synapse	Causes highest blood concentrations in reticular activating system and limbic system	
Marijuana	Decreases	Decreases		Decreases		
Belladonna	Blocks action					

Serotonin

This fits into the sex area because too much of it makes us feel content and it thereby reduces our sex drives. For this reason, drugs which increase serotonin have been used to treat premature ejaculation. (That quick male orgasm is called premature ejaculation.) If you're very relaxed, orgasm doesn't seem to be so important! With low levels of this neurotransmitter, both women and men have orgasms more quickly. But low levels can also give us an agitated feeling and make us aggressive. So a low level of a relaxing neurotransmitter, such as serotonin, can make us excited or agitated and a low level of a stimulating neurotransmitter, such as dopamine, can make us more quiet and calm.

Dopamine

This is the major neurotransmitter which excites the various parts of the brain. It is involved in most of the 'upper' feelings in the brain. It, therefore, is involved in pleasure seeking and pleasure experiencing, such as an orgasm.

If our stimulating neurotransmitters are increased in certain parts of our brains, we may become more sexual. If other brain areas are affected, our desires may be reduced or eliminated. Without a proper diet, we may not be able to make some of these essential chemicals and our internal chemistry will be negatively influenced. Many prescription drugs and most illegal drugs have upper or downer effects on our neurotransmitters.

Peptides

Peptides are potent body chemicals made from the amino acids which make up proteins. Many affect our behaviour by being, or acting as, hormones. They may also act as brain chemicals. Oxytocin, which is discussed on p. 237, is a hormone when it induces labour and begins milk production, but it has non-hormonal effects in the brain where it acts to change behaviour. Peptides are also found as pheromones (natural body scents) – which are discussed on p. 245.

Hormones

Hormones (which mean to 'set in motion') are substances made in one organ which travel in the blood and can affect other organs – including our brains. They are major players in our carnal controls. They can get us so excited over somebody that we jump into bed with them, then hate ourselves in the morning. They can even lead us to marriage, because the lust they have created makes us think we are in love. They can also turn us off – even when another person should otherwise seem attractive. So, hormones often hold the answer as to why we are hot or cold in our sexual drives (Box 8).

Our minds may want a closeness, but our hormones may push us apart. Our minds may want to stay apart, but our hormones may pull us together. We always think that we can explain why we do what we do – but that isn't always possible. In the following sections, we look at

Box 8   Small chemicals –
enormous effects

- Hormones have varied effects.
- Testosterone increases sex drive.
- Oestrogen can make us desirous.
- Progesterone can suppress the sex drive by decreasing testosterone.
- Vasopressin makes animals more monogamous, does it in people?
- Oxytocin is increased by touching. It helps us to bond together.
- Prolactin, the hormone which stimulates mother's milk, reduces her sex drive.
- DHEA increases sex drive in women, and can stimulate our pheromones.
- Pheromones are the subconsciously smelled substances which can turn us on or off sexually.
- Neurotransmitters, the chemicals which aid our nerve impulses, can increase or decrease our desires.
- Dopamine increases our excitement.
- Serotonin calms us down.

what some research tells us about how our hormones affect us. While we like to think that we are in total control of our thoughts and behaviour, reading this chapter may make you aware of the fact that our control over our behaviour is not as complete as we might desire.

In the following explanations, the reader should understand that many of the studies on which these theories have been developed have been based on studies of animals, from rats to monkeys. They, therefore, may not be scientifically 'proven' but they do give us strong indications of what might be stimulating or calming us.

Testosterone

This is the male hormone which increases sexual desire in both men and women. Men, of course, have more, but women have it too. This is the hormone which gives men their broader shoulders, hairy chests and deeper voices. It is also responsible for aggressiveness in our pursuit of sex as well as in our drive to succeed in business, war or sport. Sexually, it tends to push us toward wanting a conquest or an orgasm – whether that orgasm is the result of masturbation or intercourse. A study in Greece has shown conclusively that the amount of testosterone in the blood is a major predictor of sexual activity in men (C. S. Mantzoros *et al.*, 'Contributions of di-hydrotestosterone to male sexual behaviour', *British Medical Journal*, **310**(6990), 20 May 1995, 1289–1291).

It rises and falls in men several times an hour and the average level can increase significantly at times during a day or even at certain times of the year. As it rises, a man's aggression and sex drive rise with it, as it falls he becomes more docile. The fluctuations in a man's testosterone levels can be affected by factors within his body or by external cues. While job stress may reduce it, a pretty girl may increase it.

Most of us are familiar with PMS (pre-menstrual syndrome), which can make women a bit bitchy. The effect of the 28-day menstrual cycle tends to give women 28 somewhat varying hormone-based personalities during a month. The same is happening with men but is more on an hourly basis as their testosterone levels ebb and flow. Some, like former US President John Kennedy, needed daily supplements to keep his levels within the normal range. Men low in testosterone tend to be more depressed, easier to anger, more confused and more tired. This is in addition to their lower interest and capacity for sexual activity. Treatment with testosterone can reduce all of these factors but does not completely eliminate any depression. It does, however, clearly increase the man's desire for and ability to perform sexual intercourse (A. S. Burris 'A long term, prospective study of the physiologic and behavioral effects of hormone replacement in untreated hypogonal men', *J. Androl.*, **13**(4), July 1992, 297–304).

Testosterone is also an important hormone for women, being produced by the ovaries throughout life. The reduction of testosterone production, particularly after menopause, can reduce both sexual desire and sexual response in women. While a reduction of oestrogen production also reduces sexual response, replacement of oestrogen does not seem to change the sexual response and may even increase the symptoms which have developed due to the low production of testosterone.

Diagnosis of the problem is based on both pre-menopausal sexual interest and response and a low level of testosterone. When such a diagnosis has been confirmed, testosterone (androgen) replacement usually increases the woman's sexual interest and response (R. Basson, 'Androgen replacement for women', *Can. Fam. Physician*, September 1999, **45**, 2100–2107; P. M. Sarrel, 'Psychosexual effects of menopause: Role of androgens', Am. J. Obstet. Gynecol., **180**(3, Pt, 2), March 1999, S319–324). Female athletes, particularly endurance and strength-trained women, often show higher levels of testosterone, so working out can often increase women's sex drives. More studies are needed in this area, however.

Oestrogen

This is the major female hormone. It is responsible for developing soft breasts and curvaceous hips as well as a number of other feminine traits. It also seems to be responsible for a female desiring sex – whether it be the canine bitch in heat or a human desiring to be penetrated.

An interesting study was done at Penn State University in 1997 with boys and girls who had low levels of sex hormones. Boys were given testosterone supplements for three months and girls were given oestrogen supplements for the same period. Then, they were given a placebo (a similar looking pill but with no hormones in it). Both the boys and the girls became more physically aggressive and had more aggressive impulses when they were on the hormones. This indicates that the female hormone, as well as the male testosterone, can make us aggressive (J. W. Finkelstein *et al.*, 'Estrogen or testosterone increases self reported aggressive behaviors in hypogonadal adolescents', *J. of Clinical Endocrinology and Metabolism*, **82**(8), August 1997, 2433–2438).

We all know that oestrogen is decreased during and after menopause, but it is also decreased when a woman starves herself, such as in anorexia nervosa. It is also decreased when she refrains from sex. Oestrogen is increased by more sexual activity and by being overweight. It may even be increased by cuddling.

Progesterone

This is a female hormone which suppresses the sex drive by reducing the amount of testosterone in the body – for

men or women. When made synthetically it is a major
ingredient in female contraceptives – which makes it
doubly effective. It reduces a woman's ability to conceive
while it makes her less interested in sex. In animals, it has
been found to reduce the pheromones, the sexual smells
which the females give off making them attractive to the
males of their species. It tends to make females protective
of their young, but it can also make the females aggressive
against the opposite sex.

It is a factor in PMS because it increases later in the
menstrual cycle. Both being pregnant and nursing the
newborn also increase it, thereby reducing the woman's
sexual drive at these times. It is probably the reduced
testosterone caused by the progesterone which reduces
the sexual desire.

Prolactin

This literally means 'with milk'. It is secreted by the
pituitary gland just after giving birth and stimulates
breast-milk production. It is the hormone which increases
during pregnancy and becomes highest during nursing.
Prolactin is found in abundance in women who are
nursing. It reduces their sex drive. During the minutes
that a woman is nursing, her prolactin levels may increase
by 1,000%, then come back to normal within a few hours.

Prolactin reduces our sex drives, whether it be in the
nursing mother or a less common condition in either men
or women where the hormonal system secretes too much of
the hormone. While prolactin reduces our sex drives, it
does not reduce the sensation of orgasm. The hormone
may be increased by stress, too much exercise, changed
sleep patterns or to a lack of menstruation (amenorrhoea).
(Thin women who exercise a great deal – particularly
dancers, gymnasts and long-distance swimmers and

runners – often experience the female athlete triangle of amenorrhoea, anorexia nervosa and bone calcium loss. They may also be expected to have their sex drives reduced because of an increase in prolactin.) Men who happen to have high levels of the hormone also lose their sex drives. It tends to decrease testosterone levels and can cause impotence.

'Sexual arousal and orgasm produce a distinct pattern of neuroendocrine alterations in women, primarily inducing a long-lasting elevation in plasma (blood) prolactin concentrations.' (M. S. Exton, A. Bindert, T. Kruger, F. Scheller, U. Hartmann and M. Schedlowski, 'Cardiovascular and endocrine alterations after masturbation-induced orgasm in women', *Psychosom. Med.*, **61**(3), May–June 1999, 280–289). These results are similar to those observed in men, suggesting that prolactin is an endocrine marker of sexual arousal and orgasm. In both men and women, whether the orgasm is induced by masturbation or by sexual intercourse, there are increases in the amount of prolactin in the blood. The increase in the prolactin lasts for at least an hour and reduces the sexual desire during the time that it remains high (M. S. Exton, T. H. Kruger, M. Koch, E. Paulson, W. Knapp, U. Hartmann and M. Schedlowski, 'Coitus-induced orgasm stimulates prolactin secretion in healthy subjects', *Psychoneuroendocrinology*, **26**(3), April 2001, 287–294).

Oxytocin

This is secreted by the back part of the pituitary gland (the master gland) in the brain. It is medically used to induce labour and to increase the strength of the muscular contractions of the uterus when there isn't enough of the hormone naturally to accomplish this. It, also, is one of the factors which increases the production of breast milk.

But it seems to have other functions (N. M. McCarthy and M. Altemus, 'Central nervous system actions of oxytocin and modulation of behavior in humans', *Molecular Medicine Today*, **3**(6), June 1997, 269–275). It may even give some protection against breast cancer (T. Murrell, 'The potential for oxytocin to prevent breast cancer: A hypothesis', *Breast Cancer Res. Treat.*, **35**(2), August 1995, 225–229).

It has been called the 'touch' hormone. It is stimulated by one person touching another – men or women touching, an adult touching a child or a baby stimulating the mother's nipple while nursing. It seems that when we touch another person we become psychologically closer to them. We seem to increase oxytocin when we touch or when we are touched lovingly. The breasts and nipples seem to be particularly important as areas which, when fondled, can release oxytocin (K. Uvnas-Moberg and M. Eriksson, 'Breastfeeding: Physiological, endocrine and behavioral adaptations caused by oxytocin and local neurogenic activity in the nipple and mammary gland', *Acta Paediatr.*, **85**(5), May 1996, 525–530).

An interesting study was done at the University of Maryland on small animals called voles. When a female vole was injected with oxytocin, while in the presence of a male vole, she later preferred to be with that male. Females who were not injected did not develop such an attraction (J. R. Williams *et al.*, 'Oxytocin administration centrally facilitates formation of a partner preference in female prairie voles' *J. Neuroendocrinology*, **6**(3), June 1994, 247–250; C. S. Carter, 'Oxytocin and social bonding', *Annals N.Y. Acad. Sci.*, 12 June 1992, 204–211). Is it possible that oxytocin is somehow related to love at first sight? Is it possible that the oxytocin released while playing 'let's kiss our faces and hug our bodies' or what is scientifically called 'copulatory interactions' may bond us to our amorous partner? When we talk about a special chemistry between us, maybe there is more truth than poetry in our observation.

It is theorised that one of the responses of love making in women is that this hormone helps fertilisation by speeding the sperm up the fallopian tubes toward the ovum. Certainly, the touching during love making increases it. It is also increased during childbirth and assists in reducing the pains caused as the baby passes through the birth canal. It increases the pleasure of a woman nursing her baby. Its effects seem to be increased when it works with oestrogen, and it is reduced by alcohol and by not being touched.

According to a study at Stanford University, it, also, is involved with orgasms and reaches a very high level during sexual activity and orgasm (M. S. Carmichael *et al*., 'Relationships among cardiovascular, muscular, and oxytocin responses during human sexual activity', *Archives of Sexual Behavior*, **23**(1), February 1994, 59–79). In addition to the positive factors, it seems to make us forget – and it reduces our ability to think rationally. It seems to have a more erotic effect when combined with male hormones (androgens), which make up a part of most contraceptive pills (J. Herbert, 'Oxytocin and sexual behaviour' *British Medical J*., **309**, 8 October 1994, 891–892).

A number of years ago, America's foremost social scientist, Ashley Montagu, wrote a classic book *Touching – The Human Significance of the Skin* (Columbia University Press, New York, 1971). The magic results of touching he ascribed merely to physical closeness. Now, it looks like some of the sorcery of the touch is hormonal. Children deprived of touching tend to become mentally and physically retarded and older people deprived of touching seem to age faster and die sooner. As a parent or lover, there is probably nothing you can do to psychologically get closer to the one you love than through touching.

As noted on p. 230, serotonin is a neurotransmitter which activates the more calming nerves and can also inhibit male sexual abilities. When people are severely depressed, they are often treated with drugs which increase the amount of serotonin in the synapses. But this reduces both a male's sexual desire and his ability to ejaculate. In a Canadian study, using rats which were on an antidepressant drug, injections of oxytocin increased the males' ability to perform (ejaculate) after that ability had been lowered by the drug. However, the lowering effect of the antidepressant on the rats' sexual excitement was not raised (J. M. Cantor, Y. M. Binik and J. G. Pfaus, 'Chronic fluoxetine inhibits sexual behavior in the male rat: Reversal with oxytocin', *Psychopharmacology* (Berlin), **144**(4), June 1999, 355–362).

Another area researched at Harvard University indicates that oxytocin may inhibit the effects of morphine, heroin and cocaine (in animals) by changing the amount of the neurotransmitter dopamine in the limbic system and forebrain areas (Z. Sarnyai and G. L. Kovacs, 'The role of oxytocin in the neuroadaptation to drugs of abuse', *Psychoneuroendocrinology*, **19**(1), 1994, 85–117). These are areas affected by many mind-altering drugs – and the seats of many of our emotions. So you see, our hormonal system is rather complex – and we are just scratching the surface on which hormones exist and what kinds of actions they can aid or inhibit in our bodies. (You see that there are more questions than answers in this chapter!)

Vasopressin

This is another hormone. Its major functions are in controlling muscular contractions in our intestines and our blood-circulation system. But, it also can affect our sexual desires. It seems to work with testosterone in affecting sexual impulses, but it tends to make some male animals stay at home to satisfy their sexual desires. It seems to increase some animals' ability to remember and to think more clearly (L. J. Young *et al.*, 'Species differences in Via receptor gene expression in monogamous and non-monogamous voles: Behavioral consequences', *Behav. Neurosci.*, **111**(3), June 1997, 599–605). It also helps us to sleep more effectively by increasing our dreaming sleep, our REM (rapid eye movement) sleep. It is during this period of sleep when we tend to be more sexual. Men get erections and women lubricate.

There is evidence in animals that vasopressin in specific areas of the brain makes a male animal more of a 'home body'. While in the monogamous rodent, the prairie vole, oxytocin seems to be more important in a female's bonding, it is vasopressin which is more important in a male bonding to a female (T. R. Insell *et al.*, 'A gender specific mechanism for pair bonding: Oxytocin and partner preference', *Behav. Neurosci.*, **109**(4), August 1995, 782–789; T. R. Insel *et al.*, 'Oxytocin and the molecular basis of monogamy' *Adv. Experim. Medical Biology*, **395**, 1995, 227–234). On the other hand, the promiscuous male mountain voles, while closely related, do not have the receptors for vasopressin in their brains. This seems to keep them from being monogamous (T. R. Insel, *et al.*, 'Patterns of brain vasopressin receptor distribution associated with social organization in microtine rodents'. *J. Neuroscience*, **14**(9), September 1994, 5381–5392). In the species of voles which are monogamous, the vasopressin also makes them ready to defend their homes and mates (J. T. Winslow *et al.*, 'A role for central vasopressin in pair bonding in monogamous prairie voles', *Nature*, **365**(6446), 7 October 1993, 545–548). It is not yet known if it will make the human male more likely to sit home voluntarily – as he does for watching the Olympics on television.

During the last two decades, it has become apparent that vasopressin and oxytocin, in addition to playing a role as peptide hormones, also act as neurotransmitters. They can change the way the nerve transmissions work. This occurs in many areas of the brain, especially in those areas dealing with emotion (M. Raggenbass, 'Vasopressin- and oxytocin-induced activity in the central nervous system: Electrophysiological studies using in-vitro systems', *Prog. Neurobiol.*, **64**(3), June 2001, 307–326).

DHEA (dehydroepiandrosterone)

This is produced in the adrenal glands and is the most common hormone in the body – for both men and women. It is the substance from which most of the hormones affecting our sexuality are formed. It also rises and falls significantly during a day. While we are in the womb DHEA is the major hormone we produce. It is hundreds of times more common than either oestrogen or testosterone. DHEA rises early in life but begins to decline during our 30s.

Among the functions it may have in high amounts are: a stimulation of the immune system which can reduce our chances of contracting diseases, including cancers; the matrix from which pheromones (our unconsciously detected odours) are made; a sex-drive enhancer (particularly in women); and it may play a part in slowing the aging process. In low amounts, it may increase the chances of obesity and depression – particularly the depression which often follows the birth of a child.

In a study of women who were already deficient in adrenal hormones, DHEA replacement improved the feeling of well-being and sexuality. This may be because of the DHEA itself or because of its effect on increasing androgens, the male hormones (W. Arlt, F. Callies and B. Allolio, 'DHEA replacement in women with adrenal insufficiency – pharmacokinetics, bioconversion and clinical effects on well-being, sexuality and cognition', *Endocr. Res.*, **26**(4), November 2000, 505–11). DHEA is decreased with alcohol ingestion, stress, illness, overweight, poor nutrition and aging. It is increased by exercise, calmness and sexual activity. It can also be supplemented, but we are not certain of its effectiveness.

Phenylethylamine (PEA)

This is another hormone which makes us feel high. Its effect is something like cocaine or amphetamines – as such it should keep us high and make our natural highs, like orgasm, even better. It is somewhat high when we are happy, but is particularly high during orgasm. Its effect can be exciting, as with cocaine, and its absence can make us depressed. By the way, chocolate contains PEA, so if you don't get enough loving perhaps you can make it up with Hershey's kisses.

While it can be prescribed by a doctor, it can also be taken in small doses as chocolate or diet products made with Nutrasweet. So that box of chocolates Waldo brought your daughter may have some unforeseen consequences (Waldo, of course, wasn't aware of the small hormonal aphrodisiac qualities of his gift.) Strippers (both male and female – depending on your tastes!), romance novels or romantic and sexy films, and even poems and music which elicit a romantic twinge can stimulate PEA production.

The menstrual cycle and hormones

The first part of the cycle, the proliferative phase (9–10 days), begins as menstruation ceases. Oestrogen and progesterone were low during menstruation, but oestrogen increases during the second or ovulatory phase (1–2 days). The third phase (secretory or luteal) is characterised by large increases in oestrogen and progesterone and lasts about 14 days. The high levels of progesterone signals the pituitary gland to stop producing two other hormones (LH and FSH), so the levels of oestrogen and progesterone fall significantly. This brings on the fourth phase, the menstrual phase, which lasts about 5 days.

A woman's menstrual cycle influences her sex drive. As she comes closer to the time of ovulation, around day 14, there is an increase in male-type hormones, which increases her sex drive. Nature provides this because it is at this time that she is most fertile. At the same time, oestrogen increases which makes her more receptive and more ready to be penetrated by a man. Near the end of the cycle, women tend to be more desirous of sex than at any other time.

Endorphins

Endorphins are brain chemicals (peptides) which are considered to be 'natural opiates'. They give us an exhilarated feeling when they are present. They can be naturally increased several ways. Listening to classical music raises them. (Loud rock music lowers them.) Endurance exercise such as jogging, after about 40 minutes, usually increases them. So does touching and sexual activity. Ever notice how the pains go away before and during an orgasm?

Pheromones

Pheromones are the body chemicals which are secreted to the skin where they are sensed by another animal. The word was coined in 1959 from two Greek words *pherein* (to transfer) and *hormon* (to excite). In animals, most pheromones seem to be synthesised from DHEA. It is likely that this is also true of people. Our research has been primarily done on animals, not us humans – nevertheless, we're beginning to understand how they affect us as well. Body fluids, particularly sweat and vaginal secretions, as well as urine, faeces and saliva are likely carriers of sexually stimulating pheromones (DHEA is found in large amounts in urine). Each of us seems to have a particular odour specific to us. That is why bloodhounds are able to track down a suspect after merely whiffing an article of clothing.

In animals, pheromones stimulate sexual drives – as commonly seen when all the neighbourhood dogs are attracted to a bitch in heat. In humans, we have not identified such a 'cause and effect' result of any pheromone, but the smells we exude may turn some people on and make us more desirable.

Perfume makers in the past have attempted to make their scents give aphrodisiac qualities. If the perfume doesn't do it, the names should: My Sin, Obsession or Seduction – indicate that the buyer was interested somewhat in a roll in the hay. Perfumeries are ready to hop on the wagon and include pheromones in their products as soon as they can be identified and duplicated. This is in spite of the fact that we don't seem to smell these substances consciously. There seems to be a subliminal recognition rather than an identifiable scent. This is one of the problems in researching these substances. Already a few perfumes and aftershave lotions have been marketed claiming to contain effective genitally stimulating pheromones.

Orgasm

During foreplay and orgasm, a flood of hormones are titillating our brains making us more cuddly and excited. DHEA increases significantly and increases the neural activity in the septum of the brain which facilitates orgasm. PEA increases, as does testosterone, in most cases. There are several centres in the brain which seem to be excited and which result in what we call an orgasm. The medial forebrain bundle is stimulated by the neurotransmitter dopamine. This seems to be the major reason for the feeling which we call 'orgasm'. Perhaps not so strangely, this is the same part of the brain that is stimulated by cocaine and amphetamines. So people who don't get enough orgasms may be attracted to the chemicals which can give them a similar effect. No wonder that those illegal drugs are so popular!!

Studies of what is happening in the brain during orgasm are now being accomplished. A study of men, using the advanced technique of magnetic resonance imaging (MRI), showed that during orgasm men's blood flow was reduced in most areas of the brain but increased significantly in the right prefrontal cortex. (J. Tiihonen *et al.*, 'Increase in cerebral blood flow of right prefrontal cortex in man during orgasm', *Neuroscience Lett.*, **170**(2), 11 April 1994, 241–243). Exactly what this means is not yet known, but it certainly indicates brain involvement.

Of course, there is an increase in the blood flow in the genital area. The blood flow in men gives the erection and in women it increases the flow in both the large and small lips (labia majora and labia minora) of the female genitals (F. Sommer, H. P. Caspers, K. Esders, T. Klotz and U. Engelmann, 'Measurement of vaginal and minor labial oxygen tension for the evaluation of female sexual function', *J. Urol.*, **165**(3), April 2001, 1181–1184).

Women often are able to have orgasms only by thinking about it. 'Imagery induced orgasm' is the scientific term. A study at the College of Nursing at Rutgers University compared orgasms stimulated only by thinking about it with orgasms induced by masturbation. They showed similar effects on the subjects' blood pressure, heart rate and other physical manifestations of orgasm (for these reasons the researchers are asking for a new definition of orgasm and its causes) (B. Whipple *et al.*, 'Physiological correlates of imagery-induced orgasm in women', *Arch. Sexual Behavior*, **21**(2), April 1992, 121–123).

A number of studies have been done which attempt to locate the primary organs responsible for orgasm. Many women report that it is the stimulation of the clitoris which is primary. Others say that it is the stimulation of the vagina which is essential. But the mental health of the woman also seems to be critical to being able to experience orgasm. A study in Czechoslovakia which compared neurotic women with mentally healthy women and how they achieved orgasm found that the mentally healthy women were able to achieve significantly more orgasms. Furthermore, of the orgasms experienced, 90% of the women experienced orgasms through clitoral stimulation and

75% experienced them through vaginal stimulation. So both seem to be important (S. Kratochvuk, 'Sexual stimulation and the female orgasm', *Czechoslovakian Psychiatry*, **89**(4), August 1993, 191–194).

Our sexual desires – as we age

Most people know that teenage boys are at their highest sexual peaks in their late teens. They are quick to arouse and quick to recover and be ready for another orgasm. Similarly, most of us are aware that women tend to become more sexual in their 30s. This has prompted some to suggest that 30-year-old women should marry teenage boys – and it does happen. Her sex life might be improved – but she'd have another kid around the house to take care of.

Happily, for those of us who have passed our midlife crises, our psychological desires for sex are generally at their highest during our 50s – for both men and women. So, if we can live that long together we should be amply rewarded. Our emotions have levelled out and our psychological traits tend to become more similar. Men usually become softer and more nurturing as their testosterone decreases, while women generally become more independent and assertive as their oestrogen diminishes.

Men in their 20s are setting out to conquer the world, so they can be valued. Getting sex is a quick way of feeling appreciated – and conquering. The traditional women want to be valued by being accepted by a man.

Men in their 30s are often thinking about settling down. This is often the time that women are thinking about getting out – particularly if they have been divorced and realise that they must become responsible for their own lives. For those who have been married for several years, the temptation of having an affair rears its ugly head. If our spouse is so busy with business or children, we may find some interested adult exciting.

In their 40s, men can often settle down a bit and enjoy family life. The touching which they may have passed over in their earlier years now often becomes important and their oxytocin rushes can make cuddling very rewarding. With the children either raised or spending most of their waking hours with friends, men and women can become more truly compatible than ever before. The hormones which stimulate their sexual drives are about on a par and their life goals are more likely to be in sync. His testosterone has dropped, making him less of a satyr and her oestrogen has dropped, making her more sexually aggressive and interested. Hormonally, this mutuality becomes even more positive in the next decades.

Chemical help

Chemical help can come in the form of aphrodisiacs which would help to increase desire or substances which aid in performance, such as Viagra. Viagra is the answer many men have prayed for to increase their ability to achieve or maintain an erection, other factors are being investigated.

While it is often said that the best aphrodisiac is in the mind, humans have looked for them in magic potions from ground beatles ('Spanish fly') to crushed flowers (perfumes). A recent study from the Institute of Sexuality in Paris found that a combination of two herbs (*Muira puama* and *Ginkgo biloba*) significantly increased sexual interest and satisfaction in women. After taking the supplement, 65% of the sample made statistically significant improvements in the frequency of sexual desires, sexual intercourse and sexual fantasies, as well as in satisfaction with sex life, intensity of sexual desires, excitement of fantasies, ability to reach orgasm and the intensity of their orgasms. Reported compliance and tolerability were good. These initial findings support the strong anecdotal evidence for the benefits of Herbal vX on the female sex drive (J. Waynberg and S. Brewer, 'Effects of Herbal vX on libido and sexual activity in premenopausal and postmenopausal women', *Adv. Ther.*, **17**(5), September–October 2000, 255–256).

There are a number of studies which have investigated the effects of high blood pressure (hypertension) on sexual functioning in men. A recent study on women which compared women with hypertension, some on medication for the condition, with others who were not hypertensive showed no major differences in terms of sexuality. However, the women who were hypertensive, whether or not they were on medication, showed less ability to lubricate, more frequent pain and fewer orgasms than the women who were not hypertensive. An unexpected finding was that women who smoked had significantly fewer orgasms than non-smokers (L. E. Duncan, C. Lewis, P. Jenkins and T. A. Pearson, 'Does hypertension and its pharmacotherapy affect the quality of sexual function in women?' *Am. J. Hypertens.*, **13**(6, Pt 1), June 2000, 640–647).

Making love, not war

We are quite aware that men typically want that 'wham, bam, thank you mam!' orgasm which their testosterone is screaming for. But women want to be touched and fondled prior to and after the orgasm. It isn't that women don't like orgasms, they just need more touching. The fondling increases their oxytocin levels which then stimulate their sexual drives as their testosterone rises, and makes them desire penetration, as their oestrogen rises. Men don't understand that women react differently and are generally slower to be excited. And women think that men are merely using them as gratification givers without wanting the real essentials of loving – the touching. It is like so many other areas of our communication – we think that everyone thinks exactly like we do.

By understanding a bit about that mob of chemicals running wildly through our bodies, perhaps we can be a bit more tolerant of the ebb and flow of feelings in both ourselves and our partners. And, perhaps, if we need to be 'sexually fixed', we will seek an endocrinologist rather than a psychotherapist, or a psychiatrist rather than a psychologist.

Something to think about

While this chapter has addressed a few of the chemicals which may influence or control our behaviours, we should be struck by the millions or billions of potential influences on all of our behaviour – not just our sexual behaviour. From the days of Freud, psychologists have pretty much told us that we have learned our way into what we are. And although Freud said that 'biology is destiny', he said that long before the contraceptive pill was invented and before women's equality movements had gained any momentum. Still, our body chemicals can certainly give us the push to behave in a certain way.

As people in relationships, we must be aware that we and our partners are, and have been, influenced by many events in our lives. At the same time, we are all being influenced by our hormones and brain chemistries in 'mega-ways'. Science is just beginning to see some of the ways in which our own body chemicals and those of others are mutually influential.

To ascribe our own or our partner's behaviour only to psychological causes may be too simple. We must allow for the influences of our genetic make-ups in how we develop. We are all products of nature and nurture. Consequently, both our joys and our problems are outcomes of our bodies, our brains and our minds.

Earlier, we discussed the psychological drive for power. It certainly seems to be influenced by testosterone and probably by a number of other chemicals. We have mentioned the typical nurturing role of women and the traditional power role of men. But, if we were to compare all the men in the world with all the women of the world in any trait, we would find an enormous overlap. Whether we are measuring blood testosterone level, how fast they can run, how much weight they can lift, how much of a drive for power they exhibit or how well they do on a mathematics test – we will find a great overlap between men and women. We, therefore, can't say that 'for women this is always true' or 'for men this is always true'.

Not only are there huge biochemical differences in us, we have also had different experiences in our lives. Our differences will also be changed as we age. Sometimes becoming greater, sometimes less. (The reduction of testosterone and oestrogens, as we age, is a case in point.)

Our race, religion or social class will also have influences on us, which may force us to control our biological propensities. Does a woman's religion or ethnic situation force her to reduce any biological urge for power? Does her high social class require that she push for success when her genes would prefer a more family-oriented commitment? Would a loving man's desire to be a nurse encounter antagonism by his multimillionaire parents?

So, while the message of this book deals with intelligent discussion of our desires and our lives together, we must be aware that our relationships contain elements which influence both of us and over which we generally have no control. In the areas where some control is possible through the medical community, we take advantage of them. Depression, alcoholism, sex hormone problems, sex performance problems and a large number of other physical and psychological realities are controllable through effective medical intervention. So, when problems seem to be developing, look for effective medical help. We can't cure biochemical problems with a discussion.

More severe psychological problems relating to sex

Reasons for us not having the same levels of sexual desire may find their source in our upbringing. Was family closeness normal or a taboo in our early life? Some see sex as dirty. This is usually a carry-over from a cleanliness complex in their early years and the acquiring of the idea that our genitals are dirty and shouldn't be touched. In some cases, it stems from our religious beliefs such as the Christian dualism which separates the 'good' mind and soul from the 'evil' body. In some religions, sex is seen as sinful, dirty and against the ideal of devoting oneself to God. St Paul said 'It is best for a man not to touch a woman ...' Early sexual abuse can also be a conscious or unconscious factor. It is much more common than we previously believed.

It is difficult to move from a position in which sexual activity was dirty or exploitive to a position where it is an expression of intimacy and friendship, or from a situation in which our trust in others is violated, such as childhood incestual abuse, to a relationship in which trust is an essential element. Psychologists have done us a service in helping us to recognise that unusual behaviour often has its roots in our mind, our unconscious mind.

Other mental barriers to intimacy can be as obvious as being fatigued or stressed. Or they can be somewhat hidden in our conscious or unconscious minds where we fear rejection. Getting too close may set us up for being rejected, so we stay emotionally distant.

Sometimes, the psychological problems of one of the partners create major breaches in the sexual side of the contract. For men, the princess–prostitute (or madonna–prostitute) syndrome is sometimes evident. In this situation, the man's unconscious mind has determined that sex is bad so you only do it with bad people, such as prostitutes. For someone you really love and respect, like your mother, or the wife you have come to love, you cannot have sex. These women are too good.

One of my patients confided in me that her sexual relationship had been great before her marriage and for the first few years, but as her husband came to idolise her, he could not have sex with her any more. Being of a generous nature, he told her that she could have sex with another woman, but not with another man. However, she entered into an affair and fell in love. But her lover, whose wife had reduced her sexual intimacy, still loved his wife. My patient, being hurt, decided to stay with her husband, whom she loved, in spite of the absence of sex in their relationship.

Some women have a similar complex. Some men, or

all men, may be off limits for her because she categorises them with her father. Such a relationship would therefore be incestuous and consequently immoral.

Some men and women have other psychological problems which relate to orgasm. Their feeling is that they will lose control if they have an orgasm. Certainly a real orgasm requires an abandoning of control. Sometimes this problem is expressed by men as a fear that the penis will be trapped in the vagina. Women may express the fear that the vagina will be ripped.

Any of these problems require competent therapy – often sex therapy. Such problems can generally be eliminated. You may not want to put into a contract that 'if you are ever frigid', or 'if you are ever impotent' that the relationship is over. But, if a change in sexual desire, sexual response, sexual frequency or another sex-related problem develops, be aware that counselling is available – and should be used. The relationship will be better because of it.

Common and not so common sexual practices

Sometimes, we or our partners either have, or develop, problems (Box 9). They may be physical problems, possibly hormonal imbalances, or psychological problems. When these occur we must be able to recognise them for what they are. Often, they are not something which we have planned on. Nevertheless, they develop. Here is a little background which you may need at sometime during your relationship. Let's hope not. But because

Box 9 Variations in sexual desires and behaviours

Sexual behaviour can be observed from several points of view. We can understand normal, deviant and perverted types of behaviour by looking at:

The choice of partners:

- self (masturbation);
- a person of the opposite sex (heterosexuality);
- a person of the same sex (homosexuality);
- both sexes (bisexuality);
- several partners at once (swinging or group sex);
- a child (paedophilia) or specifically young boys (paederasty);
- an animal (bestiality).

The means of achieving sexual arousal or orgasm:

- involuntary expression (such as while sleeping, including nocturnal emissions);
- voluntary including:
- genital sex (coitus);
- manual stimulation (hand–genital);
- oral–genital stimulation (fellatio, cunnilingus);
- visual stimulation including watching male or female strippers, nude shows or movies (voyeurism) (this can be done in public or in private);
- reading erotic literature (pornography);
- inflicting pain on our partner (sadism);
- wanting pain inflicted on ourselves (masochism);
- displaying our genitals to others (exhibitionism);

- touching, wearing, seeing inanimate objects such as underwear (fetishism);
- wearing the clothes of the opposite sex (transvestitism).

The frequency of sexual stimulation desired:

- none (abstinence, chastity, frigidity);
- compulsive or excessive activity by a male (Don Juanism, satyriasis);
- compulsive or excessive activity by a female (nymphomania).

The degree of emotional commitment:

- a loved one or a person for whom we feel affection;
- a person with whom there is no relationship, such as a 'pickup', a prostitute or a rape victim.

The marriage or family status of the people involved:

- premarital sex;
- married sex;
- sex with a close relative (incest);
- sex in which at least one of the partners is married to another (adultery).

The social values expressed by the culture:

- extreme repressiveness or permissiveness;
- values which reward virginity;
- a double standard for men and women;
- free sexual expression.

some of these are quite common, you shouldn't be surprised.

As was indicated earlier, while intimacy and pleasure are considered the common and ideal reasons for sexual activities, the drive for power is often also found – particularly in activities which are harmful to society such as rape and child molestation. And while sadistic sex with a consenting masochist may be lawful in many areas, it is not considered to be psychologically healthy – in spite of what the Marquis de Sade told us.

Among the sexual actions which often have a power-drive motive are:

- Sexual abuse of women which includes: incest, rape and date rape. Date rape has been experienced by more than 50% of American college women according to a major survey (cited in D. Benson *et al.*, 'Acquaintance rape on campus: A literature review', *Journal of American College Health*, **40**(4), January 1992, 157–165). Any such abuse can harm one's self-esteem – a prime concern for one's mental health (A. Parrot, 'Acquaintance rape among adolescents: Identifying risk groups and intervention strategies', *Journal of Social Work and Human Sexuality*, **8**(1), 47–61).

- Victims of rapes (by husbands, dates or strangers) were 11 times more likely to be seriously depressed, 6 times more likely to be afraid in social situations and $2\frac{1}{2}$ times more likely to experience a sexual dysfunction (D. G. Kilpatrick *et al.*, 'Rape in marriage and in dating relationships: How bad is it for mental health?' *Annals of the New York Academy of Sciences*, **528**, August 1988, 335–344).

- Rape was once thought of as a crime which was sexually motivated. It is now seen as a power-drive crime in which a stronger man subdues a weaker woman, often an elderly woman. It is far more common than is reflected in the official crime statistics because it is so often not reported (M. Koss, 'The underdetection of rape: methodological choices influence incidence estimates', *Journal of Social Issues*, **48**(1), Spring 1992, 61–75).

- Acquaintance rape is another type of power activity being expressed on the sexual scene. Men have expressed far more tolerant attitudes towards acquaintance rape than have women (D. R. Holcomb *et al.*, 'Attitudes about date rape: Gender differences among college students', *College Student Journal*, **25**(4), December 1991, 434–439; E. Beaver *et al.*, 'Priming macho attitudes and emotions', *Journal of Interpersonal Violence*, **7**(3), September 1992, 321–333). But if women asked for the date and paid for it, their willingness was higher (T. D. Bostwick and J. L. DeLucia, 'Effects of gender specific dating behaviors on perception of sex willingness and date rape', *Journal of Social and Clinical Psychology*, **11**(1), Spring 1992, 14–25).

- Paedophilia (child molestation) is commonly found among men who have not been able to have relationships with women. They are often impotent and must have an even stronger, more dominant position in a relationship. Consequently, children, rather than adults, are the sex objects which best satisfy their power drives.

- Exhibitionists, such as male 'flashers', are also attempting to control by shocking their victims. One in three college-age women has seen a flasher. (Because it is an activity used to attempt to gain control, laughing at the flasher is the best way to eliminate his satisfaction.) Strippers, both male and female, may also be in this category. And some would say that those who dress seductively could sometimes be in this category –

however, they would be in the normal, rather than the abnormal, part of the exhibitionist spectrum.

- Pornography often leads to sexual aggression. It seems to depend on the type of pornography just how a particular person will be stimulated. For example, in a recent survey among college men, hard-core rape depictions were six times more likely to stimulate rape behaviour than soft porn (such as *Playboy Magazine*), but soft-core depictions were more likely to make a man attempt to verbally coerce a woman into bed (S. B. Boeringer, 'Pornography and sexual aggression: Associations of violent and nonviolent depiction with rape and rape proclivity', *Deviant Behavior: An Interdisciplinary Journal*, **15**(3), July–September 1994, 289–304). Women exposed to pornography may be more accepting of sexual violence and rape (S. Corne, *et al.*, 'Women's attitudes and fantasies about rape as a function of early exposure to pornography', *Journal of Interpersonal Violence*, **7**(4), December 1992, 454–461).

- A person using a prostitute may also be considered to be in a power position. While most people consider it to be a means of sexual gratification, it is also often found to be the man's sense of control which is his primary need – not his sex drive.

Problems of sexual identity

Such identity problems can be seen in transsexuals, who believe that their physical bodies do not match their psychological feelings, and in transvestites who enjoy dressing in the clothes of the opposite sex. Both of these probably have genetic and learned causes (G. R. Brown, 'Cross dressing men often lead double lives', *The Mennin-*

ger Letter, **3**(4), April 1995, 4–5). These desires never seem to leave in spite of marriage or therapy. If, after you marry, your mate decides that he or she is really the same sex as you – you have a problem. You probably forgot to put that in your marriage contract!

There was one marriage where it worked out just fine. Both partners had sex-change operations. The major question may have been who used the *his* and who used the *hers* bathroom towels.

Sexual disorders

These can be classified according to whether they stem from desire, arousal, orgasmic or pain problems.

SEXUAL DESIRE PROBLEMS

These can have physical causes, such as a lack of the male hormone testosterone, or psychological causes such as a poor marriage, work stress or a fear of sexual activity. Anxiety is the most often-reported factor. A history of sexual assault or the fear of performing inadequately can reduce sexual desire. While 'desire' problems were once primarily found in females, they have been increasingly found in males and the number of cases in males may now outnumber those of females.

AROUSAL DISORDERS

These can also be physical or psychological. In arousal disorders, the engorgement of the genitals, which should occur, is absent. *Impotence* is the commonly used term for what professionals call *male erectile disorder*. It is the lack of ability to have or hold an erection. This malady is more likely to affect the very young and the very old. It is often temporary and may occur with some partners but not others. Another possibility indicating this problem is that an erection can occur, but be lost before the act is completed. Often, it is caused by psychological problems. Many have hypothesised that the increase of this disorder in men is often the result of *performance anxiety*, in which men are afraid that they cannot measure up to what is expected. Sex in the media may have put too much pressure on the individual male. A lack of self-esteem is also often a problem (W. E. Leary, 'Medical panel says most sexual impotence in men can be treated without surgery', *New York Times*, 10 December 1992, p. D20).

The major physiological causes are heart disease, hypertension (high blood pressure) and diabetes. These causes may be interrelated because the three are often found together. Low levels of the 'good' cholesterols have also been implicated (*Johns Hopkins Medical Letter – Health After 50*, 6(7) September 1994, p. 1). These problems are the causes in 60% of the cases which have a physical basis. In another 25%, it is the side-effect of drugs, such as those which lower high blood pressure, antidepressant medications, alcohol, tobacco or marijuana. Psychological causes, such as anxiety, depression or stress cause the remaining 15% of cases. Sometimes, there is a combination of causes. Doctors have a number of possible cures available for prescription (*Johns Hopkins Medical Letter – Health After 50*, October 1994, p. 3). Viagra has been the major answer to this problem.

FRIGIDITY

This is the common term for the *female arousal disorder*. The problem can have a physiological basis such as diabetes or a low hormone level, but is more likely to be psychological. Childhood abuse, feelings of guilt or ineffective stimulation by a partner can all be causes of this disorder (B. Graber, 'Medical aspects of sexual arousal disorders', in W. O'Donohue and J. H. Greer (eds) *Handbook of Sexual Dysfunctions: Assessment and Treatment*, Allyn & Bacon, Boston, 1993, pp. 103–156).

ORGASM DISORDERS

These are of three types: premature ejaculation, inhibited male orgasm and inhibited female orgasm. The inhibited orgasms are more common among women than men; however, its incidence seems to be dropping. Oral or manual stimulation is more likely to elicit an orgasm than is penile thrusting (W. Stock, 'Inhibited female orgasm', in O'Donohue, *op. cit.*, pp. 253–301). *Premature ejaculation* is the most common male dysfunction. About one man in three states that he has problems in this area (I. P. Spector and M. P. Carey, 'Incidence and prevalence of the sexual dysfunctions: A critical review of the empirical literature', *Archives of Sexual Behavior*, **19**, 1990, 389–408). It is quite common among younger men. Some men ejaculate on seeing a partner disrobe, others during foreplay and others during the first few pelvic thrusts.

SEXUAL PAIN DISORDERS

These can affect both men and women. As with the other dysfunctions, they can be caused by physical or psychological problems. For women, an inadequate amount of lubrication is the primary cause. But both infections and allergies can also cause problems for either sex. Allergies to spermicides or to rubber are possible. Chafing of the skin of either sex can also bring pain. For many of these causes, a water-based lubricant can minimise or eliminate the pain. *Vaginismus* is the contracting of the outer third of the vagina which makes penetration difficult or impossible. It is nearly always caused by psychological problems which can include rape, sexual abuse or vaginal injuries.

Sexual problems and the marriage contract

For the sexually experienced, if everything went as it had gone before the marriage there would be fewer problems. And for the virgins, if everything went as well as they hoped, there would be no problems. But for most of us changes in sexual behaviour occur. Luckily, most of the problems can be solved if the people want to continue the relationship and make it better and stronger.

Psychological and sex therapies have come a long way. A good therapist can do wonders. The problem is that there aren't as many good therapists as people might believe. The fact that someone has a licence to practise counselling doesn't mean that competence is implied in the licence. We all know that people study psychology to throw suspicion off themselves. Many people have studied psychology because of their own problems and, because of this, they see the problems of others from their own warped point of view.

Sex therapy with a competent therapist, and often a psychiatrist who can prescribe necessary drugs or change prescriptions which have had a negative effect on our arousal potentials, can cure most of the problems of arousal and orgasm.

If there is a sexual problem, the cause of the problem needs to be addressed. It may be not enough time. It may be not enough exercise to keep up the energy level. So a marriage therapist may not be as important for your sex life as a babysitter, a dietitian or even an acupuncturist!

So, if there are problems, explore the widest possible sources of effective therapy – from psychiatrists and endocrinologists to marriage counsellors and sex therapists.

Effective communication

Why can't I get through to my mate?

Read this chapter if:

You think there isn't enough positive communication in your relationship

You or your mate don't say 'I love you' enough

You think there is too much negative or controlling communication in your relationship

You think your relationship needs to get on a more positive track

If you think something needs to be done to bring your relationship up to what it once was

You want to re-kindle your romance

You need to clarify your relationship understandings

You want to understand how to communicate more clearly and effectively

You need some help in communicating your concerns

You want to learn to listen more effectively

While 'love' or infatuation may get people into serious relationships, it is the *process* of communication which makes relationships work. It takes two mature people to be able to see the values of both communication and compromise as being essential to developing that glorious marriage to which we all aspire. Simone Signoret, one of France's premier actresses may have said it best, 'Chains do not hold a marriage together. It is threads, hundreds of tiny threads, which sew people together through the years.'

For the ultimate marriage you need:

- infatuation (this means that you 'turn each other on'); plus,
- the ability to love (the unselfish ability to help the other to be the best that he or she can be); plus,
- an honest sense of friendship and equality; plus,
- an effort on each partner's part to honestly enjoy living and to becoming 'self-actualised' by being the most that you can be; plus,
- the ability to communicate which requires being able to effectively say both the positive and the negative statements. (To honestly discuss the strengths and weaknesses of the relationship and to make compromises where necessary to make an even better marriage.)

We have chosen to be in a relationship with somebody who is important to us and whom we have grown to love. But, we have done it to meet our own needs. Of course, as we grow in the ability to love, we want our partner to be able to fulfil their own needs. We each have biological, such as sexual, needs. We each need food and shelter. We need to have a close human companion. We need success in our lives. But, these things don't all just happen. We must help ourselves and our mate to realise our potentials. We do this in our relationship through what is called communication. We want to communicate what our own needs are and we need to communicate that we are willing to help our mate in realising his or her potentials. We are in a joint project which should be far more efficient in meeting each of our goals than if we were trying to do it alone.

While we want to emphasise the process of communication, we must recognise that honest communication must be based on a vibrant relationship, or on a relationship which has the potential to be vibrant. And it will be based on two different people with the common goal of making their relationship better. *If you don't have time to talk, you don't have time for a relationship.*

When partners are equal in the relationship and both are desirous of being open so that the relationship can develop, you have the most effective type of communication. If you can keep the individual power drives out of relationship development, you are lucky that you are both mature enough to handle a modern relationship – and your romance will become more solidly based and will grow in positive ways which you had not imagined.

It is a shame that so many couples, either because of tradition or because of an imbalance of power, evolve into relationships which have a dominant partner. The power drive of the submissive person is minimised and their inferiority feelings are increased. They cannot develop into a fully functioning human being and partner. How can a real romance develop between such unequals? This inequality not only infects the relationship of the mates but can also affect the relationship of the children to the dominant person. Oftentimes, the children cannot grow out of the inferior position in which they have been raised.

Effective communication cannot do everything. It can't increase your oestrogen or testosterone. It can't penetrate into the unconscious mind. But cuddling, a non-verbal type of communication, can increase the oxytocin output and make you feel more romantic. Hearing your mate say 'I' love you' may increase your endorphins and give you a mental high.

You cannot not communicate! This is a major rule of marriage counselling. Even your silence is a type of communication. Your every action, word and tone of voice is saying something. It may be saying 'I'm hurt.' It may be saying 'I am more important than you are.' It may be saying 'I'm so happy with you.' Or it may simply be saying simply 'I'm tired.'

Having a relationship with a TV program is much easier than having one with a real live person. The TV doesn't demand closeness. It doesn't demand the attention to intimate thoughts. But being more involved with the TV than in your mate is a clear type of communication. Whether it is a soccer match or a soap opera, your intense interest in the TV screen communicates your message strongly.

Positive communication

You may have heard the story of the woman who wanted a divorce and went to her doctor friend for advice on how to hurt her husband the most. The doctor told her that for the next few months do everything for him. Make him feel like a prince. Then, when you divorce him, he will really be hurt. She took his advice, but six months later the doctor saw her and wondered how the divorce was going. 'Divorce, are you kidding? When I was nice to him, he was nicer to me. The relationship has never been better.'

In a good relationship there is a great deal of positive communication. It may be often saying 'I love you' or 'Have I told you I love you, today.' Commonly, it is the hugs and kisses, the touches as you pass each other or the kisses blown across a crowded room. As the Bard observed 'They do not love who do not show their love.' It should feel good for us to tell our partner that we care, that we approve, that we love. Let's emphasise that positive communication.

Some men find it impossible to say 'I love you' after they are married. It seems that their inferiority complexes get in their way. The fact that they haven't been able to satisfy their power drives in other areas of life makes it essential that they control their wives. But, if they give up a part of themselves by saying 'I love you', they would be giving the wife power over them. Obviously, such men are psychologically immature.

It is a shame that many men and women are so afraid of becoming vulnerable by expressing their love. The same is sometimes true in being afraid to have an orgasm. Becoming totally open to another does make you vulnerable to be hurt, if you are eventually rejected. But, it is essential if you are going to have a romantic relationship, an open partnership, a committed bond.

The nearly universal human truth is that most of us need someone who is psychologically close. The impersonal development of our modern society makes it so much more important today that it was just a few years ago. If you are mature, you should be able to say and show your affection. It should be shown often. This is essential to developing the reality of romance which this book is about.

When positive communication has moulded us together, those negatives that require problem solving will occur less. And when they occur, they will not carry the same weight as they do when people are not romantically connected. The unromantic couple tends to be two self-centred people each looking for their own needs to be met. When this is true, the deep relationship which most of us desire is impossible.

Communication

Communication is one of the most commonly talked about areas of marriage. It is important that, no matter how busy a couple is, they find time to talk to each other. In most marriages, it seems to be the husband who is the silent partner, often not interested in communicating. But, if thoughts and feelings are to be shared, they must be communicated. It is much easier to communicate happy thoughts than sad thoughts. The goals of an up-coming marriage or birth are easier to discuss than the problems of an existing marriage or the alcohol problems of your partner or your children. As a couple matures in a marriage, the partners should develop understanding, patience and the ability to communicate. This is necessary in order for the couple to set up and evaluate goals for their relationship and to understand and solve the problems which will inhibit the attainment of those goals.

Television writers, in their attempt to be funny, continually use 'put-downs' to gain laughter. Husbands deal in 'one-up*man*ship' while their wives use their 'one-ups-*woman*ship' on their husbands. And their children have mastered the sharpness of sarcasm. As you remember from the discussion of the 'power drive', the goal of such insensitivity is to make the speaker think that he or she is better than the other by pushing the other down – not exactly the stuff of which a good partnership is made!

Effective communication requires that both parties be able to express both the good and the bad as they see it – without hurting the other. We are emotional and psychological beings with a minor amount of reasoning ability. If she is feeling hurt because he forgot her birthday, he may try to explain rationally why he did. He was busy at work, he thought it was next week, but she sees it as him not thinking she is important. She is hurt and, rather than apologise, he tries to find reasons why. His reasons may be true, but he still hurt her and he should have remembered. It takes a mature person to recognise that he has been wrong. It's like fighting a fire with gasoline. Reason is the wrong liquid to fight emotional fires. Understanding and concern are the right emotional salves.

It is generally easier to communicate intimately when you are dating than later as the relationship matures – or sours. During courtship, we want the other person so much that we may even share weaknesses and insecurities as well as goals and values. It's much easier to say 'I want to be a good father to my children' than it is to actually take the time to be a good father.

An acquaintance, an important Las Vegas lawyer who lived in Southern California, after having his house built, took a month off from his lucrative law practice while he and his family landscaped the garden in their million-dollar house. The whole family participated. It was his way of having the family together working on a common family project. It was an impressive method of communicating his concern for family and family values. And the message was largely non-verbal.

It is difficult for some of us to communicate the good things – 'You look great today', 'I'm so proud of you', it is extremely difficult for most of us to enunciate the negative factors in our relationships. But, if they are not enunciated, those small sores will fester – and without the antibiotics of intelligent communication, they can turn into serious diseases and may even lead to the death of the relationship.

What we don't say can be as important as what we do say. Being quiet about something which is bothering us can lead to larger bothers down the road. Sometimes, the unsaid word can be clearly understood in the body language of the other. Women are often quite good in spotting this type of 'communication'.

It takes an emotional robot to fail to understand that, when your mate gets into bed and immediately faces the other side of the bed – something negative is being 'said'. You don't need a clairvoyant to point out that sometimes watching TV, cleaning the house or tinkering with the car are more important than having a conversation. When this happens, something is being 'said'. The all too common diet of 'TV and dinner' means that there is nothing to say, or at least one of the partners wants to avoid a more positive and deeper type of communication.

There is an old saying that 'Beauty is in the eye of the beholder'. It is not the actual object, but how that object is seen and evaluated, that is important. We might also say that '*truth* is in the eye of the beholder.' Whether we see the truth of the position that 'abortion should be allowed' or 'abortion should not be allowed', or 'we should have capital punishment' or 'we should not have capital punishment', or when we see any other idea with adherents on both sides of the issue – we have to agree that at least truth seems to be in the eye of the beholder. Most of us can easily see the truth when our partner is not communicating with us.

Gender traditions and communications

Much has been studied and written about how typical men and women communicate. Men are seen to be more

analytical, less verbal and more private. They are generally not so interested in sharing their feelings. They want
to feel that they are in control of themselves and their
world. Typically, men find it more difficult to share feelings than do women.

Women are seen to be more verbal, more emotional
and feeling, and more interested in sharing their problems
with other women – often to the detriment of the marriage. As a general rule, in our society, these are true. But
they are not universal in all societies and they are not
always true in our own society. These stereotypes
merely reflect average behaviours – not all behaviour.

The communicative and sharing woman can be both
exciting, and a relief, for the quiet or shy man. But when
that communicative woman brings up problems, such as
how she feels about their life or his shortcomings, he feels
threatened, insecure and emasculated – because the power
drive is the core of traditional masculinity. Even the
meekest of macho men will be intimidated or angered
by a threat to their power.

Quite often, men and women think similarly. Scientific researchers, for example, tend to be analysers not
problem sharers. They both think like the stereotypical
man. So, don't get caught up in the 'everything this
book says is true' syndrome. It is quite enough to
know that the average boy and girl have been socialised
differently. They have learned different ways of communicating from the time they were young. While it is
possibly a fact that there may be some average genetic
differences, they are not universal. So, while the
'average' man and the 'average' woman may differ
from each other, there is a huge overlap of thinking
abilities, reasonable behaviour and communication
styles. You need to find out just where you and your
mate are on these scales. For effective communication,
you must realise that none of us is all black or all white.

We are all various shades of grey. Which shades are you and your mate?

The strong, silent, 'everything's under control' man often believes that if there is a problem it will go away. The equally 'know it all' wife may nag and cajole and often drive away the person she is trying to get closer to. When a woman is married to a non-confrontational man, it is far better for her to calmly lay out her problems and ask that they be resolved or compromised. Traditional men are much more likely to be able to respond to a problem-solving opportunity than to an argument. A confrontational situation is more likely to bring out the 'win at all costs' attitude rather than the resolve to 'solve at all costs'.

Nagging, as a way of changing another's behaviour, puts the nagger in the power position. But loving, not power, is the essential of an egalitarian relationship. People who speak sweetly to each other are more likely to have an attentive ear listening. Nagging gets the psychologically expected response, either war or a humiliating surrender – and it will not be forgotten.

You must be mature

The realities of an egalitarian marriage require that a person be mature. An immature person cannot function effectively in a modern marriage. A modern 50–50 relationship requires people who are sufficiently mature to be able to understand that the relationship can offer more rewards than may be possible if living alone. But, living in a relationship is going to require a maturity beyond what is necessary for living alone. When you live alone, you make all of the decisions. When you live in a modern relationship, both people are equals and compromises are often necessary. You may need to give up a little now to be able to gain a greater satisfaction later. The mature person must learn to communicate effectively.

Being mature does not just happen with age. We might equate maturity with wisdom. It seems that both develop because of a combination of knowledge plus experience. I doubt that there are many truly wise or mature 20-year-olds. Most haven't lived long enough to develop the experience necessary for being truly mature. (This isn't to say that most 20-year-olds don't think they know everything!!) Sociological studies usually show that college graduates are happier in their jobs and their relationships than are non-graduates. Is this because they may have acquired some knowledge from their college courses or their reading which they can apply to their experiences and have them make sense? If you have studied psychology, you should have at least a theory or two which you might apply to your relationship situations – whether at home or at work.

Perhaps the primitive societies, which place much of their leadership and counselling roles in the hands of 'the elders', have developed a more maturity and wisdom-based society. It seems that so often in our Western societies, we may place too much store in the minds of our youth because we are envious of their physical beauty and their energy. Perhaps the hippy credo of the 1960s 'don't trust anyone over 30' has been emblazoned on many of the baby boomers!

Mature people are aware of how another person may understand and react to a statement. Positive statements, obviously, would not carry a negative message. But, being ordered around or using sarcasm and other types of 'put-downs' can cause great damage. One sarcastic remark, which may inflate the ego of the speaker, can cause immense damage to a relationship. One negative remark will cancel out a hundred positive statements. The husband of a client had always talked about how much he loved her freckles. But one day in the heat of an argument he said 'I never liked your damn freckles anyway.' She was crushed. Had he lied to her? Has he lied in other areas? Is she really unattractive to him? One stupid emotional remark and he had created a cataclysm.

The immature person is incapable of moving beyond his or her own selfishness. A modern sharing relationship is beyond such a person's capabilities. So the aspects of personality discussed in Chapters 3 and 4 come into play. You can't expect an immature person to function in a mature way.

Successful relationships must not only have a general positive level of communication but the couple should also understand and talk about the essentials of how their relationship can be better. They must have clear plans for solving the inevitable conflicts which will arise. They should discuss future plans. They should understand how and when they will be apart and when together – since more and more marriages will require time away from each other because of dual careers.

Keeping the relationship positive makes communication easier

Let's double-check where we are in the relationship. Here is a list of thoughts and actions which were probably functioning quite well when you were dating. How are they now? If one or more of these has been reduced it must be fixed. If you can't do it yourself, find a competent marriage therapist:

● *Are you still partners and friends?* Friendship is the essential ingredient in a full and happy relationship. Friendship is the positive feelings in the present, based on the shared experiences of the past, and directed by an attainable hope for the future. True friendship must be based on an equal relationship of the partners. Be available – be there whenever the other person feels there's a need for talking. Find a common meeting ground, such as hobbies and sports, to share. However, your relationship can't be better than you are as people. Consequently, you must continue to develop yourself into a whole person, develop outside interests that keep you abreast of new ideas and events. This makes you interesting. Be interested and offer encouragement to the other person in their work, and plan time together to share your interests.

- *Your relationship should be primary.* Many forces can weaken or break the strength of a marital union. Children, friends, occupations, relatives or the pursuit of worldly goods can come between two loving adults. Don't lose sight of the importance of your friendship and of the union of your marriage. This doesn't mean that you should love others any less. If you remember the discussion on *love* (Chapter 2), you understand that a person who is a true lover *just loves*. It is not as if you have 100 ounces of love and that you must give at least 51% to your mate, most of the rest to the kids and a little to everyone else. What is meant here is that your relationship should be the central core of your family life. Your children, in-laws or neighbours must be on the perimeter. Certainly there are times when one or another child will require more of your time – but keep the focus. Cultivate your emotional garden. Keep the core of your life nurtured and growing. Children grow up and move away. Jobs and neighbours change. But your relationship will probably survive these changes – so it should be strong and vibrant.

- *Respect each other's rights.* Everyone is entitled to make their own choices and their own mistakes. A partner in marriage does not 'own' his or her mate. While the marriage should be based on common goals, it is a mistake to believe that the goals and needs of one person will always totally encompass those of the other. In fact, the non-shared goals of the people in a relationship often add greatly to the dimensions of the partnership. Togetherness in a committed relationship often requires being apart sometimes. Each person requires different amounts of time that they need to spend alone or in pursuits not directly related to a job or to the relationship. A proper balance of aloneness and togetherness is essential for most effective marriages.

- *Trust each other.* Open yourselves up to each other to avoid doubts and suspicions. The depth of love is often gauged by the measure of trust. Be dependable. If you make promises, then keep them. This is the primary ingredient of mental intimacy.

- *Express and demonstrate your approval* for each other. Taking each other for granted may be expected, but the expression of approval for our mate strengthens the relationship bonds. Everyone needs approval. Your mate, being the most important person in the world, should be the first object of your demonstrated approval. When you say 'thank you', it means a lot. Tell your partner how much you appreciate him or her and tell others. Compliment your partner on his or her appearance – it's good to hear and it makes your spouse more confident and secure in the relationship. Of course, you can't be approved of if you don't deserve it. Unshaven husbands and unkempt wives don't have to look at themselves. They may portray an 'I don't care attitude' to the other person. People who are sarcastic or come out with negative comments certainly don't merit approval. So, you should be both presentable and pleasant if you would like to be appreciated.

- *Listen to each other.* Communication is meant to be a vehicle for understanding – not the fuse for an argument. As mentioned, communication can be verbal or non-verbal. Our actions, moods, tones of voice and expressions are often far more eloquent than their words. And, how often do the words say one thing but the actions express an entirely different message. Often a person says 'Get out', when what is really meant is 'take me in your arms'. Listen to the message of the actions and the unsaid words. They are far more truthful. Develop a sensitive antenna to your mate so that you are more aware of his or her needs and why moodiness occurs. Try to understand the other person from their point of view. Understand their feelings and why these feelings have developed. Maya Angelou in her book *The Heart of a Woman* reminds us that 'The most called upon prerequisite of a friend is an accessible ear.'

- *Take care of each other.* Everyone has the occasion to be depressed. The warmth of comfort by our best friend is the most effective analgesic for the pain of sorrow. We are not always 'up', so it helps to have someone with whom our problems and concerns can be shared.

- *Be physically involved with your mate.* Most of us like to be touched and caressed. Hold hands, hug, tell how much you care – keep that behaviour which you practised while dating. Physical closeness is the most easily understood sign of mental closeness. Sexual activity is good, and sex can be fun. In fact, sex *should* be fun –

not a duty. Avoid self-consciousness about sex. Don't be afraid to experiment. For a good sex relationship, both partners should be aggressive. Puritanical morals, so common in the UK and USA, have often precluded women from such aggressiveness. Remember that everybody wants to be wanted. In a sound sex relationship, both partners should indicate their desires to the other person; both should be able to initiate sexual activity. Never use sex as a weapon – withdrawing it as a punishment to your spouse, especially when it might be a good thing to share at the moment. Such a misuse of sex is often blamed as the cause of marriage failures. Someone once observed that sexual activities make up only 2% of a good marriage, but in a bad marriage, they appear to be 98% of the problem. Withholding sex is a powerful, but often misguided, way to bring up a problem.

● *Don't be afraid to forgive.* Forgiveness affirms that none of us are perfect. It eliminates the anger and the hurt and it allows us to go on. It gives us the freedom to begin again – hopefully in a more positive direction (Figure 23).

When all of these are in place you are in position to start moving forward toward more mature goals.

Romance comes from the positives in your relationship

While marriage books often deal with 'communication', they tend to dwell on how you work out problems. We will do that in Chapter 10, but here it seems important to deal

Figure 23 An ounce of prevention is worth a pound of cure.

with how we communicate, what we need to talk about and most of all – positive communication.

Happiness and contentedness don't come from re-moving the hurdles – the problems that have occurred, although eliminating the negatives is often a necessity. It comes from the warm fuzzies. It is the 'I love you' and the 'you mean so much to me' and the flowers and cookies and special thoughts. It is the spontaneous hugs in the kitchen, the hand holding in the park, the kiss in the

movies. You may remember the advice from that old song
'You gotta accentuate the positive – eliminate the negative.'

Positive communication is more important than the
negative communication required when a problem is
brought up. There is a need to share our lives – our experiences and our feelings about them. Our friendship
needs to be nourished just as any other living thing. Remember with relish the good things you have done. Positives build – negatives destroy. When we have weak egos
and poor self-esteem, it is easy to pick on the one closest to
us to raise our egos by pushing down our partner. But this
is exactly the thing you don't do to a friend, and it is an
effective way to sour a relationship. As a friend, you want
to build up your partner's self-esteem. Tell them how
happy or proud you are of them. Your partner must
have something very positive going – or you wouldn't
have chosen him or her.

Relationships, whether personal or business, thrive or
die based on what is put into them. Just as lying and
selfishness will bring a relationship to the ground,
honesty, concern and positive communication can make
it soar and prosper. Honesty is the key in terms of mate
selection and in developing an effective relationship.
Without honesty from the beginning, you cannot develop the trust which is essential in a real relationship.

Cooperating in individual or relationship goals

In today's world, people often make abrupt changes in
their life paths – or have the opportunities to progress in
a very different area than what was originally expected.

Perhaps the husband gets the opportunity for that 'dream' job in India – heading his own factory. Fifty years ago, the wife would have packed up, said goodbye to her family and friends and dutifully, and perhaps happily, settled in Bombay. But, today, that same opportunity would disrupt the wife's position as head of brain research at the university hospital where she is a full professor. Now, what do we do?

While that example may not be a common occurrence, certainly today's couples often are faced with conflicting opportunities for the partners. My daughter's experiences are perhaps more illustrative of what today's young people may face. After completing her master's degree, she was given the opportunity to teach in a university. The original candidate with a doctorate had withdrawn from the job at the last minute. The job was for only four years, unless she obtained her own doctorate. Her husband, a recently graduated accountant, followed her to Maine and took a job waiting tables. He eventually became controller for the restaurant corporation. But, he was not too happy with the way the restaurant business was being handled.

She went to New Mexico to pursue her doctorate. He followed and took another job in a restaurant. She did not like the doctoral program, so dropped out. But, he saw great potential and challenge in his new accounting business. While she would have liked to have gone to Colorado to pursue her doctorate, she felt that it was more important for him to follow what he liked. Each could see the importance of a goal or a dream of the other, and each adjusted to the desires of the other. He is now an accountant for a major company and she is happy in business.

Over the years, I have made a practice of talking to those who have successfully completed 50 years of marriage. These 'golden wedding' celebrants have one observation in common. They all agree that there must be a 'give and take' in the relationship. Understanding the options in giving and taking are essential subjects of communicating in a marriage. Where do you demand certain things for yourself and where are you willing to give up some very important desires? If the relationship is important in your life, the direction of your marriage cannot be based only on where you point your compass.

Developing and changing your relationship contract

Whether or not you want to call it a contract, marriage is a contract – just as every human relationship involves understandings which should be or must be met in order for that relationship to survive. A marriage contract is much more than just looking at how the money will be handled. The emotionally mature couple will set up what they expect out of their marriage: whether or not to have children, who will do the shopping and cooking, who will clean the house, how will vacation destinations be decided, even how the property would be split up if a divorce or death were to occur. Equally important is how they will cultivate their friendship, through such activities as quiet meals out, vacations or sharing hobbies.

The well-thought-out contract or understanding could spell out when and where discussions of problems might take place. There should also be a provision for periodic renegotiating and renewing of the expectations for the relationship. It is almost as if you have made a divorce settlement prior to the marriage, so you know what you can expect. But, what you have done is to look at some of the areas that commonly result in conflict and you have talked about them. Having done this prior to the marriage, and during the marriage, you have already been forced to communicate about areas of possible differences. This is a good start in developing a mature relationship in which the needs and wants of both parties are considered.

The intention, which was fundamental to a promise in the past, may be changed in the future. Then, discussion must occur. The intention to have children within five years may be changed because of our jobs or educational goals. Maybe children are no longer desired by one person. Maybe there was the promise to follow him wherever his job took him, but now you are a senior partner in your law firm or are firmly entrenched as the president of your own advertising agency. The change in your life priorities certainly requires negotiation.

When disagreements occur, you will need to try to solve them for the sake of the relationship – not put down your partner so that you appear to be in the power position. None of us like to be put in an inferior position in a relationship, yet sarcasm, body language and an attitude of superiority can do just that. And certainly, being an inferior is uncalled for in a relationship of equals. This requires that we be able to control our emotions to some degree with our reasoning power and intelligence.

Because our society places many more demands on us than have earlier societies, we can expect more pushes and pulls on ourselves and on our partners. For example, not having children has become a more common idea. Changing jobs often, moving often and finding additional recreational options are more common today than in the past. Add to these the fact that we live much longer than our grandparents and we can understand some of the reasons for the increases of possible conflicts in our partnerships. If we can't solve these problems with a mature 'give and take' attitude, there is always the divorce court. But, if we can solve these problems our relationship potentials can give us greater and greater feelings of intimacy and being loved. These are our most important human needs today. It is, therefore, sensible to choose a partner wisely, then emphasise the proven techniques which will keep our relationships evolving and adjusting. It sure beats divorce!!

Skills necessary for effective communication

When all is right with the world and we are deeply 'in love', we expect no bumps in the road, but if we hit a bump we usually want to avoid talking about it. No sense rocking the boat – it just isn't fun to come off cloud 9 and have to grovel in the mud of reality!

As mentioned, communication skills are necessary to convey both positive and negative ideas. However, it is much more difficult to make a mistake when giving a compliment than when bringing up a problem. 'You are sure a lot prettier than the bride of Frankenstein' may not get as positive a response as 'I'd rather have you than Nicole Kidman'. Or 'Of course I love you, you old goat – otherwise I wouldn't be here' probably isn't going to get the same warm reception as 'I really do love you'. So, for expressing a positive evaluation or bringing up a problem which is negative, there are elements of communicating that are important:

● Be rational and think clearly. Often, what we say is a rationalisation. A rationalisation is a statement that is not true but we think it is true. This is different from a lie, which is untrue and we know it is untrue.

- Communicate clearly. Is your message being sent so that it is likely to be understood the way you meant it?
- Remember that your body language is communicating, whether or not you are talking.
- Understand how your own power drive and the power drive of your loved one are involved. This means no 'put-downs' or sarcasm.
- Listen carefully. Understand the spoken language and the body language of the speaker.
- Respond appropriately. 'I love that dress on you.' 'What? This old rag.' We need to be able to accept compliments gracefully and criticism with intelligence.

Being rational

This is supposed to set us apart from the lower species – although experiments with many mammals has shown that some are quite rational in a simple way. Every therapist and every self-help book expects you to rationally apply the advice which is given. But our psychological or emotional selves often get in the way.

It is much more difficult than it might seem on the surface. Our own desires and our emotional states often make us mistake our feelings for rational thinking. In philosophy, there are two main branches of logic, inductive and deductive plus the area of semantics. Semantics deals with the meaning of the terms or words. Inductive logic deals with how probable is it that a statement is true. Deductive logic deals with whether or not the statements made hang together according to the rules for logical thinking which have been developed over the years.

SEMANTICS

This looks at the meanings of words and exactly what that meaning is. Look at the words that you use. Are you 'masterful' while your partner is 'controlling'? Are you 'relaxed' while your partner is 'sloppy?' Are you 'disciplined' while your partner is 'rigid?' The same actions can be seen quite differently by different people or by the same people as the relationship matures. Were you attracted to his relaxed 'devil may care' attitude, but are now upset because he doesn't think the house needs cleaning? Were you attracted by her competence and success at her job, but now you think she spends too much time and energy as she rises in the business world?

The point is, do you know exactly what you mean in using a word – and will that word be understood in exactly the same sense that you meant it? Have you ever heard someone say 'It's hot as hell'. That may make some sense. But, what if they say it is 'cold as hell' or 'wet as hell' or 'dry as hell?' The word 'hell' has taken on a number of quite different meanings. I once saw a six-page exposé of the use of the word 'fuck'. As we all know, the word originally meant sexual intercourse – at least that was Shakespeare's meaning. But when we say it was 'fuckin' good' or 'what the fuck' or saying 'I've been fucked' when something bad has happened to me – it doesn't make much sense semantically.

American films, in their effort to make their heroes tough, have made them semantically absurd. It is so intellectually lazy to use a 'one word fits all' approach to vocabulary. As an American, I must apologise for the abominable level of language in the media – but movies are made at a fourth to sixth grade vocabulary. So don't expect help from Hollywood in making you think clearly! Thank God that many British people still choose their words carefully from a more extensive vocabulary than is used across the Atlantic. But many UK films now mimic Hollywood's glorification of the vulgar.

INDUCTIVE THINKING

This deals with the truth or probability of a statement. If we say 'Tomorrow the sun will rise in the east', it is highly probable. If we say that 'Tomorrow a meteorite will destroy London', it is highly improbable. On the personal level, if I say 'You never think of me' the probability is questionable. If I say 'I feel that you don't often think of me', it is a more highly probable statement.

To avoid the question of truth or falsity of a statement, use 'I' statements. 'My feelings are hurt.' 'I'm angry.' 'I'm upset.' 'I feel I'm doing more than my part.' There is then no factual basis on which to respond – because you are the best judge of how you feel.

Another source of problems in finding the 'truth' of the situation can occur because of our unconscious minds – we may sometimes confuse the issues. While we think we have identified the real problem, the source of the problem may be somewhere else. We may blame an outside situation for relationship problems which originate with one or both of us. When she tries to initiate sex, he is unresponsive. He blames his being tired on his work or his tennis workout. While this may be true, the real problem may be the fact that she has been on his case for some reason, that he doesn't want to go on vacation where she has made reservations without telling him, or that her mother has been putting him down because he doesn't make enough money or doesn't want children.

This can also work in the opposite direction – a situation outside the relationship can be unconsciously brought back to the relationship. The boss is harping on, so you do the same to your partner. That's the old pecking-order theory! You can't win the conflict in one place, so you bring it back home where your ego can win.

DEDUCTIVE LOGIC

This deals with whether or not the inductive statements hang together. The classic syllogism is 'All men are mortal. Socrates was a man. Therefore Socrates was mortal.' If it is true that all people will die and if it is true that Socrates was a person, then the conclusion would be true by the laws of deductive reasoning. But what if I say 'You don't pay any attention to me. All you think about is your job. This proves you don't love me.' From the inductive idea of proof, is it actually true that you never think about me? Is it actually true that you only think about your job? Possibly the reason your partner works so much is to be able to provide for you. While you might prefer him or her spending more time at home and would settle for fewer of the goodies that the job salary provides, your partner actually may be thinking of you.

One of the rules of deductive logic is that you can only have three 'terms' in your argument. In the first example, they were: men, mortal and Socrates. In the second example, we had: you, people who don't pay attention to me, people who think only about their jobs, and love – so there were four terms. By the rules of logical argument that second argument does not hold up. To go into all of the possibilities of deductive or inductive logic would take a few more books. But, suffice to say, many marital arguments break one or more rules of logical thinking.

There are a number of factors which can make a statement wrong, questionable or invalid:

My sister Janie thinks that we ought to ... (Is your sister Janie right? Is she God? Is she really an authority in this matter?)

You're an idiot, what do you know? (The definition of idiot is a person having an IQ of less than 25 and a mental age of about 3.) Is this really the person you married? If so, who is really the idiot?)

Everybody knows that men can't express their feelings. (Does 'everyone' mean all people, the majority, all psychologists? Does it mean that no men can express their feelings?)

If you have thought out your position clearly, you don't need to apologise for it or demean yourself for asking for consideration. So you wouldn't say:

This may be a stupid request, but ...

I'm not that smart but ...

I'm not an expert but ...

Communicate clearly. Explain how and why you feel the way you do. Give illustrations without accusing. There are some barriers to communicating effectively. Here are some examples.

DOUBLE-LEVEL MESSAGES

These are not uncommon in close relationships. For example, a client went to meet his mother at the airport.

He hugged her. Her body stiffened, saying in effect 'I don't like this.' But, as he interpreted her body language to say 'take your arms off me' and stood back, she said 'What's the matter, don't you love your mother?'

Often, when we don't want to hurt a partner, we smile while we are criticising or pointing out a problem. Our words give a serious message which is negative while our face gives a positive and friendly message:

- Smiling at him while saying 'Why didn't you call and tell me you would be late?'
- Smiling at your child while saying 'You little dickens, you know you shouldn't lie' or 'You know mommy doesn't like you to kick her so I have to spank you.'

Get your whole 'self' delivering the same message. A sneer is a put-down. A look of anger gives one message while a look of approval or happiness gives another. Your tone of voice can indicate that the message is extremely important or is only a sidelight.

POWER DRIVES AND INFERIORITY FEELINGS

These are very real, sometimes at the conscious level of our minds, but nearly always at the unconscious levels. Let's look briefly at how your drive for power can reduce your ability to have your communication accepted. No one, even George Bush, likes to hear that he or she is wrong or be exposed to condescending statements or behaviour. Trying to build up our own status by putting down another person is one of the greatest indications of inferiority feelings and a lack of maturity. In any communication, we want to enter as an equal, never as a superior. Be positive rather than negative. 'I like it when you ...'

rather than 'Don't do that' or 'I don't like that'. Try to keep the negatives to a minimum – they hurt. Telling a person what they do right is much more likely to have them continue it. Do you want your mate to do more of the housework? If so, don't be sarcastic about how ineffective the effort is. You'll catch more flies with honey than vinegar.

We must be aware of how the other person will feel when we say something negative. We are psychological beings; that is, we are emotional and have feelings. So even logical suggestions, such as 'why don't we reduce the fat in the food we are eating' or 'why won't you give up smoking' suggest that the other person is not intelligent or not disciplined. We would like to think that we are rational and controlled only by the facts, but unfortunately, it is seldom true.

When you put anybody down on your way to asking for something, you are going to have to overcome two hurdles, their animosity towards you for being so superior and their reticence to give you what you want and what they may not want to give. A number of books during the last 20 years have dealt with being confrontational and asking or demanding what you want. These have made many people think that, by demanding something, they will get what they want. It often gets them a divorce.

Some 'pop psychology' tells us to get our feelings into the open – and if they hurt the other person it is their problem. That's bad psychology. While change may be good, hurt is never good. Getting your feelings out is good but if you are attempting to be understood, to become accepted or to make changes – sugar is far better than brine as a coating. One client, who had read half of a self-help book on confrontation and 'who owns the problem', confronted her husband and one of the children with very negative and untrue remarks. It made the recipients feel quite low. When her husband asked her why she was so vindictive and hurtful, she answered that she was not responsible for the way they took her remarks. It was their problem. Their divorce then became her problem.

Our power drives can hinder our communication when we appear to be the one in the driver's seat. Threatening or ordering someone to do something, lecturing them, ridiculing them – especially when passing ourselves of as being of a higher moral level – are effective if our only need is to feel superior. But, if our objective is to move the relationship along, solve a problem or bring us closer together, they are the absolute worst tactics we can use.

Listening carefully, or watching the body language carefully

These are pleasurable when positive messages are being received, but are uncomfortable when negative or disturbing messages are being heard – such as when your partner is bringing up a problem. Just as our 'reasoning' is often overwhelmed by our emotional state, so are the messages we hear. We often hear only what we want to hear – selective listening. Rather than hearing correctly the message that is actually being sent, we often spend much of our hearing time formulating arguments against what we think is being said.

Why are you listening? Is it because you really want to understand and aid in solving the problem? Are you only giving the appearance of listening so that your partner doesn't get more angry or confrontational? Whatever it is – let your partner get through the whole message before you answer. Definitely don't interrupt. Sometimes, just getting the problem exposed is all that is needed. Solutions aren't always necessary immediately.

To ensure that you have the opportunity to listen, eliminate distractions. Turn off the music or TV. Take the phone off the hook. Focus your attention on what you are going to hear. Try to understand, by asking questions when necessary or summarising what has been said. Keep your emotions controlled because it should not be an emotional situation. It should be an *intellectual* problem-solving experience.

Just being quiet doesn't indicate that you are listening. To show your partner that you are actively listening, you should repeat what was said in your own words. 'You mean ____?' What you thought you heard may not have been the message which was meant to be conveyed. Use eye contact, nod when you are in agreement or use facial expressions to show that you don't understand or question what was being said. Show your concern and keep your mind on the message.

A major problem in listening is 'mind-reading' – assuming we know what the other is thinking and feeling. If he admits to having had an affair, but says she meant nothing to him – he just needed someone to be close to because he wasn't getting it at home, she may see the other woman as a real threat. If he was truthful but she refuses to accept the truth, then criticises him for what she believes to be true, she has set up a 'straw man' which she can then knock over.

Responding appropriately

This requires that we understand the seriousness and the importance of the speaker's statement. Find out just how important this problem is. Is it *the* major problem, *a* major problem or is it just a concern which your partner would like you to think about.

Since it is important to your partner, you don't want to minimise or criticise the argument just yet. Refrain from retorting 'Why do you bring that up?' or 'Everybody does that'. When it is a problem which is being brought up, don't blame it on the speaker – attempting to make him or her feel guilty and you blameless. Remember that old power drive and how important it is for each of us to think we matter.

Don't use jokes to stop the flow of your partner's thoughts. This is supposed to be a serious discussion. Communicating a real concern is not a joke. Don't treat it as such. Definitely don't minimise the situation.

The same is very true when we are attempting to communicate our own ideas. What you mean and what you think you are saying is often not heard or understood by the person with whom you think you are communicating. For this reason, it is good to have the other person repeat what he or she thinks you have said. This is a common technique used in marriage counselling.

You: *I feel that I do too much of the housework.*

Your partner:
- *You mean that I am lazy?*
- *But that's a woman's job.*
- *So what do you want me to do about it?*
- *How can we ease your load and make it a fair share?*

It is obvious which person heard the thought being communicated.

As was indicated earlier, if one person is deprived of touching or sex or compliments, the other person may not feel that he or she is actually rejecting the partner. But the effects on the partner can be quite negative. Remember that you are the authority on how you feel.

So whether the communication is verbal or non-verbal, it is being interpreted by your partner – and your partner may not be interpreting and understanding what you actually feel. This is another reason to be able to verbalise our feelings and be clear about whether we feel loved and appreciated, tolerated or rejected. Your partner should understand how his or her behaviour is affecting you. It's not a guessing game!

Another thought on responding with quick solutions – they may not be desired just yet. It is another one of those typical male–female thinking patterns, men are typically out to solve problems. If there is a problem, let's fix it. Women often just want to get a concern out into the open. A solution may not be necessary for every problem, but being aware of the situation may be considered to be important. And there is a good chance that your partner had already considered the same solution. Just agree with your partner on the injustice he or she is suffering. What your partner suffers, you should be suffering.

Some of you saw the movie *Cool Hand Luke* with Paul Newman as a prisoner in a jail in the southern United States. When he did not do what the tough southern warden, played by Strother Martin, ordered, the warden uttered those oft-repeated lines that 'What we have here is a failure to communicate'. The real-life Strother, my next door neighbour in Malibu Lake for many years, was actually the gentlest of human beings. (May he rest in peace.) The one-way communication which the warden required is not the answer in a relationship. We must be equals, not jailer and prisoner.

We must be honest. When your partner says 'What's the matter?' and you answer 'nothing', but there is something bothering you – you are not being honest.

In conclusion

We are always communicating, whether by our actions, our words or our silence. It is the positive communication, which we did during our dating years, which keeps that romance alive. The more critical communication of concerns and problems is going to occur. To keep the romance blooming, the concerns should not be critical but, rather, constructive.

Problem solving with love and respect

Is there really a way to solve our problems?

Read this chapter if:

You want to know how to effectively solve relationship or personal problems

Your mate irritates you with his or her habits

You want to explore a new avenue to solving problems

You want to judge whether your anger with your partner is justified

You want to know how to make your criticisms more easily understood

The god or goddess you selected for your lifetime mate is not a statue. Each of us is an evolving being – evolving toward self-actualisation and, hopefully, getting closer to perfection. However, we each evolve in our own way and at our own speed. This creates some incompatibilities. Since we are perfect, we often want to change our partner to accommodate us.

Our unrealistic view of the world often makes us believe that love will conquer all and that our loving partners will accommodate us in all of our whims. We forget that we each have our own needs and desires. It is not an uncommon approach that people assume that their partner will change 'because he loves me'. It is often said in counselling circles that a man wants to be married to the woman he married on his wedding day, while a woman wants to be married to a man she has changed for the better.

If, in selecting a mate, you were lucky enough to find the absolute best person in 'the whole wide world' – that world is still going to change. That absolute best person may develop an alcohol or gambling problem. He or she may have heavy business pressures which were not there when you met and fell in love. Parenthood certainly increases some time and financial stresses for many. These shifts in circumstances may put strains on the marriage. However, making successful adjustments to them can make the relationship much, much stronger. It's how you both see the world, what goals you have together and how you handle the stresses that lead to strength or stumbling, to a robust romance or to the ruin of the relationship.

The noted Norwegian painter Edvard Munch said that 'The truth is that people at different times see things through different eyes. People are different in the morning than in the afternoon. This is one of the interesting things about our human culture.' We all recognise the reality of such changes in our needs, interests and points of view. Sometimes, these changes help a relationship. Other times, they put ruts in our road to happiness – and sometimes those ruts become chasms.

While there are two individuals in the relationship – and those individuals WILL change during the term of the relationship, the truth is that the relationship has a life of its own. The relationship will grow or diminish. The goals originally set for it may be changed. And it may, at some point, die. It is effective communication and problem-solving skills which allow the couple to control the relationship – and make it stronger and better. Disagreeing doesn't mean that you don't love the other person. We are separate individuals who are evolving in our needs and desires. We are not who we were when we first met nor when we were married.

When one member of the relationship changes, for better or worse, it throws the relationship out of balance. Honest communication can usually bring it back, and even make it better. Effective communication must make positive things happen. There should be a goal to be set, a problem to be resolved, a course of action to be clarified or a movement towards a stronger relationship. While solving disagreements is necessary in any human relationship, it is not the central element in making a marriage work. We have to have that romantic stuff to keep our hearts warm and fuzzy, then we are more likely to be able to discuss and compromise to keep the relationship upright.

Politics is the science of the possible. If you do the right things, there is a good chance that you can reconnect and begin the journey to a far better relationship and be 'happy ever after'. You can call it manipulating if you will – but we do manipulate our surroundings and our relationships. We have done it from the very beginning. Much of our dating and engagement behaviour is manipulative. We do the things and say the things which will elicit a positive response in our beloved. We got into this relationship because we both wanted it. The relationship was all-important then. It should be all-important now. When you reward your partner (with praise or other considerations), you may be able to have a partner who is more receptive to change.

Occasionally, we have ruts in the road to romance

It has been said that 'marriages are made in heaven – but so is thunder and lightning.' On the other hand, so are rainbows and moonlit nights. Your relationship can be what you want it to be, depending on how important it is for the two of you and how maturely you act in the relationship.

A recent survey by the Institute of Life Insurance found that 87% of the respondents over 29 years of age chose 'a happy family life' as the most important goal of their lives. Only 7% named 'developing as an individual' as most important. And 97% of married Americans characterise their marriages as 'happy' (*US News & World Report*, 6 June 1994, p. 12). But, that happy marriage doesn't necessarily come easily. While selfishly we might want everything to go our way, realistically there are two of us in this tango!

Every person has an image of his or her ideal mate. But, too often we spend time trying to make the person we marry *into* that ideal mate. We may concentrate so much on what this person is 'not', that we forget what he or she 'is'. We should understand that people's virtues are often a result of their defects. For example, a man who has not achieved the financial success, which some people might expect of him, may use his time to become a loving husband and father. A woman who is less than physically beautiful may have developed the pleasant aspects of her personality to a great degree and develop that rarer quality of inner beauty. On the other hand, a person who is very successful in business may have achieved that success because of an exceptionally aggressive attitude. That same attitude applied to a marriage may be more than the partner can tolerate.

Perhaps we expect too much from being married. It is unrealistic to think of marriage as constant excitement, although many are very exciting. Perhaps, when excitement leaves a marriage, it is because the couple has stopped courting and stopped planning for the future. When they were dating and engaged, they did a good many things together and had a great deal of fun. They had romance! But quite often, after they become married, these enjoyable things stop or are minimised. It seems that while a couple will do a fair amount of talking before the marriage, after the wedding it is often just watching TV which fills their shared hours. A good relationship really needs a good deal of zest and creativity on the part of the couple in order to continue to grow.

One factor which has been identified in successful marriages is the fact that the partners are able to accept the bad times, which inevitably will occur, as well as the good times. One partner may be on the upswing in his or her career and the other may be in a down cycle. This may create a problem. The couple's child-raising theories may be in conflict. This can create problems. Every marriage can expect some periods of temporary incompatibility. With intelligence, communication and possibly some effective counselling, most problems can generally be worked out. It sure is a lot cheaper and more satisfying than a divorce!

People who were able to talk a great deal when they were dating and when they were engaged, and even during their first year or two of marriage, may find communicating difficult after a couple of years. One study found that after a year of marriage, the average couple spends about 37 minutes a week in exclusive conversation with each other. That hardly seems enough to have the element of

Figure 24   You always hurt the one you love.

'friendship' which we all see as essential to our relationships (Figure 24).

Handling the day-to-day annoyances

While most of *us* are perfect, we tend to get into relationships with people with some minor faults. Irritations can
develop when our partner does something which we don't
do. Among these nasty habits are:

- leaving the toilet seat up (men) or down (women);
- installing the toilet paper with the flap outside (men)
  or next to the wall (women);
- not turning off the lights;
- hanging clothes in the bathroom, over a door handle,
  or (heaven forbid!) on the floor;
- drinking beer, cola or milk right out of the container;

- leaving non-kitchen utensils in the kitchen;
- eating (or not eating) breakfast;
- eating *your* favourite cookies or candies;
- leaving newspapers or magazines in a clutter on a table or on the floor;
- leaving dirty dishes in the sink;
- Enough?

Many of these minor irritations can turn into major wounds. They can also signal a power-drive fight for control. These habits, if known early, can be settled before the marriage ceremony takes place. Compromises can generally be easily worked out. 'I will ____, if you will ____.' If not, they should be able to be settled early in the relationship with honest problem solving.

Anger

When things are not going our way at home, at work or with the children, we will certainly get upset. Sometimes, the frustration is so great that it evolves into anger. Being truly angry at a partner is not good for the relationship. It must be acknowledged and eliminated.

What is the source of the stress which makes us angry? Is it the job, the children or your mate? Are we taking out our anger on our mate because he or she is most available as a whipping boy? Is the real source of the problem the boss or a co-worker?

Some people believe that venting our anger is good – cathartic. But, if you are the object of the anger, how does it make you feel? What is easiest for the angry person is not necessarily best for the total relationship. And the

more you use anger as an adjustment technique, the more
it becomes ingrained as a habit. If you are uncontrollably
angry at one situation or if you get angry at many small
situations, it is time to try to control the primitive psychological outlet with the intellect. Looking at the health of
the relationship, which is better – calm discussion or
throwing the telephone?

The media help to give us permission for venting our
anger – and even for hitting our partner. In earlier days,
what was the unthinkable is now allowed by the images on
the silver screen. To take a more intellectual approach, we
must first find the real source of the frustration that makes
us angry. Do you say:

- I accept (your action) or (your inaction). (No anger but
  possibly some frustration.)
- I do not accept (your action) or (your inaction). (Frustration and/or anger.)

Second, we should look for alternatives to the anger.
Anger includes blaming the other. Being constantly
blamed or confronted does not sit too well with most of
us – unless we are masochists! Alternatives can include:
discussion of the problem with our partner, competent
marriage therapy, physical recreation to take out our frustrations elsewhere. Hitting a tennis ball or kicking a soccer
ball is actually good therapy. So are mental-relaxation
techniques such as meditation.

Larger problems

Anger or excessive frustration indicate a larger problem.
Alert couples can understand when something is wrong

and should attempt to understand the source. Whether it is one big irritation or thousands of small ones, they usually have their source in only a few areas: the power and control issues, lack of mental closeness and physical intimacy, not pulling our weight (such as in housework or childcare – either differing standards of what is required- or a lack of shared responsibilities) and the financial areas (not enough money or disagreements on how it is spent).

Some of these problems, large or small, will often manifest themselves in the course of the marriage. What is your approach to handling them? Is it non-confrontational:

Don't say anything negative because it only makes things worse. Or,

The problems will eventually go away. Or,

I'll just accept it so I don't rock the boat.

Or is it more confrontational:

Let's clear the air right now. Or,

Little things can become big things, so let's discuss it now.

Both approaches to problems have their positive and their negative sides. Some little annoyances do go away. Sometimes spontaneously, sometimes just because of a simple suggestion. But the big things better be addressed. They need to be addressed while keeping your partner's power drive undented. The 'I'm right and you're wrong' approach does nothing more than boost your own ego and power feelings. We must keep in mind that it is the relationship which is our primary concern. While we can avoid a confrontation and 'let sleeping dogs lie' that sleeping dog may gnaw on you with the undesired result of argument or divorce.

Studies generally show that men are quite content with the way things are in terms of household chores – women tend to be quite upset about the same issue. They usually see more clutter and do more of the work. Not sharing the work in a two-income family is a major source of frustration and anger.

Lack of sharing in childcare for two-income families is another major problem. But whether it is house cleaning or childcare, when responsibility is delegated, the authority to do it the way that person wants must be a part of the package. If Cynthia wants Harold to take more responsibility for child-care but she continually criticises his efforts, she has not allowed him the authority needed to take on the responsibility. After all, child raising is 'her' responsibility and she only wants a little help – on her terms.

In housekeeping or child raising, as in other areas of concern for a relationship, communication on what should be the preferred way for accomplishing something should be discussed. It could be whether to dust the furniture first then vacuum, or whether to let your toddler kick you (and if so what will be the punishment so that he can learn that kicking is not acceptable), or whether to go to the Canary Islands or to Greece. The goals have to be set first.

If you turn him loose on the housekeeping and he doesn't do it the way you want, it's too late to jump on him for his stupidity. Suggest vacuuming first, or dusting first, then turn him loose. It is much easier to take an early suggestion than a later criticism.

Is it a problem for our relationship?

It is not expected that both people will want the same things at the same time – all the time. It's OK to put different priorities on the same items. He may put 'more sex' as number 1 and a cleaner house at number 20. She may put sex at number 11 and a cleaner house at number 3. You are responsible for your needs. You may not be able to get your partner to make all the changes you desire in order to have a perfect world for yourself. Whatever we each see as *needed* or *not needed* in a relationship is a legitimate concern. His number 1 concern is just as valid as her number 1 concern. Do you just bring up the 1 and 2 ranked concerns, while your partner brings up every concern from 1 to 20? There are some things we just need to accept.

We can often take care of our own needs. Wanting more time alone is easy. Wanting to see friends is also easy. But wanting more sex or cuddling in the relationship may be more difficult to achieve! Realise that you are not going to get your relationship going exactly the way you want. Your partner has some personality traits, needs and goals which don't correspond exactly with yours. The relationship must, therefore, be seen as a dynamic changing alliance in which both people function as individuals, but both contribute and gain from the union. Best friends don't have to have everything in common all the time.

Disagreement in close relationships

This is quite normal because personalities vary and individuals often see things differently. But don't let the tensions build up. Problems should be aired and worked out as they arise. What is important is to talk about the differences. It is always difficult to discuss unpleasant topics, but there are times when these topics must be discussed. In the case of marriages, it is often in the divorce attorney's office that these mountains of problems are finally brought into the open. If only each small problem had been discussed when it occurred, many marriages would have grown into satisfying relationships. When problems occur, they should be solved or at least understood, because repressed feelings will often explode and may ruin a marriage.

As the old story goes – a lady, in answering the questions about why she was divorcing a seemingly perfect mate, took off her shoe and asked her friends if they knew where it felt uncomfortable to her. Experiences on the inside of a relationship can be much better or much worse than those on the outside can understand. It may not be one huge problem but, rather, a number of smaller experiences which have made staying in the relationship questionable.

The conflict may or may not be a result of the relationship. Problems at work, with neighbours, at school or with the kids can all set a person on edge. Sometimes, talking about it helps these situations; sometimes, the person needs to be left alone. Two friends once let me in on one of their basic rules. When they were edgy, they just told the other 'I'm bitchy.' That meant they were to be left alone until things came back closer to normal.

When the problems are not solved in a family, they will show up somewhere as maladjustments to the relationships. The most common methods of handling unresolved conflicts are that:

- There is open conflict, either verbal or physical. Arguments, sarcastic remarks and spousal beatings are all quite common. Or:

- One of the couple just clams up and stews about it. As problems grow, the festering of the unresolved conflicts grows until they explode – often in divorce, sometimes in murder! Or:
- One of the spouses becomes physically or mentally ill. This may be an unconscious attempt at gaining sympathy, or it can merely be a way of withdrawing from the problems. Or:
- The problems between the spouses are taken out on the children, usually just one child.

Children are safer targets for a weak adult, so, rather than fighting with our mate, the child takes the brunt of the frustrations and anger of the weak adult. This can be shown as scoldings, put-downs or physical violence.

The hostility which often develops in relationships, even in discussions of the problems, have very negative effects on our immune systems. And when the immune systems are weakened, our chances for developing physical diseases increases – from colds to heart attacks and cancers. So negative relationships cause a hardship to our physical bodies. The flip side of this is that, when relationships are happy, the partners live longer while enjoying their lives every day.

Solving relationship disagreements and conflicts

It isn't fair, but women seem to have the job of trying to initiate and solve most relationship problems. Whether it is a biological ability or a learned psychosocial skill, it is a fact. Perhaps another reason is that, because men have had

the power and women want a share in that power, they
have to initiate the process to get some of what he's got.
While many educated and/or mature men say they want
an egalitarian relationship, they may not consciously think
of giving up some of the control they have traditionally
had. It would be like walking past a millionaire and expecting a gift of money. Perhaps, if you asked, you might
get some – but, without asking, it probably would never
even occur to him to give you some. In a truly loving
relationship, each partner would want as much for the
other as for himself or herself. But, sometimes, we must
ask.

Since you're not married to Mother Theresa, there
may be some deficiencies in the total ability to love unselfishly. A major concern in bringing up a problem is
therefore – how far can I go in terms of being assertive
and asking for what I want. Will he be angry? Will he
leave? And if so, do I care?

Recovering from the problem solving may take some
time. For some, it may take some time to heal the wounds
they think they have experienced in the therapeutic
process. Then, there are others who feel so much closer
that they want to jump in bed immediately after reaching
an agreement.

When there is a conflict, the couple must understand
the goal they are attempting to accomplish. If you don't
have a goal which both people want to accomplish, you
don't know where you're going and you won't know when
you get there.

If you don't have a clear goal, what commonly
happens is that the couple will continue in their warring
behaviour, each trying to get 'one up' on the other. There
will be a great deal of unnecessary tongue flapping, and
nothing constructive will happen. What should have been
marital becomes martial (Figure 25) – and the trenches of
war get dug deeper and deeper. The task at hand will more

MARITAL   MARTIAL

Figure 25 The difference between marital and martial is where one puts the 'I'.

likely be to be taking control of the partnership rather than making the relationship better. That old drive for power (Chapter 3) will show through as the basic force, and what the people are arguing about will only be the tip of the iceberg.

Often, as a way of communicating, a person will 'outdo' the other in the behaviour they want to change. If one leaves the dirty dishes in the sink, the other may do the same thing until the sink is piled high with dishes. The person trying to teach the lesson may be leaving a message which is relatively clear, but it would have been much simpler to say that you would prefer that the dirty dishes be washed as they are dirtied. The revenge or 'eye for an eye and tooth for a tooth' motives seem to be the major approach to problem solving in the Israel–Palestine area, but they don't make much sense in solving relationship conflicts. And the success of this tactic in the Middle East shows that it doesn't work for nations either.

One couple left notes in the appropriate areas to remind the spouse to do something. She continually left the lights on after she left the room. It bothered him, so he left notes on the light switches saying 'Please turn me out'. He squeezed the toothpaste tube in the middle which she abhorred, so she left a sign on the toothpaste 'Please squeeze my bottom'. (What an invitation, eh?)

The non-communicator who just listens, hoping that the angry fire in the partner will eventually extinguish itself, will sometimes create more problems and even more anger in the partner who wants a verbal reaction from their muted mate. But, other times, the person doing all the talking will see some solutions as he or she talks, then ask for some reaction. This is the better way.

The manner of solving conflict is very important. Disagreements don't have to be disagreeable. Each person should be willing to give up something to develop a stronger relationship. But, often, the individual's selfish needs interfere with the good of the couple. Many people find it difficult, if not impossible, to talk to each other about their problems. This is due, in large part, to the games they played while dating and during the early days of the marriage. They're afraid to bring up irritating problems because they might hurt the other's feelings. This habit becomes reinforced over the years, and becomes difficult to break.

Quite often, when a person is hurt by a mate, the injured partner will strike back in non-verbal ways. If one of the mates is found to be an adulterer, the other often seeks revenge and becomes adulterous. If a wife strongly objects to her husband's television viewing, he may seek revenge by not taking her out to dinner. But the problem has to be brought up; while this is painful, it's not nearly as painful as the events which will probably occur if the problem isn't solved.

Often the person who does not feel the problem is the one who may recognise that the problem exists. Perhaps a husband complains about the bills or swears at the traffic, as a way to indicate to his wife that he's about to blow. Or a wife, who does not touch her husband, is giving an indication that there is a mental separation that's going on and the alert husband then may be able to initiate the conversation relating to what the problem might be.

While women are generally better at being 'assertive', many women do what most men do – they keep quiet. They fume and fume until it eventually explodes – often in divorce. A number of years ago, two of my neighbours got a divorce. She filed. He was astonished. When he asked 'why?', she had a couple of hundred reasons – including the time 20 years before when he danced too close to another woman at a party. The neighbours sided with the wife, realising that the husband's 'macho' attitude would have stopped most of them from bringing up a problem to him.

If you can overcome the common obstacles to sharing and compromise, you have a good chance to solve the problem. A good rule, when there is a problem, is:

- to pick a time (have serious discussions by appointment);
- pick a neutral area, and discuss only a single problem at each session;
- be sure you listen attentively when the other is talking;
- when things are getting too heated, call a 'timeout' and take a break.

With these ideas in mind here are some more specifics.

Can you clearly state the problem?

Often there are overlapping negatives. Sort them out before you start. What is the major problem. Also, is this negotiable or is it a demand? Recognise that most things are negotiable, with each getting and each giving in some areas. Unfortunately, the selfishness which is so prevalent in today's society often makes our every wish a demand. Remember that, if the demand is not met, that may be the end of the relationship.

You must stop drinking.

You must stop gambling.

You must lose weight. You eat all the time.

Each of these situations can be the result of a strong compulsion, or addiction, which may be more psychologically satisfying than the relationship. Also, when a demand is made, there is generally a power-drive conflict even if the behaviour demanded is 'for one's own good'. The egocentric idea that 'nobody is going to tell me what to do!' often protects a weak ego which results from having an inferiority complex due to not having enough power or control in one's life.

Even with lesser problems, there will generally be a power-drive confrontation, so the way the problem is phrased is critical:

It bothers me that ...

I'm very sensitive to ...

are ways of showing that you are bothered. If the relationship is 'loving', something can probably be worked out. In fact, while you are formulating how to state the problem, you might think of several possible solutions.

Define your terms

What do you mean by the words you say? *'We should be more loving and affectionate.'* What do you mean by those terms – exactly. Do you mean that you will kiss and hug every morning and evening? Does it mean that you will go out for dinner once a week? Does it mean that you will bring a small gift to the other once a week or once a month? If you haven't defined exactly what you mean, you won't know if the 'loving' and 'affection' are being done. If, by affectionate, one of you means 'more patting on the bottom' and the other means more cookies baked or more flowers brought home, you don't have the same understanding of the behaviour which you desire.

If you want your partner to be less confrontational, how can that behaviour be changed? What does 'confrontational' mean? When is your partner more likely to be confrontational? How does this occur? Is it the spoken word, the tone of the voice or other body language?

Where is the real source of the problem? You remember that we each have parts of our minds which are both conscious and unconscious. Both our memories and our values have roots in both the conscious and unconscious parts of our minds.

When two people, who are already very complicated, attempt to discuss a problem which seems conscious but may have its roots in the unconscious mind, it is much more difficult that we might imagine. Just look at the story in Chapter 5 to see the possible dimensions of our joys and our problems (see Box 4 in Chapter 5).

You must be fair

One client of mine had the idea that compromise meant bringing up the issue over and over again, negotiating and negotiating until she got everything she wanted. No real 'give and take'. Her husband had given his house to his daughter from a former marriage because her stepmother had mistreated the daughter over the years. He also felt that he had not been treated fairly in the relationship for years. He didn't 'like' his wife – but he loved her.

The couple owned another house as community property. In order to save the marriage they tried counselling, then divorce mediation with a counsellor and an attorney. He offered to give her everything, all of the community property and half of his separate property house – the half which hadn't been deeded to his daughter. The wife wanted it all. So divorce! Over and over again during counselling it was apparent that 'marriage' meant 'house' – the house that was his separate property according to the California Constitution. He has told me many times since that it was the dumbest divorce he had ever heard of, but her desire to win the war of the separate property was paramount – and irreconcilable.

Selfishness is obviously the cause of most marriage problems. Self-centred interest (see Chapter 3) is, too often, more important than the flowering of the relationship. That common sign of immaturity, *selfishness*, is a continual enemy of the fair communication of needs and the development of a mature egalitarian relationship. We can be expected to have different viewpoints of situations and problems. Such differences don't necessarily mean that one person is 'wrong'. But, it does mean that the viewpoints have to be understood and discussed. Hopefully, then, a workable solution can be found.

Pick the right time to discuss a problem

Do some preliminary thinking about what time is right. Don't dump all your trouble into your mate's lap as soon as they step into the door, or as you are on your way to a party. If a husband has had trouble at work, maybe he shouldn't lay that on his wife as soon as he sees her. If a wife has had trouble with the children or at her job, she shouldn't throw those problems at him immediately. Just before dropping off to sleep is not a good time to talk about anything – let alone problems.

Don't begin a serious discussion when either partner has had a bad day or is tired. A wise person will read the signs of possible fatigue or other trouble. Find a good time, when neither is tired, or troubled, or in a rush to do something. Saturday morning is often a good time for a serious discussion. Both people should be well rested and there should be adequate time for a discussion.

Some very effective couples set a recurring date for discussing anything that they have not brought up. Every Saturday or the first Saturday of each month would be examples of specific times for communication. Such times don't have to be used just to bring up problems but can be used for planning vacations or other recreational pursuits such as get-togethers of family or friends.

What may have been the right time, may become the wrong time, if the discussion is getting too hot. You may need to take a break for a while, a 'timeout', then come back after you have cooled off. Timeouts are necessary when the rational discussion starts to become emotional, and anger or other stumbling blocks to rational thinking emerge. Such stumbling blocks could include such accusations as 'you always' or 'you never' or belittling such as 'you think that's a problem?' When a timeout is called by one of the partners, the discussion stops. Set a time when you can return to the discussion: five minutes, an hour, etc. No other words are said by either person – no parting shots. Go to different rooms or areas. Relax naturally. Sit down. Breathe deeply, think of a quiet place. Your blood pressure can drop 10–20 points with deep breathing! (Do not use alcohol or another drug to relax you – and don't think of what you are going to say when you get back together.) Come back together at the agreed time and agree on whether or not you are ready to continue the discussion.

Pick the right place

Find a neutral area. Perhaps the kitchen is the cook's area and the bedroom is the pleasure area, if so they shouldn't be used. The dinner table isn't too appropriate either. So, find a place which can be psychologically neutral. The living room might be a good place to talk.

Get your message across clearly and without animosity

Phrase your point of view so that it can be understood. 'This bothers me.' 'I can't seem to understand this.' 'I am hurt when I feel that ...' 'I feel rejected when you ____.'
   The tone of voice is as important as the words used. If

the voice portrays sarcasm while the words express concern, the *message* becomes sarcastic:

> *You can do better than that,* might express either encouragement or sarcasm.

> *You can do better than **that**,* might express a superiority by the speaker.

> *You can do **better** than that,* might express a feeling of confidence in the other's capabilities.

Fatigue, impatience or feelings of inferiority can often be heard in a speaker's voice, no matter what the words may say. The phrasing of the words may also indicate a feeling of inadequacy by the speaker who tries to make up for certain inferiorities by appearing to be superior:

> *Don't do that, stupid.*

> *Don't do that.*

> *I always do it this way.*

> *It might be easier if you tried it this way.*

> *Have you ever tried to do it this way?*

Each of these phrasings is trying to elicit the same response in the listener. But the first was a command and a put-down. The second was merely a command. The third was a way of showing the listener that the speaker was smarter, but not necessarily in a commanding position. The fourth allowed the listener to make the decision, but the speaker was still intimating some superiority. And the fifth option was putting the listener on an almost equal footing with the speaker by simply asking if an alternative method had ever been considered.

Constructive communication is not a name-calling contest. You can't take back the spoken word, and, since married people know the weaknesses of each other better than anybody else, they can hit pretty hard with their sarcasm. Married people are able to develop subtle or sometimes grossly humorous, derogatory and sarcastic remarks which ostensibly lower the level of the other person while raising themselves in their own eyes:

> *I don't know how I married somebody so good looking, but so dumb.*

> *I remember when you used to fill out that sport shirt from the top down rather than from the bottom up.*

> *Thank goodness the kids take after me instead of you or they still wouldn't be able to tie their own shoes.*

People with inferiority feelings often use such methods to show their high status in social situations. The problem is that each cutting remark tends to cut some of the 'ties that bind', and the friendship or the marriage will be weakened or perhaps broken as the verbal barbs push one person further and further away from the other.

Only a masochist enjoys being physically or mentally hurt. So, if you let a sarcastic remark pop out or even blame somebody for something which is true:

> *I know you've been going out with so-and-so,* or

> *I never did like your freckles anyway*

this kind of remark can hurt a person, and no matter how many times you apologise, it's not forgotten. And if they're spoken during a rage, even the mildest criticisms may be deadly. Even something like *You never come home on time*, or *You always put the children first,* can ignite dangerous fuses which lead to trouble.

Using the words 'never' or 'always' means that there are no exceptions. Is this what you really mean? Do you mean 'You are *never* romantic?' Or do you mean you are only romantic at certain times – such as when we are out together for dinner or when we are on vacation, just the two of us.

Because each of us has a basic need to feel adequate, we must be able to 'save face' in any confrontation. But, if you have developed a confrontational behaviour style which has not worked, it is time for a change to a more intelligent approach. Remember that, if you always do what you've always done, you'll always get what you've always got.

The objective of discussing a problem should be finding the solution – not enhancing one person's ego at the expense of the other. But, since it is usually easy to put down a marriage partner, it is quite common for immature married couples to engage in emotional name-calling and put-downs rather than attempting to seek an intelligent solution – as a mature couple would do (Box 10).

Studies indicate that newly married couples who eventually stayed together averaged 5 negative comments per 100 about their mates. Newly married couples who eventually divorced had about twice as many negative comments, but as the relationships evolved the negative comments became about five times greater in the doomed relationships.

Generally, the 'what's wrong with our relationship' statements become 'what's wrong with me'. That's devastating to my power drive – to my self-esteem. When you find fault with anyone, they will either give a true reason

Box 10   Speaking skills when presenting a problem

Use 'I' statements rather than 'you' statements. Describe what you experience rather than attacking your partner.

1 What is the problem?

- Tell how you feel about it (upset, angry, left out).
- Don't make the problem appear bigger than it is.
- Don't blame your partner any more than your concern signifies.
- No 'you' statements, 'you always' or 'you never'.
- Stick to the problem at hand, don't bring up old problems.

2 Stay focused on the problem, stay intellectual, don't get emotional and irrational:

- No name calling.
- No put-downs (i.e. you are childish/selfish/inconsiderate/stupid/lazy – or, worse, an arsehole/idiot/bitch).
- 'Why don't you pull your weight for a change?
- No stereotyping – all women are like that.
- No accusing 'Why do you always have to have your way?'

3 Seek solutions based on acceptance or compromise, not pleas:

- 'If you really loved me you would ...'
- 'You always have it your way.'

as to why they believe or act that way – or they will rationalise. Rationalisation is an adjustment mechanism in which we give a reason which we believe, but which isn't really true. The person you are rationalising to may believe it to be true. For example, you may blame your alcoholic father for your behaviour. But, if all the facts were known, he may have had nothing to do with why you had acted in such a way.

In trying to get your point across, don't take a 'know it all' approach. You want to appear as an equal, not a superior. Don't threaten unless you mean it. If you threaten divorce, your partner may beat you to the lawyer to file.

Keep it brief – the longer you talk the more chance there is of losing your partner's attention. *What* is being said and *how* is it said. The *what* can be made more palatable or more disagreeable depending on *how* it is said.

Watch that power drive!

It is quite common that rather than trying to intelligently solve a problem, the discussion becomes a battle of 'one-upmanship' with *Well, what about the time that you ...'* or with the retort *But you never ...* We look for the weaknesses and incompetencies in the other – pushing our own egos upward with every verbal thrust and kick. While this satisfies our own power drives, it doesn't do much for those of our spouse – and how can the relationship grow when one or both partners are having their self-esteem hacked away. Were both people such bad judges of character, or so hard up to get a relationship going, that they didn't look long enough or hard enough for a mature partner?

No one knows you better than your spouse, so no one can push your buttons harder and with more accuracy than can this person you've been living with. Being sensitive to the other when arguing is often difficult. Your emotional feeling is negative, but you need to be able to control it with your rational side so that you don't say things which will have long-term negative effects. While we may be able to handle this when the boss is negative to us, it is a tough thing to do in an intimate relationship of equals.

Patience in discussing problems is necessary. Without it, you can destroy in an hour something which might take weeks to repair. Complain, but don't blame. Blaming forces the other partner to be on the defensive. There are a number of people in marriages trying to make each other into what they want by criticising and blaming them. But, it seems that most happy marriages work because the two people build on the positive rather than emphasising the negative aspects of their relationship. They use their intellects rather than their emotional outbursts as the vehicles by which they can solve problems.

The goals are – to understand the problem and solve it. The object of the discussion or argument should not be to win but, rather, to develop a deeper understanding of each other. With this in mind, you should remember to keep warmth and a feeling of caring in your attitude. It should be remembered also that not every problem needs to be solved, but that, sometimes, a trait or a habit must be accepted. Of course, one person can't always do all the adjusting. It would be nice if your partner did everything just the way you wanted, but you are not the king – just an equal partner.

There is no single way to successfully handle conflicts. Some successful couples avoid most conflicts, some talk it out quietly, some fight loudly. It's what works for both of you that is important. However, the least harmful are

Figure 26 The only difference between stumbling blocks and stepping stones is the way you use them.

most likely to be the first two alternatives. What may seem to be a stumbling block may be a stepping stone to greater understanding and intimacy (Figure 26).

In marriages which were not well planned, the values and needs of the individuals may be so different that a solution is not possible. So either one partner gives in totally or a divorce results.

Scientific problem solving

Perhaps the classic method of problem solving is to use the scientific approach. Here, we would be using a proven intellectual method to get over the conflict hurdles more easily. The philosopher, psychologist, educator John Dewey developed a simple approach to using the scientific method of problem solving. Dewey's method dealt with general science. However, it has been applied to many areas of endeavour, such as education and counselling. While I don't believe that he considered it for marriage therapy, it does work. However, because we have the strong emotional factors in a relationship which are not as likely to occur in science, we have to consider some emotional factors in using this scientific method.

Dewey's scientific method of problem solving involves three steps:

1 What is the problem? Is it a behaviour (doing or not doing something), is it new or is it that the last solution tried isn't working? Is it an attitude? Is it related to finances or to the amount of time spent (on job, with children, on a hobby). You must be specific in identifying the problem (see p. 318). Journalists investigate in terms of: who, what, where, why and how. These may be useful questions to answer relative to clarifying the perceived problem.

2 List possible solutions – don't discuss them yet, just list them. Brainstorm for all the possibilities.

3 Choose one or two possible solutions and try them for a period of time. If one works, stick with it. If it doesn't work, try another solution.

Understanding the REAL problem

This is essential to finding a solution. The apparent problem may be that she comes home late from work often. He objects. Is he jealous that she may like the work better than him or that there may be someone else in her life? The more basic problem may be that his power drive is threatened. Her job is more important than he is. Someone else may be more attractive to her than he is. Is the real problem her tardy arrival or is it his insecurity? We like to blame the other when the problem may be in ourselves.

What are the real problems? The apparent problems may be less desire for intimacy or increasing edginess with our partner or the children. The real problems may be physical (decreased energy, unhappiness about our weight) or mental and emotional (deep unhappiness with the job or in-law intrusions).

Possible solutions

What do you generally want? More help around the house, more time alone? Specifically, what does that mean?

> *You vacuum on Saturday morning or Sunday.*

> *You shop once a week, I'll shop once a week.*

Relative to time away:

> *I want to play cards with my friends once a week.*

> *I want undisturbed reading time three hours a week, will you take care of the kids?*

It is best to make your request specific and say exactly what *you* want – not what your partner shouldn't do. Instead of saying 'stop loafing around the house', negotiate for one hour of shared housework on Saturday morning. Is our concern with how our partner is in *our* relationship or is it an 'outside of the relationship' request – the way you treat my mother, your drinking too much at parties, not asking the boss for a raise, getting more exercise.

A change should start with knowledge, which should lead to a change in attitude which should lead to a change in behaviour. The knowledge starts with exactly what the problem is and why is it bothering me? It should also include an evaluation of just how important the issue is. Is it excessive gambling or child beating or is it sometimes not coming home for dinner at the agreed-upon time without phoning.

Our attitude can be evaluated in several ways. Are we interested in keeping the relationship together at all costs? Is our attitude so domineering, because of our drive for control and power that we absolutely insist that things will go our way? In terms of a solution, do you have the attitude that you can you learn to compromise, to accept a difference or, when a difference must be changed – to change it. These options for solution should be part of an intelligent discussion. If a thorough knowledge of the problem and a loving attitude are present, the solution can be found and your behaviours should change.

In bringing up more serious problems, we may need to refer back to the guidelines set in the last chapter. They were to:

- be rational;
- communicate clearly;
- understand how your own power drive and the power drive of your loved one are involved;
- listen carefully; and
- respond appropriately.

Listening skills

Therapists typically advocate the use of improved listening techniques, such as 'active listening', in which the listener repeats what the speaker is saying in order to more fully understand the message – this often doesn't work. In working out minor problems, it has its place. But, often, the couple is talking about deeply held value positions which may be mutually exclusive. For example, if before marriage both wanted children but now that she has finished law school and is working in an interesting and challenging job, she may have changed her mind and definitely does not want children. A compromise in which they adopt a child and the husband stays home and cares for it may be quite out of the question for him.

When she says 'I feel angry when you come home from work late,' she is unquestionably criticising his be-haviour. And, while this approach may be superior to 'You selfish bastard, why can't you come home on time like my brother Ralph does,' in either case the message is that you are inconsiderate – of course, the former method is somewhat less likely to incite a riot.

What you hear may not be what he or she meant. 'I want a divorce', 'I hate you', 'You're not a good mother', may be only emotional unthinking psychological reactions to the stress of an argument. But, while you may not really mean it, words once spoken can never be recalled.

Discussing problems

It usually is best to let the person with the problem talk – uninterrupted. (Stick with one problem per discussion.) It's very important that they not be interrupted until they can get it all out. Then, some discussion can begin. What does each of you think about the problem? How serious is it? What are some possible solutions? Keep the attention focused on the problem, not on the other person's faults, since none of us like to be reminded of our faults. If you want a positive change, it is far less likely with a negative start.

It is a gross negative to make one person feel guilty. Guilt is not a necessary requirement for solving a problem. Try to agree on the first step in solving the problem, then get to work on it. If you can't solve the problems yourselves, get some counselling. Or, perhaps, you may decide you need more time to think about it so you can call a halt to the discussion and come back to it at a better time.

To be rational and intelligent you need to reduce the factors which can make you more psychological and emotional. Losing it (emotional anger), nagging, playing helpless, lying and demanding are methods which are not rational or which put you in a power position and your partner as an underling. Words, once spoken, can never be taken back. Stay rational and logical – no matter how upset you are. Such things as being tired, being uncontrollably angry, being under the influence of a drug such as alcohol or being stressed will affect your ability to be logical. So, in spite of the desire to get things over right now – wait until you are both rested and ready.

The solutions

Not every minor problem has to be solved for all eternity. It may be OK to suggest 'Would you mind hanging your clothes up?' It may be another to require him to agree to hang up his clothes the minute he takes them off, and do it for ever and ever! What can you accept and what *must* be changed? Don't assume that, just because your partner loves you, he or she is going to give up major goals for success or a favourite hobby. Too much of an attempt to control and change a spouse is not fair if it is something which has been going on for years. There are several solutions to a disagreement or conflict.

When there are problems, the options are: accept, negotiate and compromise or split up – either by living quite separate lives while living together or by divorcing. If you are living with one who is, or was, your best friend, it is far better to accept and negotiate than to give up on the relationship:

- accept – you may or may not let your partner know that an aspect of their behaviour is a problem, but you accept it and are not asking for a change;
- compromise – each gives up something, and possibly gets something;
- harmonise – each is getting what is desired;
- split up – If you make the 'change or else' ultimatum, you had better be prepared that your partner will take the 'or else' option.

Acceptance

Acceptance of a personality trait or habit of your partner does not necessarily mean that your partner is winning and you are losing. The relationship may be winning. Of course, acceptance of differences should go both ways. If only one continually gives in, we call this submitting. Submission indicates being overpowered by the other. When this occurs, there is a chance of emotional explosives being stored – just waiting for the fuse to be ignited. There is a real difference between actually accepting the differences of each other and being forced to live with them.

Most older couples' advice is 'Be ready to take the ups and downs, the give and take.' But, often today, we want instant and perpetual gratification. Still, our deepest human need in today's world is a warm deep intimate friendship. For most people, this is the fundamental to a really satisfying and meaningful life.

Compromise

This could be 'To make you happy, I'll do it less.' It could be 'I'll clean the house if you will clean the garage.' Or 'This year we will spend Christmas at my mother's house then next year at your mother's.' Or 'This year we'll go to Spain, like you want, then next year we'll go to Greece, like I want.' It should be obvious that in compromising you give something and get something.

Harmonising

Harmonising your solutions would be accomplished if he wanted more recreational time together and she wanted help with the house cleaning, and they settled on hiring house-cleaning help. Some high-income dual-career couples even have their dinners catered daily.

Splitting up

This may be required. Some behaviours *must* be changed or the relationship will not survive. Compromise is not an option. Spousal or child abuse, excessive high-stakes gambling, drug or alcohol dependence or even excessive shopping are examples of behaviours which may be so totally destructive to the relationship that they must be changed if the relationship is to survive. When a gambler comes home and has lost the house, you can imagine the stress on the partner and children. I saw this happen twice in my neighbourhood when husbands returned from Las Vegas from a weekend of gambling.

The grass may look greener on the other side of the street, but it may be crab grass just like at home! When checking out the potential mate market, the good ones have already been snapped up and their mates aren't about to let you have them. So, assuming that you originally made your selection of a mate on intelligent grounds and you were once good friends, it is a whole lot easier, and cheaper, to rebuild what you had and to make it better. Divorce only settles some things – it creates a number of other problems!

If we are going in the same direction with the same 'grand plan', we can make a number of adjustments to make the path easier for both of us. It makes much more sense to get that old romantic relationship back on track.

Seeking professional help

In a relationship, most of us are the prosecuting attorney, the judge and the jury when our partner does not live up to the role we expect. Whether it is coming home late, excessively disciplining the children or not disciplining them enough. It would be comforting to think that just the two of us could solve all our problems through intelligent discussion. The reality is that when there are two sides to the story, neither may be able to accept the position of the other. The equal partners may not understand all the possibilities or consequences or they may not agree. Counsellors have found that two people do not constitute

Figure 27   People study psychology so that they can study other
people – to throw suspicion off themselves.

a stable relationship. A third person is usually necessary to
help sort out the real meaning of what is being said by each
person and possibly to offer alternate solutions. So, if we
are to use Dewey's ideas, we may need a third person to
help understand what the problem really is, then to help
us to develop possible theories of behaviour which might
work.

Some people go to ministers or even lawyers (solicitors) for this help. Ministers usually come free of charge,
so that is a definite positive. However, ministers and
lawyers are seldom extensively trained in relationship
therapy. Throughout this book, I have never mentioned
'therapy' but always 'competent therapy'. It is a sad
commentary to say that not all therapists, even when
licensed, are competent and without their pet assumptions
(Figure 27). I would suggest that, if you have a problem,
see a qualified therapist. If your friends have a recom-
mendation, try that first. If not don't think you have to
be 'married' to the first therapist you try. If the first one
doesn't work for you, try another. Just remember that
therapy is a far better option than divorce – and it is
much, much less expensive.

In any relationship, there is 'what he says', 'what she says' and what is actually true. And what is true is often quite different from what the partners are saying. When Sigmund Freud popularised the idea that we all have unconscious parts of our minds which direct our behaviour, he was a pioneer. But, for most of us, it is nearly impossible for us to believe that our unconscious motivations can have a strong effect on our lives. It is difficult to believe that a domineering or non-loving parent can emerge much later in our life and stop us from being open and accepting of change. That domineering or non-loving parent can strongly influence our own need to feel right.

If you want to keep the relationship together, but improve it, a professional is more likely to give you competent advice than is your sister or brother. 'Get rid of the son of a bitch – there are a lot of eligible people out there who would want you' sounds good, but take a look at the singles bars and the people who have been burned in previous relationships. Those people waiting for you may not be quite as likely to get into a new relationship as you may believe. The devil you know may be better than the devil you don't know. This is particularly true as we grow older. From about 40 on up, the 'pickings' are not what they were when we were 20.

Sharing with others problems which should remain in the relationship, and with a competent therapist, tends to build a wall between the one who is talked about and the partner and friends – who will generally agree with what they hear from the partner. But what they are hearing is only one side of the story. 'Divorce the bastard' may be your sister's command. She is putting the pressure on you. Now, the fact that her marriage isn't really that great doesn't enter the picture. She is pushing your power-drive buttons. You are getting pressure, perhaps even being shamed, to end the relationship. If it's all bad –

go ahead. But what does your sister know about your true feelings and the plusses in the relationship? Her own power drive is attempting to get you to move in the direction she suggests.

Conclusion

Both you and your partner should analyse how you each handle conflict. Do you avoid it and keep silent? Do you see as trivial what your partner sees as important? Once a discussion or argument does develop, how do you react? Do you listen quietly? Do you try to understand your partner's point of view? Do you defend yourself and possibly blame your partner for the problem? Is your approach to talk and talk until you get everything you want? Then, when you recognise that there is a problem, do you keep quiet about it and keep it to yourself? Do you go to your friends and family for validation of your side? Do you call for an appointment with a therapist?

Epilogue:
Realistic romance

YES – It's possible to be happy!

YES – It's possible to love and be loved!

YES – It's possible to be in a romantic and fulfilling relationship!

To make these things happen we must understand the realities that:

- love can be defined and developed;
- we have a drive for power and control and that it must be controlled;
- developing the ability to love unselfishly can control the power drive in our relationships;
- we must keep our relationship positive – say 'I love you' often!;
- we must stay emotionally and physically intimate.

Once we understand ourselves – our needs, hopes and values – we will be able to base our life direction on reality. For most of us, there will be a drive for the power to accomplish valuable things. That's good! When our power drive is used to help us achieve personal goals, that's positive.

We must be able to keep our drive for power in a socially useful direction. It must be directed at one's power to:

- power to lead the nation;
- power to be effective in business;
- power to become self-actualised, to achieve in our chosen fields.

All too often our drive for power finds its way into our relationships where the desire to control our partner can destroy the partnership. In our relationship, the inclination to control our mate must be overcome. We can't have our power drives become directed towards having power OVER our mate. If we have learned to love in an unselfish way our drives for power will be tempered with the reality that LOVE is the solution to our personal lives – our relationships. It can also be utilised in the world beyond our home.

Being able to truly LOVE in the unselfish way which philosophers, saints and poets have described is the civilising answer to the more primitive drive for power and control. There is nothing more real than the reality of our highest self. Civilisation needs the unselfishness of having citizens who are loving. And, of course, our relationships need loving people as our partners. True romance cannot occur unless we have developed the ability to love and can bring it into our partnership. We need to devote quality TIME to the people we love. We must communicate the positives.

For romance to continue to evolve, we must each know

Figure 28 Happiness is like chasing a butterfly. The more you chase it, the more it eludes you. But if you sit quietly and turn your attention to other things, it comes and sits softly on your shoulder.

where we are going as individuals and where we are going as a couple. The journey should be joyous as we travel towards our goals (Figure 28). The reality of modern romance requires two maturing partners moving in the same direction and recognising the importance of each other – as true friends.

Horace Walpole's observation that 'life is a comedy for those who think and a tradgedy for those who feel' echoes the cynicism of Euripides, the Greek dramatist, who observed 2,500 years ago that when reality clouds our romantic feelings, we become pessimistic – about our relationship, our own meaning and our lives. But as intelligent 21st century romantics, we have the knowledge to transcend that perennial pessimism and cultivate ever-better romantic relationships – IF WE MERELY HAVE THE WILL.

Index